Web Publishing with Corel® WordPerfect® Suite 8: The Official Guide

Create a Quick Home Page

Use HTML's ready-made styles for attractive pages (Chapter 6).

Add graphic elements like horizontal lines (Chapter 7).

Create a basic home page (Chapters 4 and 5).

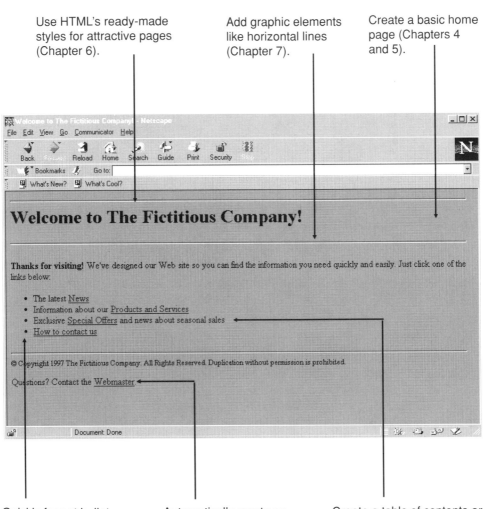

Quickly format bullet lists with HTML styles (Chapter 6).

Automatically create an e-mail link on each main page (Chapter 4) or add one yourself (Chapter 9).

Create a table of contents or main menu for your web site (Chapters 4 and 5).

Make Information Easy to Find on "Secondary" Pages

Use a variety of pre-fab HTML styles for quick formatting (Chapter 6).

Create informational links to your home page (Chapters 4 and 5).

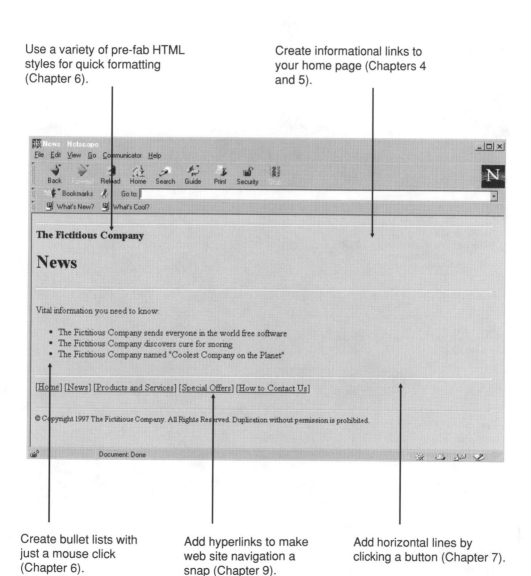

Create bullet lists with just a mouse click (Chapter 6).

Add hyperlinks to make web site navigation a snap (Chapter 9).

Add horizontal lines by clicking a button (Chapter 7).

Add Zip with Text Boxes

Save text formatting, typeface, and color with text boxes (Chapter 12).

Organize information with tables (Chapter 10).

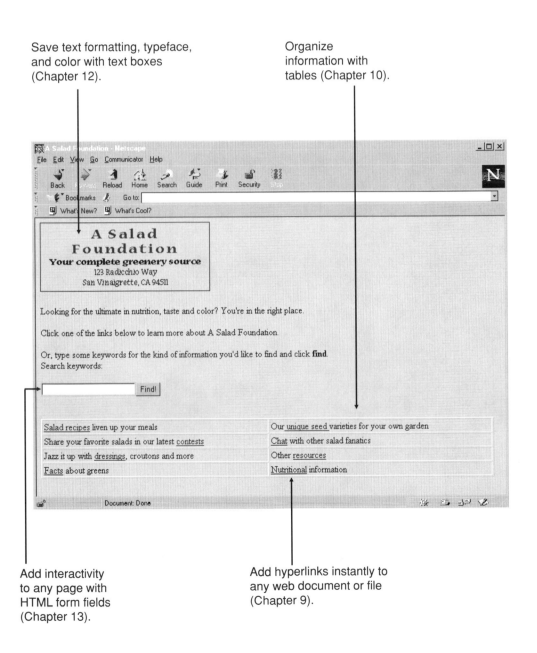

Add interactivity to any page with HTML form fields (Chapter 13).

Add hyperlinks instantly to any web document or file (Chapter 9).

Get Instant Feedback or Take Orders with Web Forms

Create complex
HTML forms easily
(Chapter 13).

Use HTML styles for
high-impact headings
(Chapter 6).

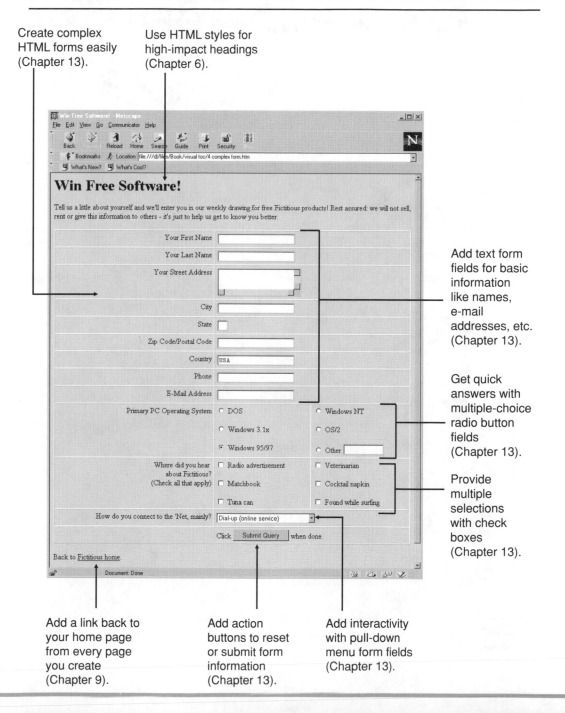

Add text form
fields for basic
information
like names,
e-mail
addresses, etc.
(Chapter 13).

Get quick
answers with
multiple-choice
radio button
fields
(Chapter 13).

Provide
multiple
selections
with check
boxes
(Chapter 13).

Add a link back to
your home page
from every page
you create
(Chapter 9).

Add action
buttons to reset
or submit form
information
(Chapter 13).

Add interactivity
with pull-down
menu form fields
(Chapter 13).

Build Attractive Web Pages
Using Specific Typefaces and Table Tricks

Preserve typefaces by specifying fonts (Chapter 12).

Tailor your tables by specifying column widths and spacing (Chapter 10)

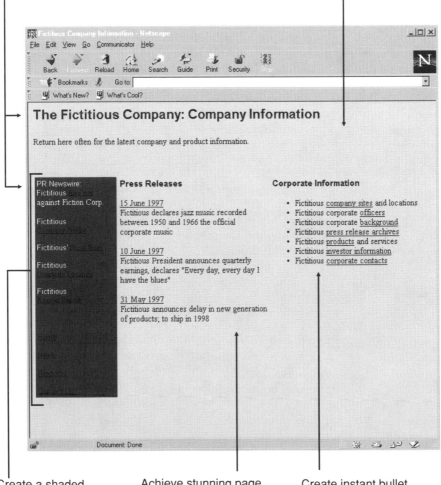

Create a shaded column (Chapter 10) of hyperlinks (Chapter 9).

Achieve stunning page design with advanced table tricks (Chapter 10).

Create instant bullet lists (Chapter 6).

Dazzle with Advanced Graphics

Use HTML styles for a variety of layout options (Chapter 6).

Use image maps to create interactive graphics (Chapter 16) in your pages (Chapter 8).

Create instant bullet lists (Chapter 6).

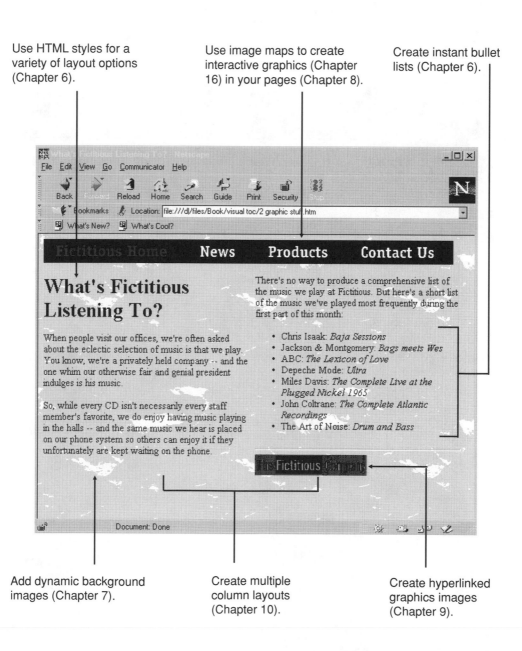

Add dynamic background images (Chapter 7).

Create multiple column layouts (Chapter 10).

Create hyperlinked graphics images (Chapter 9).

Share Your Numbers with Corel Quattro Pro

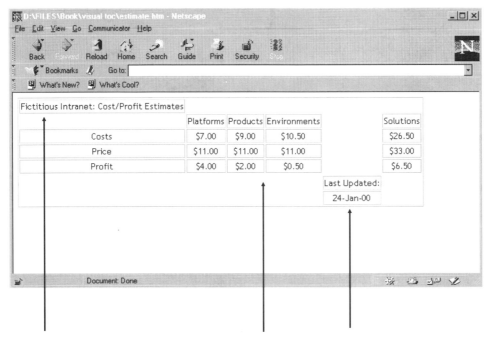

Turn Corel Quattro Pro spreadsheets into HTML tables (Chapter 15).

Use Corel Quattro Pro formulas to include spreadsheet information in your web sites (Chapter 15).

Include advanced Corel Quattro Pro features such as last-updated date/time stamps (Chapter 15).

Take Your Presentations
to the Web with Corel Presentations

Include downloadable Corel Presentations files in your web presentation (Chapter 16).

Detach the button frame into a movable "remote control" window (Chapter 16).

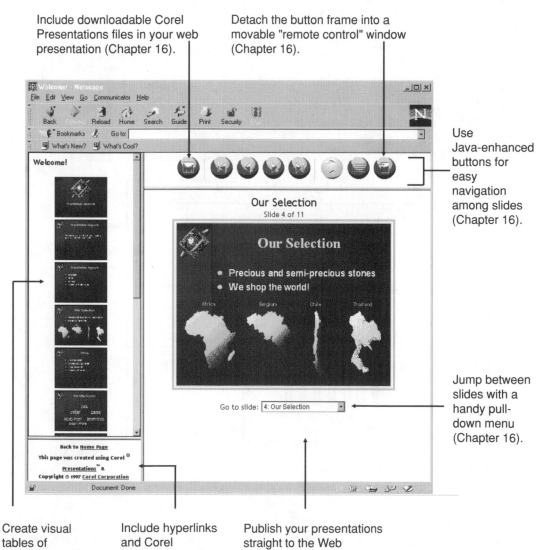

Use Java-enhanced buttons for easy navigation among slides (Chapter 16).

Jump between slides with a handy pull-down menu (Chapter 16).

Create visual tables of contents from slide thumbnails (Chapter 16).

Include hyperlinks and Corel copyright info to your home page (Chapter 16).

Publish your presentations straight to the Web (Chapter 16).

Use Java to Leap Beyond HTML Using Corel Barista

Create Corel Barista-enhanced web pages from any Corel WordPerfect Suite application (or Windows 95 application) (Chapter 18).

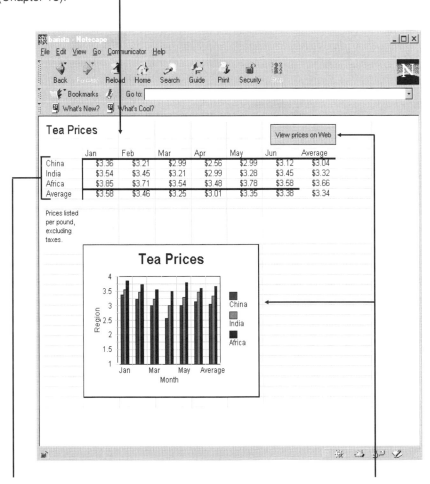

Preserve Java-supported font information (Chapter 18).

Faithfully reproduce complex Corel Quattro Pro page layouts, including hypertext buttons and charts (Chapter 15).

Web Publishing with Corel® WordPerfect® Suite 8: The Official Guide

Jeff Hadfield

Osborne/**McGraw-Hill**

Berkeley   New York   St. Louis   San Francisco
Auckland   Bogotá   Hamburg   London
Madrid   Mexico City   Milan   Montreal
New Delhi   Panama City   Paris   São Paulo
Singapore   Sydney   Tokyo   Toronto

Osborne/**McGraw-Hill**
2600 Tenth Street
Berkeley, California 94710
U.S.A.

For information on translations or book distributors outside the U.S.A., or to arrange bulk purchase discounts for sales promotions, premiums, or fund-raisers, please contact Osborne/**McGraw-Hill** at the above address.

Web Publishing with Corel® WordPerfect® Suite 8: The Official Guide

1234567890 QPM 9987

ISBN 0-07-882348-X

Publisher: Brandon A. Nordin
Editor-in-Chief: Scott Rogers
Acquisitions Editor: Joanne Cuthbertson
Project Editors: Janet Walden, Heidi Poulin
Editorial Assistant: Gordon Hurd
Technical Editor: Alan Biehl
Copy Editor: Jan Jue
Proofreader: Rhonda Holmes
Indexer: Valerie Robbins
Computer Designer: Roberta Steele
Illustrator: Leslee Bassin
Series Design: Roberta Steele
Cover Design: Arlette Crosland

To Jennifer

About the Author...

Jeff Hadfield, publishing and Corel® WordPerfect® expert, is former editorial director of *WordPerfect for Windows Magazine*, *WordPerfect Magazine (for DOS)*, *WordPerfect Magazine (UK)*, the *WordPerfect Suite Expert Newsletters*, and more. He has used Corel WordPerfect Suite and other Corel products to create electronic publications, products, and web sites. He also publishes and speaks regularly to the magazine industry on creating effective web sites and electronic publications.

CONTENTS AT A GLANCE

PART I
Essentials of Web Publishing

CONTENTS

PART II

Creating Web Pages with Corel WordPerfect

Part III

Creating Web Pages with Corel Quattro Pro, Corel Presentations, and More

PART IV

Publishing Web Pages: HTML, Envoy, and Corel Barista

Web Publishing with Corel® WordPerfect® Suite 8: The Official Guide represents the latest in a series of books dedicated to helping Corel users get the most from their software. This series provides both a solid grounding in product fundamentals and the knowledge necessary to master advanced features of the product. The author, along with Corel experts, has spent many hours working on the accuracy and scope of this book.

This edition provides an in-depth overview of Corel WordPerfect Suite 8's web publishing abilities. New users, as well as those who have purchased upgrades, will find significant value in these pages. The hands-on instruction and practical advice will help you use Corel WordPerfect Suite features to create dynamic, compelling web pages and web sites. The book reveals insider tips and tricks plus comprehensive, feature-by-feature walk-throughs to help you harness the suite's powerful web publishing abilities. You'll learn how Corel's technical leadership pays off with easy-to-use features that save you time and help your documents look their best.

The Corel Official Guide series represents a giant step in Corel's ability to disseminate information to users through the help of Osborne/McGraw-Hill and the fine authors involved in the series. Congratulations to the author and the Osborne team on the creation of this excellent book!

Dr. Michael C. J. Cowpland
President and CEO
Corel Corporation

FOREWORD

A book like this requires the talents of many people, not just the one whose name appears on the cover. As I've written this book, many have contributed their time and talents to make sure the information you read is usable, complete, accurate, and timely.

I'd first like to thank my family, without whose support this book would never have been a reality. They showed an amazing willingness to allow me to work on it in the midst of travel, household duties, an interstate move, and even holidays. This willingness was especially amazing considering our children's ages: Nick (3) and Hayley (1) let me work to the best of their ability. And most importantly, thanks to my wife Jennifer for her love, support, encouragement, and understanding (not to mention help with the appendixes). Thanks also to our parents, Glenn and Sherrol Hadfield and Dale and Jean Stringfellow, for allowing us to stay with them during our extended trips to California and allowing me to continue work on this project while we were there. Their love and support has also been invaluable.

Feedback, contributions, and help from Allen Biehl, this book's technical editor, made this a far better book than it could have otherwise been. His practical experience with web publishing plus his facility for clear explanation ensured the accuracy and completeness of this project. Thanks also to Allen for extended dog-sitting. My thanks to Dana Stohlton and Vicki Daines for their short-notice contributions to sections of this book. Thanks also to Elden Nelson, for years of friendship and professional help (not *that* kind—he's not a psychiatrist).

Special thanks to all at Corel who have been so gracious and generous with both time and resources to help me with this and other Corel-related projects. While I can never hope to list all those who have helped, I want to especially single out Cindy Howard, Paul Skillen, Vicki Silva, Michael Bellefeuille, Jackie Brinkerhoff, and Richard Whitehead for their extraordinary assistance and support. Thanks also to Michelle Pfister, Dallas Powell, Deirdre Calhoun, and Pat White. And while I'm at it, thanks to those who have continued to keep me close to the Corel WordPerfect products even with only indirect involvement in this project, including Carrie Bendza, Jeff Hunsaker, Craig Bushman, Steve Mann, and others.

But more goes into a book than just the original writing. It must be conceived, managed, planned, coordinated, designed, edited, and put up with. For these multiple contributions and more, special thanks go to Joanne Cuthbertson at Osborne/McGraw-Hill for her encouragement, support, and understanding. My

grateful thanks also to Janet Walden, senior project editor and the person largely responsible for the quality and attention to detail found within. She was capably assisted by associate project editor Heidi Poulin, copy editor Jan Jue, and proofreader Rhonda Holmes. Thanks also to Gordon Hurd for dotting I's and crossing T's, Anne Ellingsen for promotion, and the whole staff of Osborne/ McGraw-Hill.

I'd like to thank those who helped provide resources to get this project done. These include colleagues and friends throughout the publishing and computer industries. Particular thanks to Jeff Gilmore of Viewsonic, Myra Manahan of Single Source Marketing, Denise Klapperich of Dell Computers, Teresa Pulido of Creative Labs, Sonya Shaeffer of Adobe Systems.

I'd also like to extend thanks to all fellow alumni of *WordPerfect Magazine* for allowing me to work closely with WordPerfect software and teach people how to use it. And thanks to all the WordPerfect experts I've been privileged to know over the years as well for teaching me through example and patience: Gordon McComb, Daniel Will-Harris, Laura Acklen, Elizabeth Olson, Denise Vega, and more whom I can't name individually here.

If I've somehow missed someone, my heartfelt apologies. A project like this involves expertise and knowledge gained from others as well as efforts from a large, extended team, and for all this help, my deepest thanks.

Like many Corel WordPerfect users, I began using WordPerfect back in the days of version 5.0 for DOS. (If you ever get around a group of longtime users, I'm a relative newcomer.) In the mid '80s, I *sold* copies to customers at a small computer store, but I didn't *use* it intensively until versions 5.0 and 5.1. Back then, you couldn't have paid me to use a different product: WordPerfect's unparalleled speed, typographic support, and printer power allowed me to create documents and projects that outshone the competition but required very little extra effort. As my wife worked for WordPerfect Corporation, she showed me new things the program could do—and it was reason enough, I felt, to own a PC.

My views toward Corel WordPerfect haven't changed, even through all the versions and incarnations to which I've upgraded over the years. WordPerfect's strengths have remained consistent: character-level style control, comprehensive typographic support and control, extensive printer support, impressive facility with long and intricately designed documents, and more. But with version 7 for Windows 95, Corel WordPerfect developed a new strength that I couldn't do without: web authoring abilities.

While most of us were plugging away at our "day jobs"—using WordPerfect as an essential part of that work—something else was sneaking up. This sneaky development was the Internet. The Net, originally a way to interconnect government sites and universities, now sports the World Wide Web, an accessible, ubiquitous way of communicating and accessing information.

As Corel WordPerfect has developed into a suite of tools—priced so reasonably that its value is unbeatable—each part of this suite has contributed to this new facility that has become so integral to what many people do all day. Today, most of us create documents that won't just be printed. In addition, the information we create may be "published" to our company's World Wide Web site or archived to a company intranet. Corel WordPerfect Suite 7 for Windows 95 included many groundbreaking, essential tools for publishing both in print and on the Web. But with the new Corel WordPerfect Suite 8 for Windows 95, these tools provide comprehensive, best-in-the-industry ways for you to publish electronically without having to learn an arcane programming language.

This book will help you take your existing knowledge of Corel WordPerfect and its fellow applications in the suite and apply that know-how to creating documents that will be distributed on the Web. It doesn't matter if you're unfamiliar with Corel WordPerfect Suite—the instructions contained in this book will help you whatever your level of experience.

However, if you want to learn more about the basics of Corel WordPerfect Suite, I recommend two other books to you. For a quick way to pick up the essentials, try Elden Nelson's *WordPerfect 8 for Busy People* (Osborne/McGraw-Hill, 1997, ISBN 0-07-882313-7). If you're looking for a comprehensive reference work that shows you how to use every element in the suite, pick up Alan Neibauer's latest revision to his popular book *Corel WordPerfect Suite 8: The Official Guide* (like this book, this is another CorelPRESS title from Osborne/McGraw-Hill, 1997, ISBN 0-07-882327-7). Both books nicely complement the information in this book. You won't learn the basics of Corel WordPerfect here. You will, however, learn both basic and advanced techniques for creating web pages using the tools in Corel WordPerfect Suite 8.

The web tools in Corel WordPerfect Suite 8 are amazing. If you purchased one of the initial copies of Corel WordPerfect Suite 8, you hold in your hands the guide to harnessing its power. You own a set of software tools that can help you realize just about any web publishing goal. Soon after the initial release of both Corel WordPerfect Suite 8 and this book, Corel will release a Professional version of the suite. This Professional version will contain even more software and tools to help web publishing professionals get the job done quickly and easily. As of this writing, registered customers will receive an updated version of Corel WordPerfect Suite's initial release as well. The update will include Netscape Communicator (including Netscape Navigator 4.0 to update Netscape Navigator 3.0) tightly integrated with CorelCENTRAL to help you communicate, collaborate, and find information using the Internet.

No matter what version of the suite you own, this book will help you master the essential tools for creating web pages. As you browse this book, you'll notice that it's divided into four main parts. These sections correspond to the three main steps in web publishing:

1. Planning your site and web pages

2. Creating your web site and pages

3. Publishing your web pages

You'll learn more about each of these steps in Chapter 2. In the meantime, take a look at how the main parts in this book reflect these key steps.

Part I will first give you the bare basics of the World Wide Web. It's not an exhaustive treatise on the Web's origins and future. Instead, it's a chance for you to gain perspective about web publishing. You'll then learn about the web publishing process as well as some tips for planning your web site and web pages (step 1 in web publishing). Then you'll get a quick overview of how Corel WordPerfect Suite and its main components assist you in achieving your web plan.

Part II teaches you step-by-step how to create web pages using Corel WordPerfect. Since Corel WordPerfect is the suite tool most people use most often, you'll notice this is the largest section in the book. You'll learn about every single aspect of web page creation using Corel WordPerfect—from automated, basic page creation to inserting sounds and Java applets in your pages. And since the experts at Corel reviewed every page in the book, you're assured of getting comprehensive, accurate information.

Part III shows you how other applications in Corel WordPerfect Suite 8 help you publish documents to the Web. You'll spend quite a bit of time with Corel Quattro Pro and Corel Presentations. Then you'll learn how the other applications in the suite can help you as well.

After Parts II and III show you how to create web pages—the second step in web publishing—you'll learn how to publish those pages in Part IV. You'll learn to publish your pages to plain-vanilla HTML as well as to Java-enhanced, layout-rich HTML pages using Corel Barista. You'll also learn the basics of publishing to Envoy.

Don't forget to look to the end of the book for additional information that can help you learn more about web design and publishing and even troubleshoot Corel Barista documents. Appendix A lists some web sites that expand upon or supplement material you've learned from this book. Although in Chapter 4 you'll learn about the special web page backgrounds that ship with Corel WordPerfect Suite, you'll also discover more web page background graphics, included with the suite, in Appendix B—sorted by the types of pages for which you might use them. And in Appendix C, you'll find some common questions and answers to help you better understand Corel Barista and how to use it. Finally, in Appendix D, you'll find the Corel Barista file format reference—direct from Corel Corporation. It provides technical information to help advanced users understand and troubleshoot Corel Barista pages.

Now that you have a general idea of what this book contains, here are some important signposts to look for. Special tidbits of information will pop up now and then to help you on your web publishing projects.

Insider Tip

Watch for these Insider Tips for exclusive, insider information that will help you become a power user, provide unique perspectives, or just share insights. Culled from the experts and Corel insiders, this is information you can't get elsewhere.

TIP: *These short tidbits provide you with shortcuts, tricks, and hints to make your work easier.*

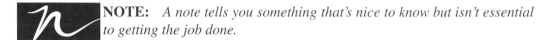

NOTE: *A note tells you something that's nice to know but isn't essential to getting the job done.*

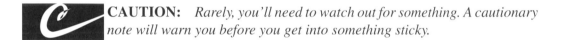

CAUTION: *Rarely, you'll need to watch out for something. A cautionary note will warn you before you get into something sticky.*

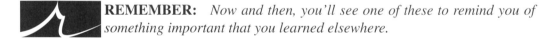

REMEMBER: *Now and then, you'll see one of these to remind you of something important that you learned elsewhere.*

You'll find complete illustrations and step-by-step instructions as well. Each of these contributes to the best compilation of how-to information you'll find anywhere. In fact, each step has been checked by Corel Corporation experts to ensure its accuracy before you read this official CorelPRESS book.

Now it's time to start learning about web publishing with Corel WordPerfect Suite 8. Dive in! It's not as intimidating as it might seem, and you'll be proudly displaying your web site and snazzy web pages in no time. I'm also anxious to hear from you: Did you use the book to create a web site? Send me its URL so I can admire it, too. Is there something you'd like to see in future editions? Let me know. And if there are any tips you'd like to share with other readers, send them along and I'll try to include them in any future editions. You can reach me via e-mail at **hadfield@iname.com** or at **jhadfield@worldcom.att.net**. In the meantime, best of luck with your web publishing, and I hope to see your work on the Web!

PART I

Essentials of Web Publishing

Basics of the World Wide Web

1

Make no mistake, publishing on the World Wide Web is a major undertaking. Or, to be more precise, publishing *well* on the World Wide Web takes a concentrated effort.

Corel WordPerfect Suite makes it easy for you to publish on the Web. However, while it makes the mechanics of web page creation easier, *you* still have to decide on the goal of your web site.

I've spoken with hundreds of people who create or plan web sites. Some have created sites for small businesses, others have planned multimillion-dollar web "stores." To be successful, they required a clear vision of what they wanted to achieve and how they were going to use the World Wide Web to accomplish their goal.

Before you can envision what you want to achieve, you need to make sure you understand the basics of how the Web works. That's what this chapter is all about. After we review some of the basics of what the Web is and how it works, we'll talk about some general approaches to creating a web site (or creating web pages). You'll learn some important things to consider when you're planning a web project. (Chapter 2 covers how Corel WordPerfect Suite can help you with the steps of planning and designing your site.) If you're already familiar with how the Web works, feel free to skip ahead.

How the World Wide Web Began

The World Wide Web is the natural—almost accidental—progression of a couple of key technologies. The first technology is the Internet. The second technology is the underlying protocols for the Web itself—HTML, HTTP, and DNS—which led to URLs.

TIP: *You don't need to know arcane technical details to understand how these technologies affect your work on the Web, and we won't talk about them here. If you want to know more about the Web, and more about the specific details of any of these technologies, you may want to consult a book on HTML and the Internet or check the Net itself. See Appendix A for some web sites that can tell you more about the Internet's history. And for a few books that can teach you more about the Net, see the list at the end of this chapter.*

The Origin of the Internet

While the Internet has become well known in the past few years, it originated in the 1960s as a U.S. Department of Defense project called ARPANET (Advanced Research Projects Agency Network). ARPANET was designed to allow researchers to share information so they could avoid duplicating efforts on crucial government projects. As the years went by, this network grew to wider usage—from academic to business use. Probably the most notable changes in the network's use came from a National Science Foundation network upgrade in the 1980s that dramatically improved this network's speed, widened its scope to universities and more government resources, and changed ARPANET's name to the Internet.

Don't be confused, though—the Internet is not one computer controlling links to all other computers—it's not like the hub of a bicycle wheel that every spoke must touch. Instead, it's a network where any computer can be connected to another through a series of interconnected, smaller networks. Some describe the Internet as a "network of networks" spread around the world.

During these years of growth, the Internet was somewhat of an elitist resource. Researchers, government technicians, and students felt that it was their resource, and their resource alone. They used it as a place to exchange technical information and to associate with others who had similar interests. These early Internet days saw this community becoming an insular one, largely focused around one use of the Internet (before the Web came along).

The one area these users congregated around was *Usenet*—a virtual "bulletin board" system where hundreds, if not thousands, of electronic discussion areas sprung up for every area of interest.

NOTE: *In the old days, the Internet was used mostly for e-mail, Usenet newsgroups, file transfer protocol (ftp), gopher, and telnet. E-mail remains the single biggest use of the Internet, but the Web is now a close second. Web browsers such as Netscape Navigator have integrated Usenet "news reader" and ftp abilities. Use of telnet (a resource for logging into remote networks) and gopher (a menu-driven list of Internet resources) is now relatively rare.*

When the ARPANET was changed to the Internet, it was designed to allow growth and to become a public network, something that any citizen could access.

The World Wide Web enabled the Internet to reach that kind of exponential growth. Much to the surprise of the original ARPANET community, in only the last ten years or so, the Internet has become an incomprehensibly huge network of linked computers around the world.

The Growth of the Web

The World Wide Web couldn't have happened without the Internet, and the Internet wouldn't be as widely known or used without the Web. The Web is based on three ways computers talk to each other. You don't need to know *how* they work, but you do need to know what they mean and can do.

The first is a *uniform resource locator* (URL). If you've ever typed a web address, such as **www.corel.com**, into a web browser, you've typed a URL. (Pronounce it "U-R-L," not "url," as in "duke of.") It's simply an identifier that tells your network where to go to find the web page you've requested. Each individual network provides a list—kind of like a phone book—that contains each of these names with their corresponding, cryptic number addresses on the Internet. Your web browser receives this information and displays the page you want to see. Earlier in this chapter, you saw the acronym *DNS*, for *domain name server.* DNS is the capability that allows you to use a plain-English name to find a site on the Web—at least, it's relatively plain English, compared with remembering and typing in a string of digits to represent an Internet Protocol (IP) address. (The domain name in the example given earlier is "corel.com.") When you type a URL, your browser looks in the domain name server you have specified by your Internet connection, much like you'd look up a phone number in the phone book. Your browser checks the DNS for the number that matches the name you typed, then looks on the Internet for that address.

TIP: *If you're creating a new site for your company, you'll need to see if the domain name you want to use is available, and then register it with the Internet's governing body, the InterNIC. To register your domain name, check with the InterNIC at* **rs.internic.net***.*

The second way computers talk to each other is by means of *hypertext transfer protocol* (HTTP). HTTP tells your web browser that you want to use the hypertext protocol to view the document at the location you've typed. And if you haven't specified a document name, your browser will usually look for a file called *index.htm* at the location (or URL) you've specified. Of course, webmasters (people in charge of a web site's operation) and web server administrators can change the name of this default file to whatever they choose—the default setting is usually *default.htm.* Netscape servers default to *index.html.* Some people prefer *home.htm, homepage.htm,* or something else.

HTTP is the protocol for HTML web pages, just like ftp (file transfer protocol) is the protocol for transferring files across the Internet. In the past, when you typed an address into your web browser, you had to type **http://** before the rest of the address (for example, the "www.corel.com" part). Now most browsers don't require this. (If you're like I am, it's difficult to remember whether you're supposed to type the forward slashes or the backward slashes, so this little feature saves a lot of time.)

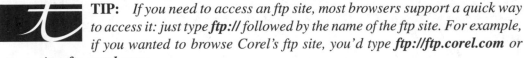

TIP: *If you need to access an ftp site, most browsers support a quick way to access it: just type **ftp://** followed by the name of the ftp site. For example, if you wanted to browse Corel's ftp site, you'd type **ftp://ftp.corel.com** or just **ftp.corel.com**.*

The third key standard is constantly evolving: *hypertext markup language* (HTML). HTML was originally a subset of SGML (standard generalized markup language), a text-only format designed to allow for complex formatting in documents used among multiple programs and platforms. Today, HTML has evolved to include many of SGML's features.

HTML is a tag-based way of specifying how a document should be formatted and, most significantly, how it *connects to other documents or files.* HTML files are basically plain ASCII text files with extra *tags* surrounded by angle brackets (<>). HTML tags are much like the codes you see in Corel WordPerfect when you use the Reveal Codes feature.

For example, using Corel WordPerfect's Reveal Codes feature, you might see [BoldOn] and [BoldOff] codes surrounding text that appears in **bold** on the screen and when printed. In an HTML document, boldface text starts with a <b> tag and ends with a </b> tag. When you view an HTML document in a text editor or open it in Corel WordPerfect as an ASCII text file (instead of an HTML file), you can see these tags scattered throughout the document. But when you open the document in a web browser such as Netscape Navigator, the browser interprets the tags much like Corel WordPerfect interprets WordPerfect codes and displays the formatted document on the screen.

Note in Figures 1-1 and 1-2 the similarities between Corel WordPerfect's formatting codes and the HTML tags. Remember, Corel WordPerfect will place all of these HTML codes in the document for you, so you don't have to remember any of them. As with using Reveal Codes, knowing how HTML codes work is mostly useful when you need to troubleshoot problems.

The "HT" in "HTML" is the key to the Web's power—*hypertext.* Hypertext, or connections to other documents, means that the Web can literally be a web of interconnections among documents anywhere in the world.

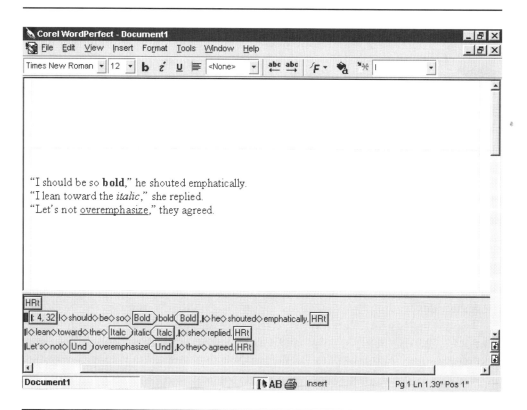

FIGURE 1-1   Corel WordPerfect's Reveal Codes feature. Note the paired codes' resemblance to the HTML tags shown in Figure 1-2.

```
AT&T WorldNet Service - [Source of: file:///D|/FILES/Book/34801f1.htm]          _ □ ×

<HTML>
<HEAD>
<META NAME="Generator" CONTENT="Corel WordPerfect 8">
<TITLE></TITLE>
</HEAD>
<BODY TEXT="#000000" LINK="#0000ff" VLINK="#551a8b" ALINK="#ff0000" DGCOLOR="#c0c0c0">

<P><STRONG>Some bold text.</STRONG>

<P><EM>Some italic text.</EM>

<P><FONT SIZE="+3">Some big text.</FONT>

<BR WP="BR1"><BR WP="BR2">
<TABLE BORDER="1" WIDTH="100%" CELLPADDING="1" CELLSPACING="1">
<TR VALIGN="TOP"><TD>And a table.</TD>
<TD>And a cell.</TD></TR>
<TR VALIGN="TOP"><TD>And another row.</TD>
<TD>And one more cell.</TD></TR></TABLE>

</BODY>
</HTML>
```

FIGURE 1-2   An example of HTML source code

The Web Today

Today, the Web is surprisingly well known. Major commercial online services such as CompuServe and America Online (AOL) have repositioned their services as gateways to the Web. Magazines, television networks, and businesses have a presence on the Web. Millions of people worldwide are connected to the Web and use it almost daily to communicate with other people, look up information, and find entertainment.

Every day, more people are turning to the Web to find information for travel, shopping, services, and information. And every day, more businesses are creating a presence on the Web—whether as an informational resource about a company's services or as a virtual storefront where people can buy the products a company sells. Industry analysts predict nothing but exponential growth for the Web in the years ahead.

The Web is becoming a "virtual community," to use Howard Rheingold's phrase from his book of the same name, where people turn for answers to their questions and seek solutions for almost any need. They're looking for businesses to provide quick information to help them with more than computer-related needs. They're looking for resources that will save them time and money as they look for information, shop, or just browse a virtual mall.

Connecting to the Web

How do all these people connect to the Web? Most use a personal computer—but even that's not necessary with the advent of products that allow you to cruise the Net using your television. However, since you're using Corel WordPerfect Suite to create your web pages, you'll need to get connected via your PC.

High-Speed Links

If you're working as part of a large company, educational institution, or government agency, there's a good chance that your organization has a high-speed link to the Internet through your existing local area network (LAN) or wide area network (WAN). If you can take advantage of that, do so—it's by far the best way to connect to the Web. Check with your system administrator, network administrator, or MIS department if you're unsure about how to connect using your organization's network.

Modems

Many people connect to the Internet using a modem. For example, I've connected to the Web using a reliable Hayes Optima 288 modem, as well as a US Robotics/Megahertz PC Card modem. These are just two of the reliable brands out there, but they're great examples of what you need before you can connect.

Internet Service Providers

You might also choose to use a local Internet service provider (ISP). For many people, a local ISP is the best choice because:

- Local ISPs provide reliable, high-speed access through a local phone number.

- A local ISP can help you "host" your web site, providing web server space and expertise so you don't have to master the technical subtleties of web server maintenance.

- Local ISPs are often reasonably priced.

- Some local ISPs can help you register and establish your own domain name—for example, instead of your web site address appearing as **www.localisp.net/yourbusinessname/index.htm**, it could appear as **www.yourbusinessname.com**.

While it used to be hard to find a local ISP, now it's as easy as looking in the yellow pages of your phone book. ISPs are often listed under "Internet Providers" or "Computers." If your area has a local computer tabloid—like *MicroTimes* or *Computer Currents*—that is often a good place to look. In fact, many local entertainment or "alternative" weeklies include advertisements for ISPs. You may also want to check your newspaper's business section.

There are some national ISPs that offer similar services as well as the advantage of local dial-up access in cities throughout the United States and Canada. These include AT&T WorldNet, NetCom, and Concentric Networks (included in the suite).

Commercial Online Services

For others, a commercial online service is the best choice. Commercial online services include CompuServe and America Online (AOL). They offer a variety of pricing plans for access to the Internet and the Web, as well as access to content that's only available on their services. They offer local, dial-up access in cities throughout the United States, Canada, and the world.

Traditionally, CompuServe has catered to a more technical or professional audience, offering similar web page hosting abilities to a regular Internet service provider. Its new interface, CompuServe 3 for Windows 95, is designed to make finding information on the Internet as easy as within CompuServe's resources and special-interest forums (see Figure 1-3). CompuServe is now based on HTML-format documents, like the main Table of Contents for CompuServe's proprietary information and content (see Figure 1-4), as well as links to information on the Web. One advantage CompuServe has over AOL is that you can choose the web browser you want to use—you're not locked into only one limited browser, even though AOL now allows you to use a special version of Microsoft Internet Explorer.

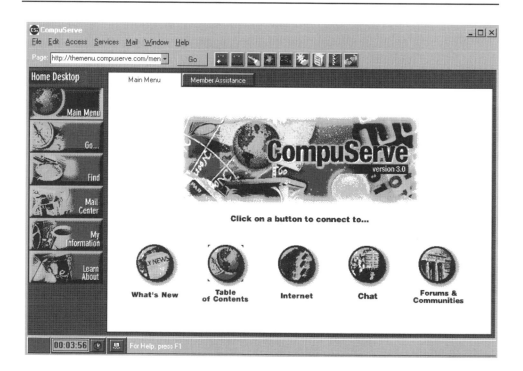

FIGURE 1-3   CompuServe 3 for Windows 95

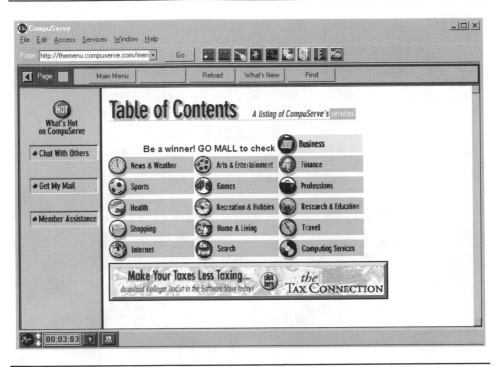

FIGURE 1-4   CompuServe's Table of Contents—an HTML document

America Online is a fast-growing, mass-market service that provides some resources and tools for web publishing. Each member even gets some space on the AOL server for his or her home page. Like CompuServe, America Online groups its information and links to the Web in general categories to make browsing easy (see Figure 1-5). However, America Online's proprietary web browser is incompatible with some of the more advanced web pages. Also, AOL's huge growth has taxed its ability to provide reliable access and service to its subscribers.

Whichever service you choose, Corel WordPerfect will help make the mechanics of web publishing easier. Now that you have a general understanding of the Internet

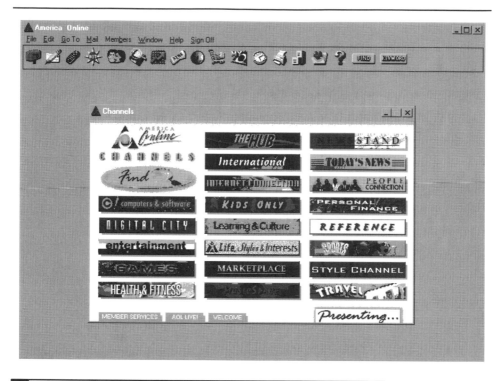

FIGURE 1-5 America Online's "channels"

and the Web, it's time to learn how to decide what to publish on the Web. In the next chapter, you'll learn some important items to consider before you create your web site—including deciding on the goal of your web site.

This chapter provides only a rudimentary introduction to some key web concepts. If you're interested in learning more about the Web and how it works, including information about web servers, net security, and more, you may want to pick up one of these books, all from Osborne/McGraw-Hill:

- *The Internet for Busy People, Second Edition*, by Christian Crumlish (1997)

- *The World Wide Web for Busy People*, by Stephen L. Nelson (1996)

- *The Internet Complete Reference, Second Edition*, by Harley Hahn (1996)

Osborne/McGraw-Hill also offers related books on more advanced topics. Check your local bookseller or visit **www.osborne.com**.

Basics of Web Publishing

2

his book will show you how to create web pages and even a basic web site. The best part is that you can create professional-quality, cutting-edge web pages that actually help your business—all with the tools you already possess in Corel WordPerfect Suite 8.

In this chapter, you'll learn about the basic process of web site building and then learn about the first step in the process: *planning.*

Building a Web Site

Creating a web site—even if it's just a home page with a few pages linked to it—follows this basic process:

1. You *plan* the web site's goals, content, and structure.

2. You *create* the web pages and the structure.

3. You *publish* those pages to the Web.

Part 1 of this book (Chapters 1 through 3) deals with step 1. Chapter 1 provided a good overview of the Web and related technology. This chapter will help you answer fundamental questions before you begin creating your site. Chapter 3 will explain how the powerful tools in Corel WordPerfect Suite 8 will help you realize your vision.

Part 2 (Chapters 4 through 14) teaches you about *creating* web pages (step 2 of the process). It deals with the cornerstone of Corel WordPerfect Suite: Corel WordPerfect. In version 8, Corel has turbocharged Corel WordPerfect's Internet and web features to make the product a web page authoring tool that's second to none. And because a lot of the information you're planning to put on your site may already be in Corel WordPerfect format, it's also the best tool for converting your existing documents to web formats.

Part 3 (Chapters 15 through 17) also shows you how to create web pages. But this time, you'll learn how to take advantage of the powerful tools in the other suite applications, including Corel Quattro Pro, Corel Presentations and other Corel WordPerfect Suite components.

The last section, Part 4 (Chapters 18 and 19), helps you with the final step in the process: *publishing* your web pages. You'll learn about using the integrated web publishing tools to create HTML pages, Java-enhanced HTML pages with Corel Barista, and Envoy pages. But for now, turn your attention back to the first step in the overall process: planning your web site.

Planning Your Web Site: Goals

Since you're reading this book, you're interested in creating a web site for your business or personal projects. You might be creating one to help your customers find things they want to buy from you, or you may be creating one for your employees to find company information more easily. Whatever your purpose, creating a web site is like undertaking a road trip. If you have no destination in mind, you may have an interesting trip…but it's unlikely you'll achieve any particular goal. In fact, it's much like this passage from Lewis Carroll's *Alice's Adventures in Wonderland*, in which Alice asks:

"Would you tell me, please, which way I ought to go from here?"
"That depends a good deal on where you want to get to," said the [Cheshire] Cat.
"I don't much care where—" said Alice.
"Then it doesn't matter which way you go," said the Cat.
"—so long as I get *somewhere*," Alice added as an explanation.
"Oh, you're sure to do that," said the Cat, "if you only walk long enough."

You could make a web site with no particular objectives in mind…and maybe you'd end up playing croquet with flamingos, as did Alice, instead of creating market presence and increasing your business revenue. But if you *plan* your web site with your goal in mind, you'll be able to create a site that helps you achieve your goals. You can discover these goals by answering some basic questions next.

Establishing Goals and Guidelines

When money and the future of your business are at stake, you need to have a clear idea of what it is you're going to communicate.

To make the best use of your precious assets of time, energy, and money, ask yourself the following questions before you begin any major web undertaking. Each question will not apply to every project, but they will help you establish clear goals and guidelines to help you see the big picture as you build each piece of a new web site. Having these goals and guidelines will help you ensure that each page contributes to your web site's overall objectives. When you build a web site with this clear focus, it will be more effective.

1. What Do You Want from Your Web Project?

How will you know if your site has succeeded if you don't know what results you were seeking?

For example, if you're creating a web site that lists the courses, faculty, and resources available in, say, the communications department at your university, you may feel that the goal is simply to make a greater amount of information more readily available to a larger number of people. With this vague a goal, you may want to ask some of the next questions in order to make your objective more measurable—and make it easier to see when you've succeeded. (And when you've succeeded at a goal, well, that's just a good excuse for an office party.)

In another example, you might be creating a site that's going to place all of your company's product information on the Web as well as general company information. What's going to be the benefit of this information being more readily available? How will you justify the expense of the web site? Perhaps you're planning to save money by abandoning product guides that are out of date by the time they are printed. Or perhaps you're planning to reach a new set of customers who are on the Web and are looking for the kind of products you offer.

Here are some other examples:

- A government agency might make its reports—formerly available for the cost of printing—available on the Web in order to comply with a legislative or management edict to make information more readily available.

- An advertising agency may want to make samples of its work in print, electronic, and broadcast media more accessible to potential clients in order to land more accounts.

- A local cleaning company may want to advertise its competitive services and rates to its potential clientele in order to increase its work.

What you want out of your web project is the most important question you will answer. You will need to have a goal—and hopefully a measurable one—so that you can tell when your site has succeeded. And if you set a goal that's renewable—one that you can adjust as time goes by—you can measure its success for years to come. Whether your objective is based on revenue or marketing, the answer you provide to this first question will tell you how to position your company, its products, and your web site.

2. Who Will Use Your Web Site?

Before you begin to design your web pages, you must know who it is you're planning to have visit the pages. Will it be existing customers? Will it be potential customers? How much familiarity will they have with the Web? How much familiarity will they have with you? What do you know about them (their demographics and psychographics), and what kind of images, colors, and messages will appeal to them?

For example, readers of HotWired may differ from readers of The New York Times online. And Lexus shoppers may respond to a different approach than Levi's shoppers. In Figure 2-1, note how the home page for The New York Times' electronic publication echoes the design of the printed newspaper. Its design focuses on news and the established, reliable look of the country's "paper of record." Now contrast this with Figure 2-2. HotWired, the electronic counterpart to *Wired* magazine, uses bright colors and less staid design to appeal to a technologically savvy crowd. Note the other sites in the HotWired family listed as links in the left column. Compare this layout, created to appear in color, with the New York Times on the Web, which uses mostly the black and white found in a print newspaper.

Now compare Figures 2-3 and 2-4. In Figure 2-3, you can see how auto manufacturer Lexus designed their site to cover current sponsorships (the animated golfer), maintaining current Lexus owners' loyalties as well as informing and persuading potential buyers. Note how they've appealed to their affluent target audience with touches like "Centre of Performance Art," which uses the International English spelling of "center," and the animated concierge. In Figure 2-4, while the buyer of Levi's clothing may own a Lexus, Lexus buyers aren't the audience of this site, which is aimed at a younger crowd. The clincher? "Happy Holidays" written across a model's bare stomach. It's unlikely Lexus' concierge will submit to the same stunt.

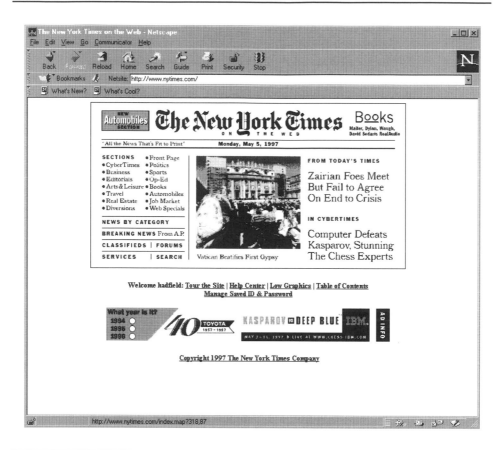

FIGURE 2-1   The home page for The New York Times on the Web

3. Why Do They Want to Visit Your Site?

When you build a web site, it's important to remember your audience—your customers. You must keep their needs foremost in mind. They must find value in your pages or they won't come back.

The secret to electronic success on the Web is to give people a reason to visit your site—as well as a reason to return. Those who are successful on the Web provide

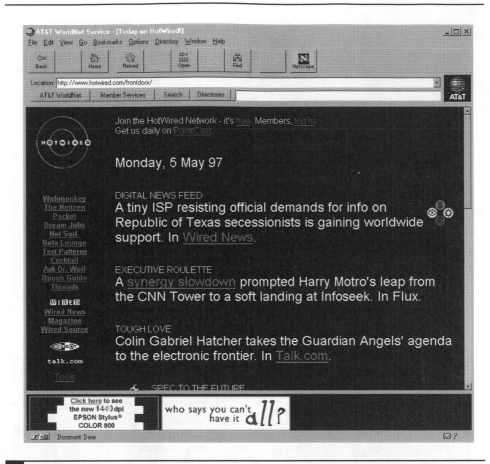

FIGURE 2-2   HotWired's home page

information that's of value to the web surfer—not just information that supports a corporate directive.

For example, Delta Air Lines strives to create more than just a "what a wonderful airline we are" promotional site. Instead, they seek to add information that's useful to all visitors—whether or not they fly Delta regularly. This includes information on major destinations worldwide for business and leisure visitors. Of course, for those who fly Delta, complete flight information is available. And Delta recently introduced special web benefits for their frequent flyers—including the ability to

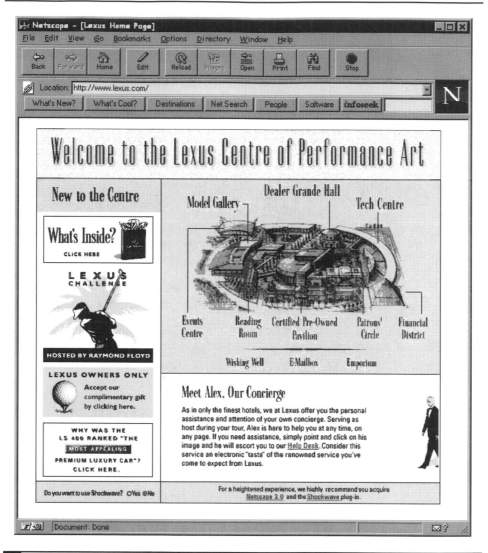

FIGURE 2-3 Lexus' home page

check frequent-flyer point balances and redeem awards on the Web. (Their URL is **www.delta-air.com**.)

Delta's successful site serves each of its audiences well: the casual surfer who stumbles across the site looking for something of interest, the web denizen who's looking for travel information, and the dedicated Delta traveler who wants to book a flight or find specific information about Delta, its service, or its programs.

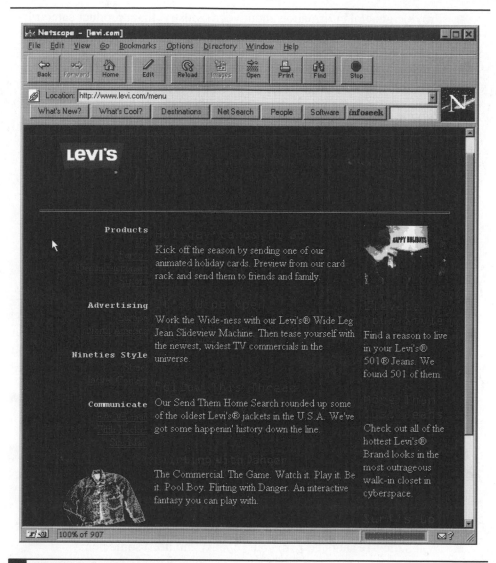

FIGURE 2-4   Levi's home page

You might also consider some other approaches:

- Partner with a company that provides information that's related to your products in some way. Provide links and exchange information to add value to each other's sites.

- Provide demonstrations or product information on your site.

- Provide general information about your industry, main product categories, or related public-service information. (If you're not a public-relations professional, ask your company's PR department, or take a PR professional to lunch, and find out about the value of establishing your company as an expert in its field.)

- Provide special, web-only offers. For example, Express, the women's clothing chain, offers web-only coupons on its site, **www.express.style.com**.

- Provide interactive opportunities. If you have the technological expertise, you can create interactive games as does the Disney site (**www.disney.com**). But interactivity may extend to a simple, e-mailed web form that enters participants into a weekly drawing for a free product. Or it might even be a discussion area.

4. When Will People Visit Your Site?

Answering this question doesn't mean analyzing the time of day when your web server will be most taxed. Instead, you need to remind yourself of the product sales cycle—again assuming you're in this web thing to build your business. Since your business grows when people buy your products, you need to know when people will visit your site. Will they visit your site:

- When they're gathering general information about products like yours?

- When they're comparison shopping for product features?

- When they're getting ready to make a decision and want to find out about price and availability?

- When they're ready to buy (and close the sale)?

- When they're annoyed with your product and need some help?

If you work for a car manufacturer such as Lexus, you would probably be able to provide valuable information for people who are gathering general information, comparing features, and needing help with the products. But you would probably leave pricing, availability, and purchase help to your local dealers—who hopefully would have web sites, too.

If you're selling software, you could provide all the preceding information and probably even allow people to download the software if they have a credit card. In fact, most products can be ordered online by use of a credit card, even if they need to be shipped (for example, music CDs at **www.cdnow.com** and books at **www.amazon.com**).

5. Where Will People Learn About Your Site?

It's easy to fall into comfortable patterns when you're promoting your web site. For example, a local company who runs ads in the newspaper may think that adding a URL to all their newspaper ads will do. Or the newspaper itself may simply add the URL to their masthead. While both of these practices are good, neither is sufficient for success. Your web site will need promotion a bit more creative than that.

Entire books have been written on successful web site promotion. A few key ideas will suffice here to get you started. First, don't neglect your existing promotion and advertising. Stick your URL everywhere—from advertisements to business cards, from T-shirts to invoices. This will help you educate your existing customers and your traditional, potential customers.

But you'll also want to reach others. Regardless of your product or service, odds are you'll want to reach just about every qualified person who's using the Web. You can do that by registering your site with all the major search engines. You can register by hand, or use off-the-shelf software such as Submit It (also available as shareware at **www.submit-it.com**). Unless you're operating on a shoestring budget, you'll want to use one of these automatic registering tools to help you in promoting your site, rather than manually registering your site with each search engine.

Insider Tip

If you're of even relatively sound mind—and you value your time—you won't try to register your site with each of the major search engines or Net resource listings all by yourself. You will take advantage of the modest fee charged for shareware such as Submit-It, which walks you through the creation of a basic description of your web pages and then automatically submits your descriptions to these search engines. Although these programs are time-savers, you will want to do research on sites that are specifically focused on your type of information and discover what it would take to get listed on those as well.

6. How Will People Use Your Site?

By now your vision of your web site's purpose should be getting clearer. But there's one more element to consider as you plan for your site: *how* people will use your site. In this case, "how" means a few things:

- Will people access your site from their homes? From a state-of-the-art PC running Windows 95 or from a 386 running Windows 3.1?

- Will people access your site using a fast, T1 connection from their corporate workstation, or will they generally use a modem?

- Will people be using only one hardware platform? (In other words, would they use PCs running Windows, Macintosh machines, or even UNIX boxes?)

- Will people be using the latest web browsers, such as Netscape Communicator's Navigator 4.0 module? And will they be using only one type of browser, or several?

The answers to these questions will help you begin to plan the layout of your site's pages. You'll be able to determine if, for example, your pages can afford the luxury of using a lot of graphics because all of the people visiting your site will be using high-speed connections. Or you may not bother creating graphically intensive pages because you know most of your site's visitors will be dialing into the Internet via modem.

TIP: *You'll learn more about using text and graphics on your web pages in Parts 2 and 3 of this book. As you develop your pages and site, you'll want to balance your plans with your technical ability and time to execute them—as well as how long it will take you to maintain them regularly.*

You've answered some key questions about what you want out of your web site—what, who, why, when, where, and how. It's now time to take a different approach to one of the most important elements of any product (including your web site): *marketing* it.

Effective Web Site Promotion: The Four P's

If you had to slog through Marketing 101 in college, mention of the "four p's" might resurrect some bad memories—or maybe just a faint taste of cold pizza for breakfast. Warning: don't compare this section to your old textbooks. This isn't particularly faithful to the traditional four p's of marketing (product, price, place, and promotion). And if you didn't take Marketing 101, don't sweat it: just read on.

It's important to think through every project, and a web site is no exception. To help your thinking, you might want to take this classic marketing paradigm and apply it in a new way as follows. It will help you approach your plans from more than one perspective.

1. What's Your *Product?*

Whether or not you're providing a tangible product, you can offer whatever you sell over the Web. But you had better define that product well before you attempt to promote or sell it electronically. (Of course, you should probably define it well to be successful in general.)

Earlier in the chapter, you saw a couple of examples of tangible products. It's fairly straightforward to see how you might sell an electronic product—like software or shareware—over the Web: get credit card information, process it, and deliver the software or a password. It's almost as easy to see how to sell a physical product: take the order and payment information, process it, and deliver the product via mail, express services, or your own shops (like FTD does).

> **NOTE:** *Ask your Internet service provider or web hosting service for information about setting up a web storefront. Or if you're hosting your web site yourself, many off-the-shelf products are available to help you take and process orders, such as Netscape's Commerce Server.*

But what if you offer a service? If you're a consultant, the product you sell is probably the results you help your clients receive—not the advice you give. This subtle distinction will help you sell your product online: you won't want to belabor the details of the services you provide. Instead, you could focus on client success stories (get permission first to use names!). Their results are your product.

2. What *Prices* Will You Charge?

Sound simple? It's not. Endless hours in conference rooms, board rooms, and across tables in bagel shops have been spent debating this issue. At its heart is this: should you discount your prices on the Web, keep them the same, or charge a premium? Here's the kernel of each argument:

- *Discount your prices* on the Web because web shoppers demand the best prices. Because you don't have to maintain a facility for your customers to visit, they expect that your overhead will be cheaper and demand bargain-basement prices.

- *Keep your prices the same* because web shoppers recognize the value of convenience. You also won't want to siphon away customers from your existing sales channels—retail locations, mail order, and so on—or anger any of your business partners.

- *Charge a premium* for web-ordered products because web shoppers are getting the product more easily and conveniently than they would otherwise. And if you can deliver the product to them right then, without a wait, then that definitely demands a premium price.

Each argument has some validity. But the answer is a combination of all three. People will expect to pay no more than your regular prices unless you're providing some kind of premium service. If they order on the Web, can you get them their product faster? Then you might consider a slight premium. Otherwise, people know that web shopping—if your site is worth the silicon it's running on—saves you time and money because it's automated. So they'll often expect a discount. But remember that although they expect a discount, it's more important that they *perceive* a discount, not that you lose your shirt.

To set your prices appropriately, watch your competition and the market to make sure you're in line with what's out there. And never forget to listen to what your customers want. Call them, read their e-mail messages.

NOTE: *Read* The One to One Future: Building Relationships One Customer at a Time *by Don Peppers and Martha Rogers, Ph.D. (Doubleday Currency, 1997) for more information on using electronic media—like the Web—to successfully market to your customers and deliver them the exact products they want.*

3. In What *Place* Will You Be on the Net?

On the Web, *place* doesn't refer to the physical location of the server on which your web pages are stored. In fact, most people don't even have a clue (or care) where your server is. On the Web, your place is your *presence* on the Net. And a big Net presence is the web equivalent of a giant, anchor store in a busy shopping mall.

REMEMBER: *Earlier in this chapter you learned about submitting your web site's information to major web search engines: don't forget this important step!*

Unlike the real world, on the Web you *can* be several places at once. You don't need additional leases, building permits, or more store fixtures. Instead, you will create a virtual presence where you erect as many signs as possible, each leading your customers to your web site—no matter where they started. How do you do this? Since the Web is a collection of documents interconnected with links, you can connect with other sites—and they with you—through these links.

Actively pursue *link exchanges.* There are some formalized link exchange programs—which may or may not benefit you. As with most automated programs, they can save time and deliver some results, but the most effective use of your time and the greatest results will come from your own efforts.

Do a little *competitive analysis.* Find out who produces products that complement but don't compete directly with yours. Contact these companies and offer to exchange links with them. Cooperate to build each other's businesses. If you can offer some benefit to them, most sites will be willing to swap links with you.

The ideal situation is when your company and your web site offer information that's valuable to another site. For example, if you provide information about, say, Las Vegas hotel accommodations or sightseeing in Canada, travel agencies and even full-service credit card/travel service companies may be interested in having you contribute information to their site—with full credit and prominent links for you.

No matter how you arrange to exchange links, you'll meet the most success when you create a situation where sharing or swapping links benefits both you and your new web business partners.

4. How Will You *Promote* Your Site?

This chapter has covered several aspects of web site promotion already. You already know that you need to register with search engines and find other sites with which to swap links. But don't overlook the obvious way to promote your new site: through your existing avenues of promotion.

Do you have business cards and letterhead? Add your URL to them. Make sure every piece of paper that leaves your business has your URL on it. If you're currently advertising in a magazine, newspaper, or even on a community bulletin board, include your URL. Think of your new web site this way: *Today, a web address is as much a part of your business address as your phone number.* Over the last ten years or so, fax machines have become so ubiquitous that no business is without fax capability. A web site will soon be the same.

Be warned, though: your best audience for your web site is *already* on the Web. You're biting off a huge piece of the marketing enchilada, so to speak, if you're planning to educate your customers to the benefits of the Web, convince them to connect to the Web, then to visit your web site. If none of your target audience is on the Web, then maybe you need to find one that *is*.

NOTE: *You can also promote your web site through paid advertisements on other sites. However, web advertising is a tricky, volatile arrangement wherein both prices and standards of measurement change more quickly than a two-year-old's temperament. If you're set on using paid ads for your site's promotion, you need to consult a professional agency with experience in interactive media promotion.*

Once you've promoted your site and plastered your URL on everything but your office cat, you may be tempted to relax. Don't. Instead, maintain your promotional efforts but turn your attention to another aspect of effective promotion: promoting the benefits of *returning* to your site.

The best customers, as any successful business professional will tell you, are repeat customers. These repeat customers or repeat visitors are the lifeblood of your web site as well. You need to give web visitors a reason to return to your site regularly so that you can talk to, market to, and sell to them again and again.

Insider Tip

Internet technology like that provided in Corel WordPerfect Suite 8 can provide unprecedented abilities for you to listen to what your customers have to say. As you get their feedback through e-mail or web forms, you have the ability to fine-tune your site to fit their needs exactly. For more ideas about using technology to effectively market your products and services, consult these excellent books, both by Don Peppers and Martha Rogers, Ph.D.: *The One to One Future: Building Relationships One Customer at a Time* (mentioned earlier) and *Enterprise One to One: Tools for Competing in the Interactive Age* (Doubleday Currency, 1997).

If you've answered all the questions so far in this chapter, you've probably got a pretty good idea why people would want to come to your web site. But as with any other promotional effort, on the Web people love certain things:

- They love to feel they're being listened to.

- They love to get something for nothing.

- They love getting something that feels exclusive.

Each of these is both a reason to visit and to return to your site. Can you offer opportunities for people to tell you what they think about your new products? Can they tell you about what types of products they'd like to see? Can they tell you why they're visiting, or about themselves?

And, most importantly, can you give them an incentive for telling you who they are? Perhaps you might give away a prize every day, week, or month. Or you might offer to send them a special electronic product they can't get elsewhere.

Besides contests, people love giveaways—and if you give away something to them regularly, they'll return. Perhaps you can offer a special electronic goody, a new one every few days, that's theirs for just visiting your site. Or maybe you offer a few questions they'll need to answer before they download the new freebie—just to help you get to know them better. (If you ever doubt that people love giveaways, visit a trade show booth—like one at the giant computer show, Softbank COMDEX. People will listen with great intensity to exorbitant marketing claims just for the chance of winning a free T-shirt.) For example, Amazon.com, the online bookseller, offers frequent contests with prizes ranging from books to computer hardware (Figure 2-5).

Insider Tip

Many experienced webmasters recommend that you change *something* on your site at least every two or three days. Daily is nice—but most people don't have time to return every day. When you change something on your site—especially your home page—every couple of days, the *perception* of your site being dynamic and up to date is nearly the same as changing it every day. Some recommend making noticeable changes—a new offer, prize, or news item—on your home page on Mondays, Wednesdays, and Fridays. Weekly is acceptable. Updating your site anything less than weekly is unacceptable if you hope to get reasonable results from your site.

Besides feeling important (through feedback mechanisms that trigger automated e-mail responses, if not personal replies) and feeling valued (through your giving them free stuff), people like to feel like they're *in the know*. You can help them feel this way—part of the in crowd—by providing them information they can't get elsewhere. You don't have to be a news agency to provide this. Do you have a research department? Do you publish any kind of industry statistics? Do you track any information that you can safely share with the world?

For example, if the Fictitious Company manufactures flummox capacitors, they probably monitor the world supply of flummox ore. They might offer a daily update on the wholesale price of that ore, or perhaps even the levels of flummox reserves in the world. As any public relations professional will tell you, this kind of information helps you promote your company as the expert in your field—and helps your company's name become related with the industry you want to dominate.

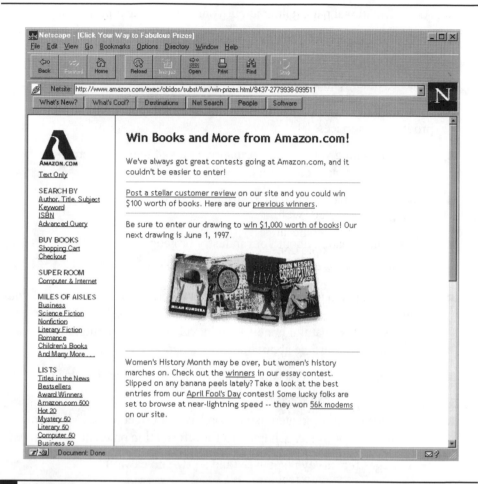

FIGURE 2-5   Amazon.com offers a nice range of prizes to promote site interactivity—and to encourage visitors to add value to the site (www.amazon.com).

Ideas for Site Structure and Contents

Now that you know what you want to achieve with your web site, you can decide what elements your site needs to realize these goals. As you plan the structure of your web site, you'll need to decide what pieces it will contain. Your web site's possible contents are as different as your possible goals, but here are a few ideas to get you started:

- An informational page telling about your company and products.

- A "how to contact us" page with e-mail, address, phone, and fax information.

- Links to other related sites or partners.

- Links to news or other information that relates to your company's products or services.

- Pages containing your own information that's of general interest—to both current and potential customers.

- Links to affiliated companies, distributors, or franchisees (or links to their content).

- Links to information about your industry or geographical area.

- Links to search engines.

- Links to related magazine articles or other information that helps sell your product. For example, an apiary might point to articles that show the health benefits of natural honey. Or a bicycle repair shop might link to a cycle magazine's article about bike maintenance.

- Pages that contain purchasable products (or even gift certificates for a service) and that support secure transactions.

- Special form pages (created using Corel WordPerfect 8's HTML form tools) for purchases (see Chapter 13 for information on creating forms).

- Form pages for survey responses (and a prize giveaway).

- A page of what's new on the web site.

- A page of survey results and a contest winner profile.

- Pages of product information (benefits and features).

- Pages of customer information.

- Customer case studies and testimonials.

- Your company's press releases.

- Coupons that people print and bring into your store (Express does this at **www.express.style.com**).

- Form pages for mail-in or fax-in orders.

- Updated, full price listings and product availability.

- Links to downloadable software.

Insider Tip

If you're linking to software someone else has created—and you've gotten their permission to do so—you may want to consider linking to the file's location on *their* server, not on yours. Why? Simple: if you store a file on your web site, you'll need to remain vigilant to make sure it's always the latest version. If you link to a file stored elsewhere, in many cases they'll update the file consistently with the newest version. If the filename changes, you can use a utility such as Corel's WEB.SiteBuilder to ensure that your web site's links are up to date. That's much easier than keeping watch on all the file versions available so you can copy them to your web server.

Once you've decided what pieces you'll need, you can build a structure. In Chapter 4, you'll learn about building site structures using Corel WordPerfect's automated tools. But it's a good idea for you to sketch the structure on your own beforehand.

For example, one of the most crucial decisions you can make has to do with your *home page*—the central page from which all other pages in your site will be accessed. You'll need to strike a balance between *depth* and *width*. In other words, you will want to provide enough depth—vertical structure—to your site that people will always have something to discover. But if you provide too many levels to your web site, it will be needlessly complex and people will have difficulty finding the information they need. Also, you will want to provide just the right amount of width, or horizontal structure. Provide a variety of choices on your home page—enough to help people find the information they need. But if you provide too many choices, people will be confused and may avoid making any choice at all. The ideal balance of width and depth provides a handful of choices on the home page—and only a handful of levels below.

Justifying Your Site

One of the hardest parts of building a web site is justifying the expense. Now, with Corel WordPerfect Suite, creating the contents and even the structure doesn't cost anything beyond what you've already spent on first-class business software. In fact, with Corel WordPerfect Suite 8 Professional's WEB.SiteBuilder, uploading, organizing, and maintaining your web pages is a snap as well. But you'll still be investing your own time and effort. And you'll most probably be spending some money on having someone host your web site and handle the web server end of things. You may even spend some cash on additional web server services.

To justify this expenditure in time, effort, and money, you will need to consider several factors. These issues will remain the same, no matter whether you're justifying it all to your boss, to your business partners, or even to yourself. Here are a few areas you may want to look at as you find ways to build a solid business case for the expense:

- Can you estimate the number of people who will learn about your products or services? If so, is it a reasonable expense as part of your marketing budget?

- Do you plan to sell products or services? Can you make a conservative guess as to how many you will sell?

- Will placing information on your web site *save* you money? Can you place technical support information, frequently requested data, or other information on your web site? Will this information save your support operators, sales staff, or others time and effort? Will it increase your customer responsiveness?

- Will creating an *intranet* (a mini-Internet that's accessible only inside your company) help your company be more responsive to customers, coordinate among departments, or sell more products?

- Finally, will creating a web site—or placing additional information on it—give you a competitive advantage? Will you be positioning yourself ahead of the competition (or even just catching up to them)?

No matter which of these you find appropriate to your web site and its goals, if your web site's expenses don't make business sense—but you feel strongly that you need to be on the Web—consider using the tools you already have in Corel

WordPerfect Suite to create the site. Unless it takes you away from another activity that provides income, the Web is so important to business today that you can't afford to ignore it.

Insider Tip

Many businesspeople who have successfully built web sites find the most effective way to launch them—and justify their expense—is to integrate them into existing strategies. For example, if you're working to increase the availability of technical support documents and product information sheets to your customers, the Web is an integral part of a strategy that might include voice-response systems and fax-back services. If the Web fits into what you're already doing, it's more likely to deliver tangible, measurable results.

Now that you've sharpened your vision of what you want your web site to be, contain, and achieve, it's time to learn what Corel WordPerfect Suite can do to help you accomplish it.

How Corel WordPerfect Suite
Works with the Web

WordPerfect (the word processor) has a distinguished history of "firsts," among them that it was the first word processor to support web page authoring with its free Internet Publisher add-in for WordPerfect 6.1 for Windows (integrated into later versions of the software). Because Corel knows that the Web is important to every business, web and Internet capabilities are integrated into every application in the suite.

What's in the Suite

Let's look at the features provided by the two versions of Corel WordPerfect Suite 8. Table 3-1 lists the products in Corel WordPerfect Suite 8 and Corel WordPerfect Suite 8 Professional. (Note: Exact components may vary upon final release.)

Corel WordPerfect Suite 8	Corel WordPerfect Suite 8 Professional
Corel WordPerfect 8	Corel WordPerfect 8
Corel Quattro Pro 8	Corel Quattro Pro 8
Corel Presentations 8	Corel Presentations 8
Corel Photo House 2.0	
	Corel Paradox 8
Envoy 7 (viewer)	Envoy 7 (full product)
CorelCENTRAL with integrated Netscape Communicator 4.0 (when available)	CorelCENTRAL with integrated Netscape Communicator 4.0 (when available)
	Corel Time Line
Fonts, clip art, and photos	Fonts, clip art, and photos
Software Development Kit (SDK)	Software Development Kit (SDK)
Bonus applications including QuickView Plus, Internet access, etc.	Bonus applications including QuickView Plus, Internet access, etc.

Comparing Corel WordPerfect Suite 8 and Corel WordPerfect Suite 8 Professional

Note: If you use Corel WordPerfect Suite 8 Professional in your corporation, your suite may also contain a license for Novell GroupWise.

TABLE 3-1

TIP: *Even if you're familiar with the suite, be sure to spend at least a few minutes looking over this section. If you're like most people, it's easy to focus on the part of the suite you use the most and to forget about the parts you use less often.*

Both versions contain useful, straightforward tools for creating, converting, publishing, and maintaining web pages and web sites. Each application gets a Java boost from Corel's exclusive Barista technology, too. Corel Barista helps you go past what you can do with plain-vanilla HTML and create web pages with layouts that more closely resemble a printed page. Getting started with web publishing is a snap with the Internet publishing features found in Corel WordPerfect 8, Corel Presentations 8, and Corel Quattro Pro 8. Polish your pages with loads of bonus clipart, photos, and fonts. Finally, "bonus" applications (like Envoy, Corel Photo House, and more) complete the suite's full complement of web site tools to help you produce cross-platform, layout-rich documents and to create, design, and maintain web sites.

Corel WordPerfect Suite 8 is designed especially for professionals working in a small business or home office. Corel WordPerfect Suite 8 Professional contains all the applications in Corel WordPerfect Suite 8 except for Photo House. It costs a bit more and is specifically designed for power users or for people using it in a large company. Of course, the additional power in the Professional suite is for anyone who needs the extra capabilities it offers (specifically, Corel Paradox 8 and Corel Time Line).

Insider Tip

Because Corel WordPerfect Suite 8 was ready for prime time *before* Netscape was ready with their new Netscape Communicator package, the initial shipments of Corel WordPerfect Suite 8 are planned to ship without Netscape Communicator. However, they will contain a way to get the software once it's released so it can be integrated with the suite. At the time this book was written, Corel WordPerfect Suite 8 Professional would wait for release until Netscape Communicator was ready—a delay of a few months. Later shipments of Corel WordPerfect Suite 8 (the regular version) will contain Netscape Communicator, fully integrated with CorelCENTRAL as it will be in the Professional suite. Corel WordPerfect Suite will contain all the

Insider Tip (continued)

Personal Information Manager (PIM) features in CorelCENTRAL. These include calendaring, scheduling, the suitewide Address Book, and a Cardfile. The Professional suite version of CorelCENTRAL will contain all these features plus web browsing (Netscape Navigator 4.0), e-mail (Netscape Messenger), web page authoring (Netscape Composer), collaborative discussion groups (Netscape Collabra), and desktop real-time conferencing (Netscape Conference).

Corel and Open Standards

Corel WordPerfect Suite 8 features collaborative tools based on *open standards.* Open standards mean that the documents you create can be saved in formats that can be read using a wide variety of software applications and platforms (see Figure 3-1). Other Corel products in the suite, especially CorelCENTRAL with Netscape Communicator, are also based on these open, widely accepted standards.

Open standards, such as POP3 e-mail, mean that you can collaborate and communicate with anyone, anywhere, using any software. Corel doesn't develop "standards" that are theirs alone. Instead, they rely on specifications put forth by standards bodies such as the "W3" (short for World Wide Web) consortium and others—groups that aren't tied or beholden to any specific applications vendor or computing platform.

That's why each application in Corel WordPerfect Suite 8 supports standard file formats like HTML. HTML has become the *lingua franca* for sharing information with anyone using any kind of computer or software. Each application supports e-mail software standards like POP3 and SMTP (standard mail transport protocol)—common, Internet-based ways of communicating.

As a side note, Corel WordPerfect is the only word processor that supports standard generalized markup language (SGML) without a costly, burdensome add-on product. Corel WordPerfect's SGML abilities come built in to Corel WordPerfect Suite 8 and are smoothly integrated into the word processor. SGML has become a standard for formatted, archived documents regardless of computing platform (it's the original markup language that spawned HTML).

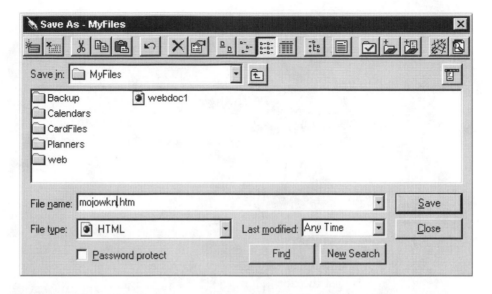

FIGURE 3-1   Corel WordPerfect Suite supports open standards like HTML through tight integration, even when you're just saving a file.

About Each Suite Component

Although this book focuses specifically on creating web documents, web sites, and web-related projects, the latest version of the suite includes strong tools to help you organize your work as well. CorelCENTRAL integrates with each suite application to help you track your time, your contacts, and other essential data. Unlike any other suite organizer, it integrates Netscape Communicator to help you put that information to work as you gather information from the Internet and share it with others.

In case you're not familiar with the general capabilities of each component of Corel WordPerfect Suite 8, take a look at Table 3-2.

 NOTE: *Descriptions of features and components of the suite are based on the U.S. English version. Other territories may have slightly different versions.*

Component	Description
Corel WordPerfect 8	This word processing program offers new features like the shadow cursor and updated web abilities to make quick work of Internet-related documents.
Corel Quattro Pro 8	This spreadsheet program helps you analyze and present data. Spreadsheets can link to the Internet to help persuade and explain using data.
Corel Presentations 8	This combines bitmap and vector drawing tools with business presentation abilities. Use it to create graphic images and effective presentations on the computer screen, on paper, or on the Web.
Envoy 7	This electronically distributes documents with formatting intact. This new version supports links to the Web and among Envoy files. Envoy helps you preserve page size, graphic quality, and font fidelity in electronic documents.
Corel Paradox 8 (Professional suite only)	Use this new version of the popular relational database software package to create data manipulation tools and data storage applications, or to help manage your business information.
CorelCENTRAL	Use this (with the integrated Netscape Communicator) to manage your personal information. You can access your Address Book, schedule, calendar, and more from any suite application. With Netscape Communicator you can also find information and share it using collaborative tools like e-mail and web-based conferencing.

The Main
Suite
Applications
and
Components

TABLE 3-2

Component	Description
Corel WEB.SiteBuilder (Professional suite only)	This makes designing, creating, and maintaining web sites easier. Its visual interface displays a web site's organization in a tree format. It also includes templates and styles to help you portray a consistent, professional image.
Corel Photo House 2.0 (Regular suite only)	Use this to quickly edit photos (even remove red-eye!) and web graphics.
Corel Time Line (Professional suite only)	This professional project-management system helps you coordinate complex projects, resources, and tasks.
Corel Barista	This exclusive Corel technology lets you publish documents to Java-enhanced HTML. This special format, readable in virtually any browser, preserves more page formatting than plain HTML. It's integrated into Corel WordPerfect 8, Corel Quattro Pro 8, and Corel Presentations 8.
DAD (Desktop Application Director)	This unique utility places in the Windows 95 taskbar special icons to applications and abilities of Corel WordPerfect Suite 8.
Corel Versions	This helps you track versions of documents among multiple people, places, and revisions. It's integrated into the Windows 95 environment.
Corel VisualDTD	If you're creating structured documents using SGML, you'll not only know what a Document Type Definition (DTD) is, but you'll also appreciate this utility. Corel VisualDTD helps you lay out document structures visually and creates DTDs painlessly.

The Main Suite Applications and Components (*continued*)

TABLE 3-2

Component	Description
Fonts	These TrueType and Type 1 fonts, organized by style and appearance, are only useful in web documents if you use them to create web graphics or you publish your web pages using Corel Barista or Envoy.
Clipart images	Choose from thousands of images to use in your web documents. Use the included thumbnail reference book to help.
Photos	Use these professional stock photographs in your web documents.
Software Development Kit (SDK)	This helps you develop applications that tap into Corel WordPerfect Suite's abilities. Electronic documentation is included.
Bonus applications	Extra-value programs such as QuickView Plus, Bitstream Font Navigator 2.0, Internet access, and more.
Grolier Encyclopedia	

The Main Suite Applications and Components (*continued*)

TABLE 3-2

About the Suite's Internet Features

Corel WordPerfect Suite and Corel WordPerfect were the first business software products to include tightly integrated HTML and web publishing tools. Each application in the new Corel WordPerfect Suite includes Internet tools appropriate to the application's most common use. For example, Corel Paradox doesn't really create layout-rich web pages—but you don't expect it to. For that, you turn to Corel WordPerfect 8.

Each major suite application reads and writes HTML and can link to the Web or to other Internet resources. Corel WordPerfect Suite 8 offers everything you need to become a powerhouse web publisher—broad Internet support mixed with unique web tools.

Web Features in Corel WordPerfect 8

There is almost no HTML layout tool that isn't supported in Corel WordPerfect 8—from forms to nested tables, from sounds to embedded Java applets. But the best

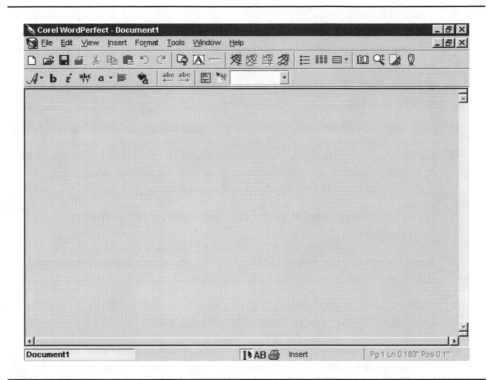

FIGURE 3-2   Take a sneak peek at Corel WordPerfect's web editing environment. In later chapters, you'll learn more about the tools and special property bars that help you create web documents quickly.

part of Corel WordPerfect's web support is that it provides all Corel WordPerfect's power in its familiar interface (and the interface itself is even better this time around). Version 8 provides one-click access between Corel WordPerfect's standard editing environment and a special web page environment (see Figure 3-2) that puts web tools at your fingertips along with Corel WordPerfect's features. You can even use the Web Page Expert to create basic pages and even sites.

When you're done creating or converting Corel WordPerfect documents for the Web, the Internet Publisher makes it easy to publish documents to HTML, Corel Barista, or Envoy. Here are a few highlights of Corel WordPerfect 8's web support:

■ *Comprehensive HTML forms support* makes it easy to get visitor feedback and to make your site interactive. You can gather information using web pages with advanced abilities such as radio buttons, check boxes, drop-down lists, and more. (See Chapter 13.)

- *QuickLinks* automatically recognize text as you type it. If the phrase starts with "www," "ftp," "http," "mailto," or the like, Corel WordPerfect automatically converts the text to a hypertext link. It can also turn phrases you specify—like "contact us"—into hypertext links (in this example, an e-mail link to the webmaster or a hypertext link to your contact information page). (See Chapter 9.)

- *Java applets* can be embedded into any web document. (See Chapter 12.)

- *Supports all HTML table features,* including shading and relative row/column sizing, except the little used and not widely accepted COL and COLGROUP HTML tags. (See Chapter 10.)

- *Hypertext linking* is now even easier and supports target frames. (See Chapter 9.)

- *Supports a wide range of HTML graphics features*, such as positioning, size, border space, and so on. (See Chapters 7 and 8.)

- Uses *columns* to turn column-based Corel WordPerfect page layouts to table-based HTML documents. (See Chapter 10.)

- *Unique SGML and XML support* is integrated throughout the program. With a mouse-click during installation, you can install comprehensive support and special tools for standardized documents. (See Chapter 12.)

- You can *edit an existing HTML document* in a way no other word processor can. When you've installed the SGML abilities, HTML does not change when you load an HTML document. Using these SGML abilities, you can edit HTML from forms to frames, from common to arcane without gumming up the page's original HTML tags. (See Chapter 12.)

- *Supports international standards* by means of SGML features that provide a graphical interface to create structured documents. Government agencies and major industries increasingly demand open, cross-platform, nonproprietary document formats. Corel WordPerfect 8 is the *only* major word processor to offer this extensive SGML support. (See Chapter 12.)

You'll learn more about Corel WordPerfect's web abilities in Part 2. It covers creating web pages with Corel WordPerfect in depth.

Web Features in Corel Quattro Pro 8

Corel Quattro Pro isn't just a spreadsheet. Instead, it's a tool designed to help you make sense of numbers—not just for yourself, but also as you present them to others. It's a powerful analysis tool, even though it can do all the cool financial, algebraic, and statistical calculations as well. Of course, it will create charts and graphs with only a few clicks.

These abilities are reflected in Corel Quattro Pro's web abilities, too (see Chapter 15). Each of these basic abilities is web enabled. Here's a quick look at some of the new, key features in Corel Quattro Pro 8:

- You can *link spreadsheet cells* to other spreadsheet cells or web documents stored *anywhere* on a local network, intranet, or on the Internet (see Figure 3-3). They'll automatically update themselves to ensure you have the latest information. Corel Quattro Pro's HTML import abilities have been enhanced to preserve more of the original web document's formatting.

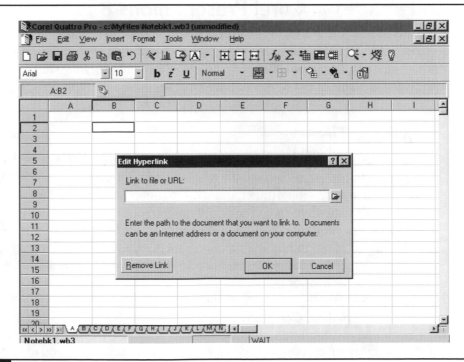

FIGURE 3-3   Corel Quattro Pro adds web abilities to all its core functions. You can even link spreadsheet cells to locations on the Internet.

- Corel Quattro Pro now includes an easy-to-use *Internet Expert*. This special tool makes publishing both spread sheets and notebooks (files that contain multiple spreadsheet "pages") simple.

- *You can write (or "save as") HTML files* to distribute spreadsheets across intranets and the Internet regardless of whether others have Corel Quattro Pro or are even using Windows 95.

- If you want to *share Corel Quattro Pro documents across the Internet,* again, regardless of whether others use Corel Quattro Pro or Windows 95, you can publish your spreadsheets to Corel Barista. Corel Barista not only preserves the spreadsheet information, but also uses Java technology to preserve formatting and graphic elements like charts in the HTML document.

- If you need to *look up something quickly on the Web,* you can launch your browser with just a click.

Web Features in Corel Presentations 8

Corel Presentations 8 has two key functions for web publishers. First, it's an illustration package that makes creating graphics for use on web pages a snap. Second, it's an excellent presentations package that can publish your slides to the Internet just as it would to the screen or for 35mm slides.

Insider Tip

Although Corel Presentations includes drawing tools, if you're planning to create professional illustrations and want a package that's dedicated to professional drawing and illustration, CorelDRAW 7 may be worth a look. Corel has redesigned the interface and added many new features to make web graphic creation easier.

Here's a quick look at new Internet features contained in Corel Presentations:

- Now it's as easy to *share your presentations via the Web* as it would be via the computer screen, paper, or 35mm slides. New features allow you to publish your slides using HTML, Corel Barista, or to special, web-based shows. Since pages are published complete with navigation buttons, web visitors can see the slide show as if it were an onscreen presentation.

- As in Corel WordPerfect, you can *QuickLink* to web pages, ftp sites, e-mail addresses, and other Internet resources.

- Corel Presentations' easy-to-use, integrated *Internet Publisher* (see Figure 3-4) steps you through publishing slides, presentations, or graphics to the Web with enhanced HTML, Corel Barista, or Envoy.

- Pages published to HTML can include *sounds* and *ActiveX* controls. While you're creating the presentation, a new *HTML layout view* lets you see what it'll look like on the Web, complete with new navigation controls.

- *Show It!* places slide shows on the Web, complete with full animation, transitions, sound, video, and more.

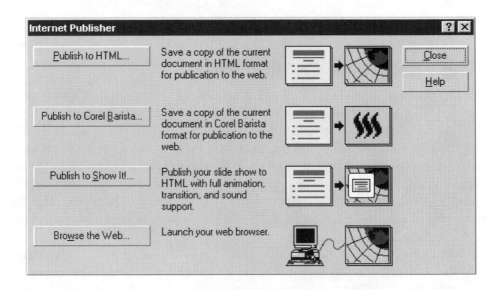

FIGURE 3-4 Corel Presentations integrates web publishing into both its drawing abilities and its presentation abilities. The integrated Internet Publisher makes it easy to create presentations for web distribution.

Web Features in Corel Paradox 8 (Professional Suite Only)

Corel Paradox 8 is a database application for industrial-strength data manipulation and storage. In its newest version, it includes some key features to help you add database capabilities to your web pages and web sites. For example, now you can create dynamic HTML pages that are updated automatically with Corel Paradox tables or reports—as web visitors request them via their browsers.

Corel Paradox also contains two special pieces of web server software. You can use both to create an intranet or a web site on the Internet. The first, the Personal Web Server, is an instant, out-of-the-box web server. You don't need to know how to program anything—just plug it in and go. If you already have a site, you can use the second piece of software—the Borland Web Server Control. This software needs some programming; it's controlled by a custom set of OLE automation methods and properties. (If you don't know what that means, don't worry about it—it's a fairly advanced feature that you probably won't need to use.)

Finally, like other core suite applications, Corel Paradox can import HTML documents so you can use them as data sources.

Web Features in CorelCENTRAL

This application is available after initial release and in Professional Suite only. CorelCENTRAL is part of the glue that holds Corel WordPerfect Suite together. It's truly a *central* place that suite applications—and you—turn to for information. It links address information, calendars, and schedules to projects, people, and things. In this role as personal information manager, CorelCENTRAL is fully web enabled. From entries in the Address Book and cards in the Cardfile database, you can link directly to web sites or other Internet resources. If you want to share your calendars or reports of personal information on the Web, you can easily publish them using Corel Barista 2.0.

But CorelCENTRAL doesn't stop there. Since it's integrated with Netscape Communicator, it contains state-of-the-art web abilities. Netscape Communicator provides CorelCENTRAL with the ability to not just view information on the Web, but also to collaborate, communicate, and conduct business over the Net. Here's a quick look at some of the features (for details, see Chapter 17).

- You can *communicate* with others using advanced e-mail features (Figure 3-5). There's a built-in HTML editor to create e-mail messages that can contain all HTML formatting. Of course, you can send and receive messages and organize them however you like using folders.

- *Coordinating* with others is easy, too. Netscape Communicator helps you assign and track tasks, to-do items, meetings, and appointments over the Internet.

- Netscape Communicator helps you electronically *collaborate* with others no matter where you are. It frees you from the limitations of physical space—none of you has to be in the same place. Instead, you can hold electronic conference calls where you collaborate using an electronic whiteboard. You can hold virtual discussions using Netscape's award-winning Collabra technology.

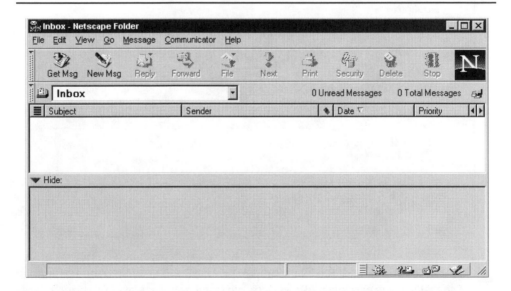

FIGURE 3-5 Netscape Communicator's e-mail module, Netscape Messenger, makes it easy to create and receive e-mail. You can jump to any other module using the Component bar, seen here "docked" in the lower-right corner of the window.

Of course, Netscape Communicator contains Netscape Navigator 4.0, the latest web browser that supports cool web features like HTML style sheets and more. See Figure 3-6 for a view of one of the beta versions of this software.

Netscape Communicator is seamlessly blended with CorelCENTRAL's abilities to both integrate and link among calendar items, Address Book entries, tasks, and more. Like other suite components, it uses industry accepted, open standards for e-mail messages (HTML) and Address Book entries.

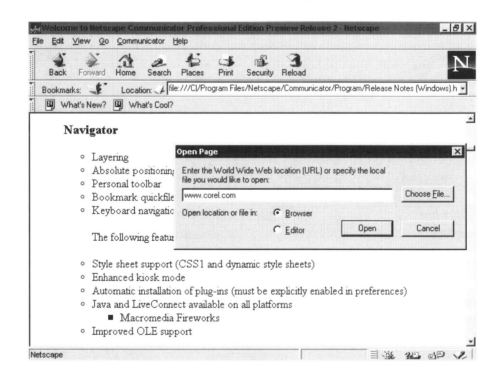

FIGURE 3-6   Netscape Navigator 4.0 provides the latest in web browser abilities. Note that you can even open files in Netscape Composer, Netscape Navigator's HTML-editing counterpart.

Total Web Site Control with Corel WEB.SiteBuilder (Professional Suite Only)

As you can tell from its name, Corel WEB.SiteBuilder doesn't just have *some* web features: it *is* web features. It's an updated version of the software found in Corel's webMaster suite. It makes creating, publishing, and maintaining web sites a snap.

Corel WEB.SiteBuilder completes the web creation package in Corel WordPerfect Suite. While other suite components provide document creation abilities and layout-rich publishing tools, Corel WEB.SiteBuilder complements these page and site creation tools *plus* provides tools to help you upload and maintain files on your web server.

When you're building web pages and web sites, you can use Corel WEB.SiteBuilder's prefab templates to ensure a consistent look on your site. It complements Corel WordPerfect's Web Page Expert to help you create instant site structures. In fact, you can build entire sites by dragging and dropping a premade component from one window to another.

Once you've designed the site, if you've used a predefined style, you can update the entire site simply by applying a new style. Changes are made automatically. And while you're maintaining the site, Corel WEB.SiteBuilder will help you check for outdated or "dead" links.

TIP: *When you're installing Corel WordPerfect Suite, be sure to install all the web features if you're planning to use them. If you don't install them and you change your mind, you can always run the Setup program again to add them. Be sure to add all the HTML templates and filters, Corel Barista, and Corel WEB.SiteBuilder.*

Of course, Corel WordPerfect Suite contains more web features than there is space to list here. You'll find new, web-ready commands in the cross-application PerfectScript macro language. And you'll find new features that help you link to, get information from, and publish to the Web.

But enough introduction. You've learned about planning your web site and web pages, and you've even learned a little about what Corel WordPerfect Suite can help you do (everything). It's time for you to get started creating web pages. Next, you'll learn about using Corel WordPerfect to create web pages (in Part 2). Part 3 will help you create web pages using Corel Quattro Pro, Corel Presentations, Netscape Communicator, CorelCENTRAL, and more. Finally, once you've created your pages, you'll learn in Part 4 about publishing those pages to web-ready formats like HTML, Corel Barista, and Envoy.

PART II

Creating Web Pages with Corel WordPerfect

Instant Web Pages and More

4

To create web pages in the "old" days, you had to know the ins and outs of HTML and do all your troubleshooting using arcane codes and tags. Now Corel WordPerfect Suite offers a wealth of automated tools to help you create both web pages and web sites. Compared to building a web page straight from HTML, using Corel WordPerfect's tools is like making bread with a mix and a bread machine instead of from scratch.

Some of these powerful automated tools, called *PerfectExpert projects*, work across all programs and documents in the suite. They feature a wealth of instant, good-looking documents, which you can use as is or as springboards for customizing. In this chapter, you'll learn how to use the suite's PerfectExpert features to load Corel WordPerfect's automated web page builder, the Web Page Expert. You'll then learn to use the Web Page Expert and even the convenient PerfectExpert tools. Finally, you'll learn to customize your web pages and publish them to HTML format.

Starting PerfectExpert Projects

Since the PerfectExpert projects work across all programs and documents in the suite, you will see them in every Corel WordPerfect Suite application. Just choose File | New. You'll see the New dialog box, shown in Figure 4-1 (the Create New tab is displayed by default when you open this dialog box).

The New Dialog Box

The New dialog box makes it easy for you to get a jump start on the PerfectExpert projects. Since you're reading the section of this book that discusses creating web pages with Corel WordPerfect, odds are you chose File | New from Corel WordPerfect. If you did, you'll see the list of Corel WordPerfect–oriented projects as a default. But you don't have to stick with the projects associated only with your current application. To see other projects, choose from the drop-down menu above the list of projects.

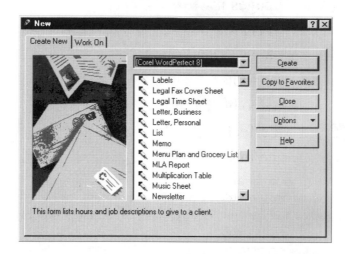

FIGURE 4-1 When you choose File | New in any Corel WordPerfect Suite application, you'll see this dialog box to help you get a quick start on the PerfectExpert projects.

TIP: *Another way to jump to this dialog box* without *having to open a suite application is from the Windows 95 Start menu. Choose Corel WordPerfect Suite 8, then Corel New Project.*

But the best part of the New dialog box is this: you can work on any project regardless of the application you're using. There are several project categories common to all applications that appear on the drop-down list after the projects that are grouped by application. (The application names appear on the list surrounded by brackets, as shown in Figure 4-1). Some of the common project categories include budgets, business forms, investments, and time management.

When you've selected the category you want, scroll through the list of associated projects. Then select a project and click on Create. In a moment, you'll learn how to use this to jump quickly to Corel WordPerfect's Web Page Expert. But first, let's look at the other components on the Create New tab of this dialog box.

TIP: *You don't have to decide if you want to work on a project from the one- or two-word title. At the bottom of the dialog box, a brief description appears as you highlight each project.*

Accessing Frequently Used Projects

Below the Create button is a handy button—if you want to have quick access to projects you frequently use, highlight that project and click on Copy To Favorites. A shortcut will be created in your Favorites folder.

NOTE: *In Windows 95 parlance, a* shortcut *is a small file that points to another file—so you don't keep duplicate files on your hard drive, but can refer to them from different locations.*

To access your Favorites folder—and the projects you have copied there—choose File | Open. Then choose Favorites | Go To/From Favorites (or click the button on the File Open dialog box toolbar that looks like a file folder with a checkmark on it).

Tailoring the Projects to Fit Your Needs

As with most other pieces of the suite, you can customize just about every aspect of these projects. You can even change the premade projects that ship with the suite. Click on the Options button to see the pop-up menu, shown here, which lists the various ways to customize the projects:

From this pop-up menu, you can view and change project properties—including both the project name and its description. You can also add projects—it's a simple way to create automated documents (a special expert, or wizard, walks you through the process). Of course, you can remove projects as well as copy them or move them among categories.

You can also create, rename, and remove categories. Or you can create Corel WordPerfect templates or edit existing ones (*templates* are boilerplate documents—formatting and information that you use more than once—that can even include some automation). If you'd like the New dialog box to appear each time you start Corel WordPerfect, check the Show This Dialog At Startup option. And finally, if you want to create or change your Personal Information—information about you that's automatically loaded into templates and other automated projects—just choose the final option in the list.

The Work On Tab

You'll also notice that the New dialog box contains another tab—the Work On tab. The Work On tab (see Figure 4-2) displays the files most recently opened by use of Corel WordPerfect Suite 8. Check the files you want to open and choose Open.

Like the Create New tab, the Work On tab provides you with more flexibility than just a list of recently opened files would. You can use the Open As Copy option to open any of the files as copies of the original. Or you can choose Browse to use the suite's File Open dialog box to find the document you want to open.

But perhaps the most useful part of the Work On tab's abilities is the preview window. To activate the preview window, check the Preview Document check box

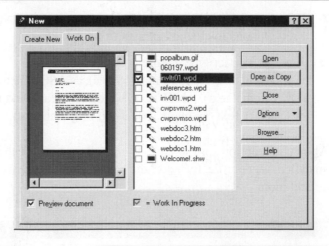

FIGURE 4-2   Use the Work On tab for instant access to recent documents

on the lower left of the dialog box. The left pane becomes a viewer window allowing you to preview any document.

Insider Tip

You're not limited to the default viewer display. Right-click (click the right mouse button instead of the left) on the viewer window for a list of additional options. Here's what they do:

- Tear Off creates a separate window for the viewer pane—more useful on high-resolution displays (1024 x 768 and above).

- Content displays the file's contents only as text—without any formatting.

- Page View displays the file's contents with page formatting intact—and squeezes the entire page into the viewer window.

- Size brings up a submenu that allows you to resize the document within the viewer pane (if you've already chosen to "tear it off"): to its Original Size, to fit the Window, or to fit the Window Width (without margins).

- Find allows you to search for text within the document without opening it.

- Print lets you print the document without opening it (choose Print Options to change settings first).

- View As also lets you choose how the document is viewed—in its original format (Native), as ASCII Text (DOS-format text), ANSI Text (Windows' default text format), or Unicode Text (an international text-only standard).

About is an option for the curious—it tells you about the viewer, the installed viewer file formats, the version of the viewer you're using, and more.

Now that you've learned about how Corel WordPerfect Suite helps you quickly start projects and open recent documents, here's a brief look at what to expect from Corel WordPerfect's Web Page Expert.

Installing the Web Page Expert

Corel's PerfectExpert provides you with a powerful set of tools for web page creation. But they're not installed into the program by default.

You'll have to install the Web Page Expert using Corel WordPerfect Suite's Setup program. It's pretty easy to do, but takes a few minutes (luckily, you don't need to reinstall the whole program). Make sure you've inserted the suite CD-ROM in your CD-ROM drive, then read on:

1. From the Windows 95 Start menu, choose Corel WordPerfect Suite 8, Setup and Tools, Corel WordPerfect Suite Setup.

2. Choose the default options on each screen (just press ENTER) until you see the Installation type window:

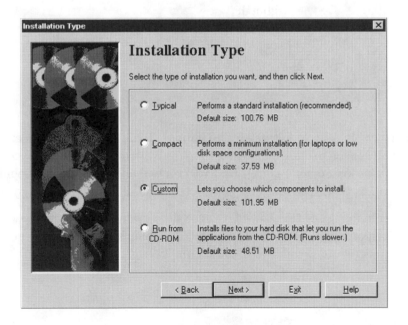

3. Choose Custom, then click the Next button.

Now comes the fun part. Since you've already installed Corel WordPerfect Suite, you don't need to reinstall it. But in order to avoid installing the whole suite over again, you'll need to uncheck all the checked options, shown below in the Custom Installation dialog box:

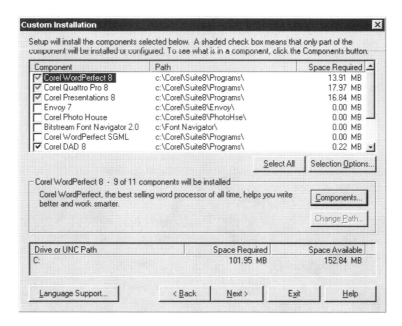

4. Uncheck each of the preselected options. To deselect shaded checkboxes, you'll need to click the selection twice—with a short pause between each click (don't double-click). The program will tell you that you shouldn't skip essential parts of the application, but tell it to skip them anyway.

5. From the list of Corel WordPerfect 8 components, choose the PerfectExpert Project Files option. You'll then see a list of PerfectExpert project groups, with two of these groups checked by default:

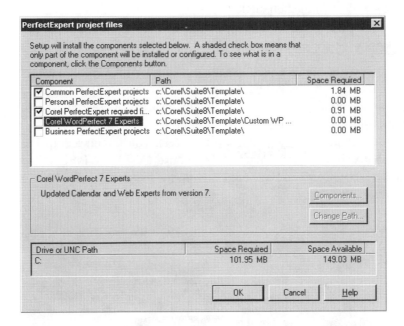

6. Select only the Corel WordPerfect 7 Experts option. (Unselect the others.)

7. Choose OK to return to the Custom Installation window.

 TIP: *If you haven't already installed Corel Barista, covered in Chapter 18, you might want to choose the Accessories: Corel Barista option while you're at it.*

8. Choose <u>N</u>ext, then <u>I</u>nstall to begin the installation process.

When the installation finishes, you'll have the Web Page Expert ready to go. You'll learn how to fire it up next.

Instant Web Pages with the Web Page Expert

The easiest way to create a web page using Corel WordPerfect Suite is to use the Web Page Expert. This expert works as if it were the office guru, leaning over your shoulder and "holding your hand" through the process of creating a basic web page.

To choose the web project you want to create, choose File | New (or get to the New dialog box in whatever manner you prefer). You'll then see the PerfectExpert window that was shown in Figure 4-1. Choose Custom WP Templates from the drop-down list, select Web Page Expert from the list that appears, then click on the Create button.

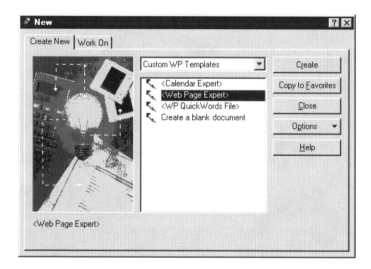

Getting Started with the Web Page Expert

The Web Page Expert—also known as the Create Web Page QuickTask—is the easiest, fastest, and most painless way to create web pages with Corel WordPerfect. When the Web Page Expert gets down to work, it may warn you with the message "Please Wait: Loading Web Page template." You'll then see a full screen view of a sample web page and the first Web Page Expert window (see Figure 4-3). From here on, it's simply a matter of filling in blanks in a series of windows.

Choosing a New Folder for Your Web Page

As you can see in Figure 4-3, the first thing the Web Page Expert will ask you is to name a new folder or subdirectory where you want your web page stored. Corel WordPerfect asks you to name a new folder so that it can keep close track of all the files that contribute to the web page you're creating. This is important: if all the files you need are in one folder, you can upload all the files in that folder to your web site without having to hunt around your hard drive for all the files you need.

[Web Page Title]

Type a brief paragraph explaining the purpose of this web page.

Contents

My Hobbies and Interests

My Personal Background

My Professional Information

Last Updated on June 2, 1997 by

> **Web Page Expert**
>
> This Expert will help you create a web page that you can publish on the Internet.
>
> To begin, type the name of a NEW folder where your web page will be saved.
>
> New folder name:
>
> c:\myfiles\website
>
> Next >
> < Previous
> Cancel

FIGURE 4-3   The first screen in the Web Page Expert. Note the blank web page template in the background.

You can enter the name of your web page's new folder in two ways:

- In the New Folder Name text box, type the full path of the folder you want to create. For example, you might type **c:\myfiles\web1**.

- If you want to browse the folders on your computer to choose the folder you want to create, click the file folder button to the right of the New Folder Name text box.

You'll then see the Select Location dialog box—which works just like the Corel WordPerfect Suite File Open dialog box. (If you need assistance using the File Open dialog box, choose Help | Help Topics or press F1.) Choose the folder you want and choose Select.

Once you've entered a new folder name, choose Next or press ENTER to move on to the next step.

 NOTE: *If you type the name of a folder that already exists, you'll get the Folder Already Exists dialog box. Choose OK to return to the Select Location dialog box and have another chance to enter a new folder name.*

Entering a Page Title, Your Name, and E-Mail Address

After you've chosen a new folder for your web page files, Corel WordPerfect will prompt you for a name for the web page, your name, and your e-mail address:

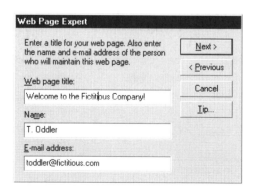

As mentioned earlier in the book, you will want to have a good idea of what you're planning to do with the page before you start it. Here's the reason: Corel WordPerfect wants to know the name of the page before you've even started it.

The Web Page Expert creates a personal home page, but it's easy to customize the page to create a company or business-related web page. The examples in this book will concentrate on creating company web pages.

To complete this next step of the expert:

1. In the <u>W</u>eb Page Title text box, type the name you want to give the web page. For example, you might type **Welcome to the Fictitious Company!** Press TAB to move to the next text box.

TIP: *Choose the <u>T</u>ip button to see Corel WordPerfect's hints on naming your web page. Corel WordPerfect suggests that you choose a descriptive name, not something vague and wordy. Choose OK to return to the Web Page Expert.*

2. In the Na<u>m</u>e text box, type your name if you're going to be maintaining the page. If someone else will be maintaining the web page, type that name instead. For example, you might type the name **T. Oddler**. Press TAB to move to the next text box.

TIP: *In both the Na<u>m</u>e and <u>E</u>-mail Address text boxes, Corel WordPerfect will automatically fill in the blanks with the default personal information stored in the Corel Address Book. If you're happy with what Corel WordPerfect has already typed for you, just skip ahead to step 4.*

3. In the <u>E</u>-mail Address text box, type your e-mail address if you're going to be maintaining the page. If someone else will be maintaining the web page, type that e-mail address instead. For example, you might type the address **toddler@fictitious.com**.

4. When you've completed all three text boxes, choose <u>N</u>ext or press ENTER to move to the next window.

TIP: *If you want to change a previous entry in the Web Page Expert, just choose <u>P</u>revious to return to the previous screen.*

Creating Your Home Page's
Table of Contents

Corel WordPerfect creates a table of contents on your home page with a list of categories, or subpages. These categories will appear as links that connect to the related pages Corel WordPerfect automatically creates and places in the proper directory for you—all you have to do is add the information you want on each page.

Corel WordPerfect presents you with three default pages:

- My Hobbies and Interests

- My Personal Background

- My Professional Information

In addition to these three categories, you can add any of your own, then choose which you want to use. For example, since the Fictitious Company example is a business page, not a personal home page, you might want to uncheck all three of the default categories and use some of your own, like these (see Figure 4-4):

- How to Contact Us

- Products and Services

- Special Offers

To tell the Web Page Expert which of the default categories and subpages you want to use and to add new subpages and categories:

1. In the Table of Contents box, uncheck the boxes next to whichever of the three default pages you don't want to use.

2. Choose Add. Corel WordPerfect will display the Add a Page dialog box.

3. In the Page name dialog box, type the name of the page you want to add to your table of contents and press ENTER or choose OK.

4. Repeat steps 1 and 2 to add as many categories as you want.

For example, if you were to create the sample home page for the Fictitious Company, you would first uncheck each of the three default categories, then choose Add three times to add the three business-related categories shown in Figure 4-4.

Welcome to the Fictitious Company!

Type a brief paragraph explaining the purpose of this web page.

Contents

How to Contact Us

Products and Services

Special Offers

Last Updated on June 2, 1997 by T. Oddler

> **Web Page Expert**
>
> Select or add the pages that will appear in the table of contents of your web page.
>
> Table of contents:
> - ☑ How to Contact Us
> - ☐ My Hobbies and Interests
> - ☐ My Personal Background
> - ☐ My Professional Information
> - ☑ Products and Services
> - ☑ Special Offers
>
> Add...
>
> Next >
> < Previous
> Cancel

FIGURE 4-4   Choose the default pages you want to use or even create your own

Corel WordPerfect will automatically check the boxes next to the categories you create. If for some reason you change your mind about a category you've added, just uncheck the box (you can't delete a category once it's listed).

Insider Tip

Corel WordPerfect will place the categories you create in alphabetical order, whether you want them that way or not. To avoid having your pages reordered, you can think of clever ways to name your pages so they're in the order you want them. Or you might place a number at the beginning of each category so they'll be sorted in numerical order. Or just wait until the Web Page Expert is finished; then cut and paste the categories where you want them.

To move on to the next window in the Web Page Expert, choose <u>N</u>ext.

Choosing Design Elements for Your Home Page

Here's the most fun part of the Web Page Expert: customizing its design. While you're limited to the design elements Corel WordPerfect provides, it offers such a variety of them that you may not need any others. Of course, you can always change any of these elements once you've selected them (you'll learn how in the next chapter as well as in Chapter 11). The Web Page Expert will help you choose a color scheme, background, and text justification for your home page from the dialog box shown in Figure 4-5.

Choosing a Color Scheme

Your home page's color scheme will include colors for the page background, text, and text links.

To set a color scheme for your web pages, simply choose the color scheme you want from the Color <u>S</u>cheme drop-down list. As you select each color scheme, Corel WordPerfect will automatically update the web page in the background so you can see what colors it includes. You can also refer to Table 4-1 to see the color of each element in each color scheme.

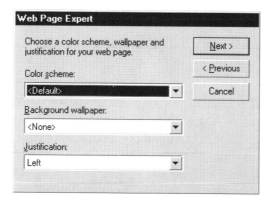

FIGURE 4-5   Choose the color scheme, background, and text justification you want for your home page

Scheme	Text Color	Link Color	Background Color
<Default>	Black	Dark Blue	Light Gray
Black	White	Yellow	Black
Dark Blue	White	Yellow	Dark Blue
Cyan	Black	Yellow	Cyan (Light Blue)
Dark Gray	Black	Yellow	Dark Gray
Green	White	Yellow	Green
Khaki	Black	Yellow	Khaki (Green)
Maroon	White	Yellow	Maroon
Mauve	White	Yellow	Mauve
Purple	White	Yellow	Purple
Steel Blue	White	Yellow	Steel (Gray) Blue
Wallpaper Dark *	White	Yellow	Black
Wallpaper Light *	Black	Dark Blue	White
White	Black	Dark Blue	White
Yellow	Black	Dark Blue	Yellow

Colors of
Each Element
in the Web
Page Expert's
Color
Schemes

* These schemes are designed for use with either dark or light bitmaps to use as "wallpaper," or page backgrounds.

TABLE 4-1

NOTE: *If you're planning to set a background bitmap for your home pages, choose either the Wallpaper Light or Wallpaper Dark color schemes. If you choose another scheme, the background color will be hidden by the background bitmap you choose.*

When you're ready for the next step of the Web Page Expert, press TAB to move to the next dialog box.

Setting a Background Bitmap

If you've explored the Web at any length, you've probably encountered a web site that uses a small, tiled bitmap image as a background for its pages. Corel WordPerfect's Web Page Expert makes it easy for you to do the same kind of thing using any background image from its library. (You can also choose images that aren't in the library, but you'll learn to do that in the next chapter.)

Corel WordPerfect's library offers a wide range of images for just about any kind of home page. Look at Table 4-2 for a description of each background bitmap image, its default color scheme (Wallpaper Light or Wallpaper Dark), and the file size.

The file size of each of these GIF (Graphics Interchange Format) images is important. Why? When your page is viewed, smaller background images mean your page will display that much faster—and your page is more likely to be read, not skipped. As a general rule, you want to strike a good balance between compact file size and the most effective image for your design.

Insider Tip

Corel WordPerfect automatically changes the color scheme to match the recommendation. But you don't have to use what Corel WordPerfect recommends—for example, you may prefer the Wallpaper Light color scheme with both the Blue Terra and Cotton wallpapers. Just select your wallpaper, then change the color scheme to your liking.

To choose a wallpaper, or background, for your web page, simply make your selection from the Background Wallpaper drop-down list. Then press TAB to move to the next box. As you select each, the choices you make will be reflected in the web page shown onscreen.

Setting the Text Justification

The final design element you can adjust on your web page is the text justification. You can choose to align all the text to the left, center, or right of the page. Most web pages use left-aligned text because it's the most common format; however, center- or right-aligned text may also be appropriate, depending on the look you want to create.

You specify the text alignment or justification you want by choosing from the Justification drop-down list. Then, choose Next or press ENTER to move to the next Web Page Expert window. The choice you make will be reflected in the onscreen web page.

Bitmap Name	Description	GIF File Size (KB)	Corel WordPerfect's Recommended Color Scheme
Blue Terra	Light and dark blue stone-like image	17	Wallpaper Dark
Cotton	Crisp, slightly wrinkled blue fabric	18	Wallpaper Dark
Green Bark	Dark green and brown tree bark	35	Wallpaper Dark
Hatch	Light papyrus-colored textile	10	Wallpaper Light
Lace 1	Light lace-like texture	8	Wallpaper Light
Lace 2	Off-white detailed lace on white background	108	Wallpaper Light
Marble 1	White stone with dark gray marbling	9	Wallpaper Light
Marble 2	Bluish gray stone with small, black mottled spots	38	Wallpaper Dark
Natural	Brown granite with light brown spots	1	Wallpaper Light
Oil 1	Blue and turquoise swirls, much like a psychedelic light show	9	Wallpaper Light
Oil 2	Brown shades, landscape-like swirls	10	Wallpaper Light
Paper 1	White, blue, and gray wrinkled paper	14	Wallpaper Light

Corel WordPerfect's Background Bitmap Images, File Sizes, and Default Color Schemes

TABLE 4-2

Bitmap Name	Description	GIF File Size (KB)	Corel WordPerfect's Recommended Color Scheme
Paper 2	Brown hand-pressed paper with orange, blue, and cream fibers	44	Wallpaper Dark
Paper 3	Brown paper with pressed, textured fibers	16	Wallpaper Dark
Pine	Light-brown wood grain	27	Wallpaper Light
Polyester	Cream-colored texture	15	Wallpaper Light
Poplar	Very light, almost white, wood grain	19	Wallpaper Light
Rock	Slate-like gray texture	4	Wallpaper Light
Sky 1	White clouds on blue sky	32	Wallpaper Light
Sky 2	Scattered clouds on dark blue sky	38	Wallpaper Light
Stucco 1	White and light brown splatter texture	5	Wallpaper Light
Stucco 2	Scraped adobe texture	7	Wallpaper Light
Tile	Gray tile with heart/floral pattern, like a kitchen or bathroom	16	Wallpaper Light
Water	Stylized waves in shades of blue	13	Wallpaper Dark
Wrinkle	Pinkish background, red and black highlights	27	Wallpaper Dark

Corel WordPerfect's Background Bitmap Images, File Sizes, and Default Color Schemes (*continued*)

TABLE 4-2

Completing the Web Page Expert

Now that you've completed all the information the Web Page Expert has asked for, you'll see this final Web Page Expert window:

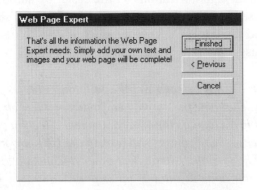

To complete your work with the Web Page Expert and begin customizing and adding information to your web pages, choose Finished.

REMEMBER: *If you're dissatisfied with any of the choices you made in the Web Page Expert, you can choose Previous to go back and modify any of your entries.*

Once you've told the Web Page Expert you're finished, it will show you a window telling you it's saving the web pages you created.

Corel WordPerfect then will show you a warning message to remind you that you *must* save your pages using Publish to HTML before you can distribute them via the Web. Although the files the Web Page Expert creates have "htm" extensions, they're still Corel WordPerfect-format documents. Since the Web only understands HTML documents, you must be sure to publish your web pages to HTML before you upload them. This is covered in "Publishing Your Web Page Expert Web Pages to HTML," the last section of this chapter.

Customizing Web Pages Created with the Web Page Expert

Although the Web Page Expert has stopped holding your hand, your web page work is not yet complete. Corel WordPerfect has created a web page structure for you, but you must still add the information, or content, to each page. (Here's where your detailed web site plans can come in handy—if you already know what you want to communicate, creating the pages is much easier.)

You will need to modify the main page and each "content" page. Corel WordPerfect makes these modifications a little easier by automatically loading the Web Editor (discussed in more detail in Chapter 5). The Web Editor loads a special toolbar, menus, and more to give you one-click access to many commonly used web-related features.

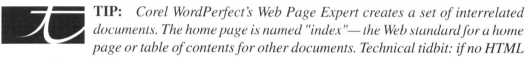

TIP: *Corel WordPerfect's Web Page Expert creates a set of interrelated documents. The home page is named "index"— the Web standard for a home page or table of contents for other documents. Technical tidbit: if no HTML file name is specified, a web browser will look in the URL, or directory you type for a file named index.htm or index.html. The other documents the Web Page Expert creates are linked from and back to this index page.*

Adding Information to the Home Page

You'll first need to add information to the home, or index, page. Corel WordPerfect makes it obvious what you need to change by inserting a placeholder or "dummy" paragraph that reads "Type a brief paragraph explaining the purpose of this web page" (see Figure 4-6). You may also want to change or add other text or graphics. (You'll learn more about these tools in Chapter 6, where you'll learn about formatting text, and in Chapters 8 and 9, where you'll learn about using graphics in your pages.)

For example, you may want to add a copyright notice to your web pages. Most copyright notices read simply "Copyright © 1997 The Fictitious Company." You may want to check with your company's lawyers or consult your country's copyright office for details.

To replace the placeholder text with your own text:

1. Highlight the line that reads "Type a brief paragraph explaining the purpose of this web page" by moving the mouse over any word in the line and triple-clicking (clicking three times in rapid succession).

2. Type the text with which you want to replace the placeholder text. As you begin typing, the highlighted text will be automatically deleted.

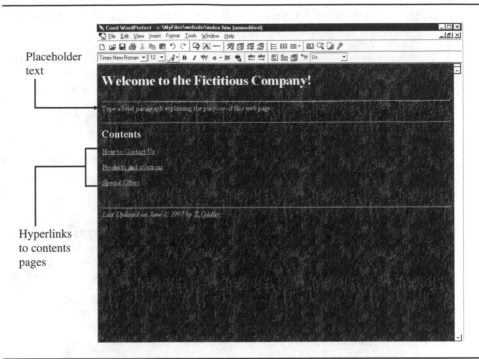

Placeholder text

Hyperlinks to contents pages

FIGURE 4-6   A completed home page for the Fictitious Company, complete with background wallpaper

Adding Information to the Contents Pages

Each of the contents pages you've created will need some attention as well. But Corel WordPerfect makes it easy to get to each page (and back to the home page). It's also provided placeholder text to show you where you need to add your own information to each page.

To view and modify each contents page, click on the appropriate underlined hyperlink on the home page (see Figure 4-6). Corel WordPerfect will switch to the contents page you selected. Each contents page has placeholder text—one for a brief description and one for content, both text and graphic.

To add your information to each contents page:

1. Highlight the line that reads "Type a brief paragraph explaining the purpose of this web page" by moving the mouse over any word in the line and triple-clicking (clicking three times in rapid succession).

2. Type the text with which you want to replace the placeholder text. As you begin typing, the highlighted text will be automatically deleted.

3. Highlight the line that reads "[Insert text and images here]" by moving the mouse over any word in the line and triple-clicking.

4. Type the text with which you want to replace the placeholder text. As you begin typing, the highlighted text will be automatically deleted.

Figure 4-7 shows a completed sample contents page. When you're done making your changes to the page, you can follow the hyperlink back to the table of contents or index document. To return to the main home page, click the "Return to Table of Contents" hyperlink at the bottom of the page.

Repeat the steps above for each page you created using the Web Page Expert. When you're finished adding information, you're ready to publish your pages to HTML.

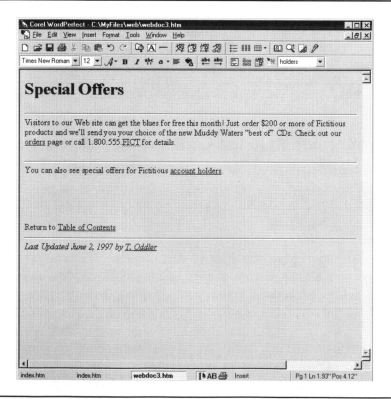

FIGURE 4-7   A sample contents page. Note the underlined hyperlink back to the table of contents page.

Publishing Your Web Page Expert Web Pages to HTML

When you've completed all your web pages, you must use Corel WordPerfect's Publish to HTML feature to place them all in the proper format for the Web. (For more details on publishing your documents to the Web, including HTML, Corel Barista, and Envoy, see Part 4.)

To publish your pages to HTML, click the Publish to HTML button on the toolbar or choose File | Internet Publisher | Publish to HTML.

CAUTION: *You must publish each page individually to HTML. Version 7 of the Web Page Expert automatically published each page, but could sometimes be confusing. Instead of worrying about using the proper method, you can simply publish each page individually.*

Corel WordPerfect will display the Publish to HTML dialog box, shown here, asking you to answer a few questions. (For more details on these options, see Chapter 18.)

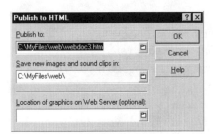

Insider Tip

Whenever you make changes to any page you created with the Web Page Expert, use the Publish to HTML button on the toolbar to update your pages. It will automatically update the "Last Updated" message at the bottom of each page.

Previewing Your Web Pages

 If you'd like to preview and test your web pages in your default web browser, usually Netscape Navigator, you can choose the View in Web Browser button from the toolbar. Corel WordPerfect will automatically load your page in your web browser. You can then see exactly what your Web Page Expert-created pages will look like in a real web browser.

When previewing your pages in your web browser, you can test for layout, links, and even typos before you send the pages to their final destination. But it doesn't make sense to test the speed at which your pages load. Remember that you are still loading the pages from your hard drive—or at least from a local area network (LAN), in most cases. Keep in mind that those viewing your pages may be viewing them across dial-up connections, using modems. So if you've added a lot of graphics, you may want to wait until you have your pages uploaded to your Internet Service Provider (ISP) before you test for download speed.

That's it! You're finished using the Web Page Expert to create, fill in, and publish web pages. Your pages are now ready to be placed in a network directory for your intranet or sent/uploaded to your Internet Service Provider to be placed on your web site.

NOTE: *In the Professional version of Corel WordPerfect Suite 8, Corel is expected to integrate new, somewhat updated Web Page Experts into their powerful PerfectExpert projects. If you're using the Professional version or an updated version of Corel WordPerfect Suite 8, you will most likely access these new web projects from a web group in the PerfectExpert. To launch a new PerfectExpert project, choose File | New. Or, from the Windows 95 Start menu, choose Corel WordPerfect Suite 8, then Corel New Project.*

But Corel WordPerfect has other automated tools that make web publishing easy. In the next chapter you'll learn more about the Internet Publisher and the Web Editor.

Creating Web Pages with Internet Publisher and the Web Editor

5

Corel WordPerfect provides a rich environment for creating web pages. The best part: Corel WordPerfect works the way you're used to—even when you're creating web pages. In fact, it has a special working environment—with specialized menus, a toolbar, and functions that help you create web pages quickly. This specialized environment is called the *Web Editor* and is part of the family of web tools Corel WordPerfect offers in its Internet Publisher.

Internet Publisher can help you with each aspect of your web publishing project. In fact, you might want to take a look at it now. In order to access Corel WordPerfect's Internet Publisher, choose File | Internet Publisher. You'll see Corel WordPerfect's Internet Publisher dialog box, as shown in Figure 5-1.

Internet Publisher is the focal point for each step in the process of creating web pages. The four buttons in the Internet Publisher dialog box correspond to four major tasks you'll perform when creating web pages:

- *New Web Document* takes you directly to the web templates included with Corel WordPerfect—the Web Page Expert (explained in Chapter 4) and the Blank Web Page template (see "Loading the Web Editor" next).

- *Format As Web Document* converts existing Corel WordPerfect documents into HTML format. See Chapter 14 for more information.

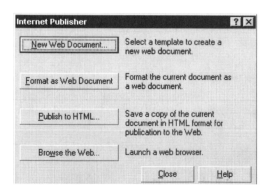

FIGURE 5-1   Corel WordPerfect's Internet Publisher main dialog box

- *Publish To HTML* saves your pages and all associated files (graphics, sounds, and so on) in formats compatible with the Web. This step prepares your pages for uploading to a web site. This is discussed in more detail in Chapter 18.

- *Browse The Web* launches your default web browser, usually Netscape Navigator, to allow you to explore the Web or to test your web pages.

Internet Publisher helps with each of the major tasks you perform with the World Wide Web: creating web pages, converting Corel WordPerfect documents to web pages, publishing documents to the Web, and browsing the Web. Each of these will be discussed in their respective chapters. But the most important option to you is the first one—New Web Document. When you choose this option and then choose the Blank Web Page template, Corel WordPerfect loads its Web Editor so you can easily produce customized web pages. Let's look at the Web Editor now.

Loading the Web Editor

When you want to create a web page from scratch, Corel WordPerfect provides a way for you to have all the web tools ready and waiting without spending a lot of time setting up your working environment.

Corel WordPerfect is also designed to eliminate surprises while you're working on a web document. When you're working on a web page, Corel WordPerfect can show you only the tools that will have an effect on the page's final form in HTML, rather than provide you with its full complement of formatting and word processing tools. For example, Corel WordPerfect doesn't offer page numbering in the web authoring menus, even though it's a standard feature of the program. (See "The Web Editor's Special Menus" later in this chapter for a comparison of one menu heading, Format, in normal Corel WordPerfect use versus using Internet Publisher's customized web authoring menus.)

The easiest and quickest way to set up your Corel WordPerfect working environment to create web pages from scratch is by taking advantage of the program's predefined suite of web-specific tools: the Internet Publisher, the Blank Web Page template, and the Web Editor. Here's how you start:

1. Choose File | Internet Publisher.

2. From the Internet Publisher dialog box, choose <u>N</u>ew Web Document. You'll then see the Select New Web Document dialog box, as shown in Figure 5-2.

3. Choose Create A Blank Web Document.

4. Choose <u>S</u>elect or press ENTER to load the Blank Web Page template and Web Editor, with its web-specific menus and toolbar.

You'll then see a blank document with a gray background, which tells you you are working in Web Editor mode. You can now create any web document you choose. (For more information about creating web documents, converting existing documents, or using Corel WordPerfect's web tools, see the rest of the chapters in Part 2.)

Quick Web Formatting with the Web Editor

"Web Editor" is Corel WordPerfect's way of describing the special set of tools it provides to make web page creation simple. While Corel WordPerfect offers numerous features and tools, not all of those features translate to the Web. So, when you're creating a web document, Corel WordPerfect switches to its Web Editor mode. This special mode provides two things:

- Quick access to commonly used web features

- Tools applicable only to web (HTML) documents—it hides Corel WordPerfect's other tools

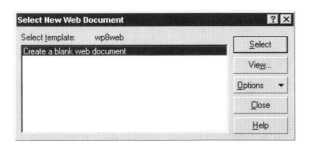

FIGURE 5-2 The Internet Publisher's Select New Web Document dialog box enables you to choose a template for your new web document. To create a new web page from scratch, choose Create A Blank Web Document—the Blank Web Page template and Web Editor will load automatically.

Although the Web Editor hides some of Corel WordPerfect's tools, it doesn't skimp on tools to help create web pages. For example, when you create a table, before you publish your document to HTML, you have access to the full complement of Corel WordPerfect table functions, from using formulas to rearranging and joining cells. (For more information about tables, see Chapter 10.)

> **NOTE:**   *The Web Editor also is automatically loaded when you open an HTML document. In the Convert File Format dialog box, be sure to choose HTML (usually the default choice) from the ___Convert File Format From___ pop-up menu and choose OK.*

Remember, the Web Editor loads automatically when you tell Corel WordPerfect to create a new web document from the Internet Publisher's Select New Web Document dialog box (see Figure 5-2). Once you've opened a blank web document or switched to Web Editor view, you'll see a blank document screen with a few key differences. This screen, shown in Figure 5-3, is the Web Editor, designed for building web pages.

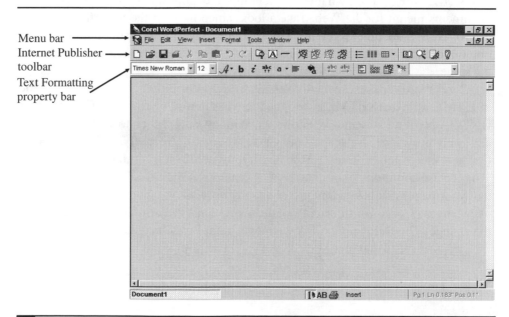

Menu bar
Internet Publisher toolbar
Text Formatting property bar

FIGURE 5-3   Corel WordPerfect's Web Editor resembles a normal document screen, but has a gray background and contains special menus and tools for web page building.

Gray is the default background color for web documents in Netscape Navigator and therefore in Corel WordPerfect's Web Editor. Notice that a toolbar with web-related tools is loaded automatically. Skim through the pull-down menus: you'll notice those have changed, too.

 With Corel WordPerfect 8, you can toggle between the regular Corel WordPerfect interface (Page view) and the Web Editor environment. Just choose <u>V</u>iew | We<u>b</u> Page or <u>V</u>iew | <u>P</u>age. You can also press the Change View button, which appears on the toolbar regardless of the mode you are working in.

The next section will take you step by step through the Web Editor's features.

Exploring the Web Editor

The Web Editor places key web tools in easy reach. It has three main groups of tools: special menus, a special toolbar, and a special property bar.

The Web Editor's Special Menus

The Web Editor's pull-down menus offer only selections that will help in formatting documents meant for the Web. Take a look: since most of the tools that you can't use for HTML documents are in the Fo<u>r</u>mat menu, you'll probably notice the most obvious differences there (see Figures 5-4 and 5-5). While the menu headings remain the same, the items listed within each menu change.

Corel WordPerfect, especially version 8, supports all major formatting abilities of HTML. But since HTML is designed to work across platforms (PC, Macintosh, UNIX), operating systems (Windows 95, Windows 3.1, Macintosh OS, and so on), and web browsers (Netscape Navigator, Microsoft Internet Explorer, America Online's integrated browser, and so on), it must settle on a common set of features. This lowest-common-denominator set of features is the safest set to use to ensure that your pages can be read by just about any browser.

Many of Corel WordPerfect's pull-down menus remain largely unaffected by the change. The following pull-down menus remain unchanged:

- <u>E</u>dit
- <u>T</u>ools
- <u>W</u>indow
- <u>H</u>elp

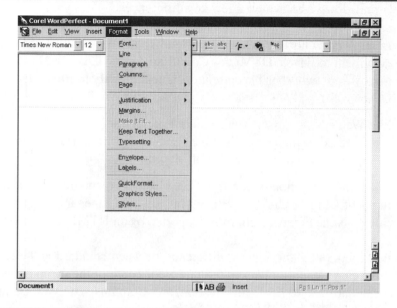

FIGURE 5-4   The standard Format menu with the full list of its formatting features

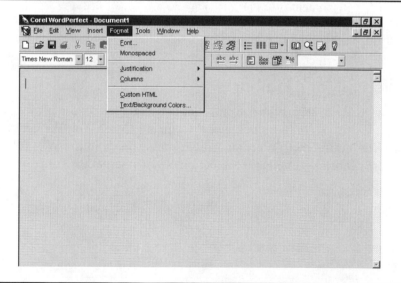

FIGURE 5-5   The Web Editor Format menu with the specialized list of features. Some features are hidden; others are added to the menu.

Other pull-down menus have a few key differences:

- In the Web Editor's File menu, the Send To item can publish the current document to Envoy, HTML, or Corel Barista (see Chapter 21). The Envoy item publishes the current document directly to Envoy (see Chapter 20).

- The Web Editor's Insert menu adds a Line Break (CTRL-SHIFT-L) item to the standard menu items. The Line Break is special to HTML, but is similar to Corel WordPerfect's Soft Return.

- The Graphics option on the Web Editor's Insert menu hides the standard items of Drag To Create, Vertical Line, Custom Line, and Graphics Styles. None of these options is supported by an HTML standard.

As was mentioned, the biggest difference between standard and Web Editor menus is the Format menu (Figures 5-4 and 5-5). Three of the menu items remain from the standard menu: Font, Justification, and Columns. The Web Editor menu adds three more:

- Monospaced

- Custom HTML

- Text/Background Colors

The Web Editor's Toolbar

When you load the Web Editor, Corel WordPerfect's standard toolbar changes to place key web tools only a click away. Compare Corel WordPerfect's standard toolbar with the Internet Publisher toolbar that appears in the Web Editor, both shown here. Table 5-1 explains each button on the Internet Publisher toolbar.

Corel WordPerfect's standard toolbar

Corel WordPerfect's Internet Publisher toolbar

Button	Name	Description
	Clipart	Insert a clipart image from the scrapbook
	Text Box	Create a text box
	Horizontal Line	Insert a horizontal line that stretches between the left and right margins
	Browse the Web	Launches your default web browser
	View in Web Browser	View a copy of your document in your default web browser
	Publish to HTML	Save a copy of your document in HTML format
	Hyperlink	Create a hyperlink, insert a bookmark, or edit either
	Insert Bullet	Begin a bulleted list or convert selected text to a bulleted list
	Columns	Define columns (using HTML tables)
	Table	Insert a table by clicking and dragging to specify the size you want
	Spell Check	Check spelling
	Zoom	Zoom in or out on your document

Corel
WordPerfect's
Internet
Publisher
(Web Editor)
Toolbar

TABLE 5-1

Corel
WordPerfect's
Internet
Publisher
(Web Editor)
Toolbar
(*continued*)

Button	Name	Description
	Change View	Change to Page view from Web Editor view
	PerfectExpert	Launch the PerfectExpert

The Web Editor's Property Bar

Like the Internet Publisher toolbar, the new Text Formatting property bar that also appears in the Web Editor places text formatting tools at your fingertips:

The property bar uses pull-down menus to provide you with quick access to key formatting functions. This bar changes more subtly from the standard one—in fact, they're identical except for one thing: the regular Font/Size pull-down menu lists only HTML styles. Table 5-2 explains each button on the Web Editor's Text Formatting property bar.

Button	Name	Description
	Font	Choose a typeface (note the neat preview window as you bring the cursor over a font name)
	Size	Choose the font size
	Font/Size	Choose an HTML paragraph or heading style
	Bold	Bold the current selection or text following

The Web
Editor's Text
Formatting
Property Bar

Button	Name	Description
i	Italic	Italicize the current selection or text following
abc ↑↑	Monospaced	Change the current selection or text following to monospaced text
a ▾	Font Attributes	Apply font attributes to the current selection or text following
≣	Justification	Change justification (choose from a pop-up menu)
🎨a	Font Color	Choose the font color
abc ←	QuickFind Previous	Find the previous instance of last searched-for text
abc →	QuickFind Next	Find the next instance of last searched-for text
▤	New Form	Insert a web form at the insertion point
10010 01101	Create Java Applet	Insert a Java applet
▤	HTML Document Properties	Specify the HTML document's properties, including title, background, etc.
✳✳ #	Insert Symbol	Insert a Corel WordPerfect symbol or typographic character
[▾]	Prompt-As-You-Go	Select commonly used phrases

The Web
Editor's Text
Formatting
Property Bar
(*continued*)

TABLE 5-2

The Web Editor's Text Formatting property bar makes it easy to access all the formatting tools you use most often to create text. In other chapters, you'll learn how the property bar changes to place the tools you need at your fingertips when you work with other types of information (graphics, forms, etc.). You'll learn more about how to use each text formatting tool later in this chapter.

Creating Web Pages

When you're building a web site, once you've decided on its general structure, you'll need to have some pages to put in it. You can get these pages in two ways: by building them or by converting them from existing documents. (See Chapter 14 for more information on converting Corel WordPerfect documents to HTML web pages.)

You will probably create from scratch most of the main pages you'll need for a web site—a home page, main pages in each area, and pages you'll update. You can also create the web site's structure from scratch—or use the Web Page Expert to build it for you quickly.

Before you create even a model web page for your site, you'll probably want to decide what structure to use by doing two simple things:

- Decide what general areas or topics you want to include

- Decide how they'll relate to each other

For example, for The Fictitious Company's web site, you might have decided you need the following topics:

- A way to contact company departments, such as the webmaster, sales, and product support

- Information about Fictitious products

- Information about Fictitious services

- Customer support information about Fictitious products

- News about Fictitious sales

- Sale prices for web visitors

- Press releases

- Company news

- What's new on the web site

- General corporate information

- Downloadable samples or demos

- Answers to frequently asked questions about the company and products/services

- Job listings

You might then decide to group these topics into four main areas or headings: Using the topics and headings you've created for the Fictitious Company, you can create a general sketch for the web site (see Table 5-3).

■ News	■ Special Offers
■ Products and Services	■ How to Contact Us

Once you've made a basic sketch of the structure you want, you're ready to begin building the web site structure using Corel WordPerfect. As mentioned, you can either build the structure from scratch, or use the Web Page Expert to create a basic structure you can modify later. You may want to try the Web Page Expert first.

Insider Tip

Because Corel WordPerfect's web formatting is so easy to use, you don't have to worry about having all the formatting exactly as you want it when you build the basic framework for your web site or web pages. It's often easier to concentrate on building the framework first. You can then apply a basic look to each page after you've completed the structure.

News	Products and Services	Special Offers	How to Contact Us
What's new on the web site	Information about Fictitious products	News about Fictitious sales	E-mail to webmaster
Company news	Information about Fictitious services	Sale prices for web visitors	E-mail, phone, fax for sales
Press releases	Customer support information about Fictitious products		
	Downloadable samples and demos	E-mail, phone, fax for customer support	
Job listings	General corporate information		

A Sample Web Site Structure for The Fictitious Company

TABLE 5-3

Building a Home Page and Site Structure Using the Web Page Expert

Perhaps the Web Page Expert's greatest strength is its ability to quickly build a web site structure complete with links between pages. A structure built by use of the Web Page Expert will automatically be updated and published when you choose Publish To HTML.

To create the sample web site structure shown in Table 5-3, just follow the next steps. You can easily adapt them to your web site and your plans.

Loading the Web Page Expert

You can launch the Web Page Expert straight from the PerfectExpert. (To learn other ways of launching the Web Page Expert, consult Chapter 4.)

1. Choose <u>F</u>ile | <u>N</u>ew. You'll see Corel WordPerfect's PerfectExpert dialog box.

2. From the PerfectExpert's category pull-down list, choose Custom WP Templates category.

3. From the projects list, choose Web Page Expert.

4. Choose <u>C</u>reate or press ENTER to launch the Web Page Expert.

Once the Web Page Expert is running, you'll want to concentrate on two key areas: the location of your web files and the main topic pages you want to create.

Choosing a Location for Your Web Files

You will want to choose a new folder (subdirectory) for your new web pages. Even if you didn't want to, Corel WordPerfect would make you choose a new folder anyway. Keeping track of everything is much easier if you keep the files for your web site separate from your regular documents.

TIP: *The new folder you create can be in your usual document folder (MyFiles). You may find it easier to create a new folder in your usual document folder because that's the default folder when you open a new document. You may want to name your new folder something like "Web1."*

REMEMBER: *Corel WordPerfect will automatically create another folder inside the new one you create when you choose Publish To HTML. The files you create using the Web Page Expert will have an .HTM extension, but will be in Corel WordPerfect format until you publish them to HTML.*

To enter the name of your web page's new folder:

1. In the New Folder Name text box, type the full path of the folder you want to create. For example, you might type **c:\myfiles\web1**. Or, if you're interested, you can browse the folders on your computer to choose the folder you want to create, click the file folder button to the right of the New Folder Name text box. Choose the folder and choose Select.

2. Choose <u>N</u>ext or press ENTER to move on to the next step.

REMEMBER: *For detailed instructions on using the Web Page Expert, see Chapter 4.*

Once you've chosen the location for your web pages and work files, you'll need to put placeholder text in the next dialog box in order to move ahead.

Inserting Placeholder Text

You don't need to worry too much about what you enter in the next Web Page Expert dialog box. You can always change your entries later. Since you're creating this example for The Fictitious Company, fill in the blanks here with text for the example. If you're creating your own pages, just replace the sample text with your own.

To insert placeholder text and e-mail information:

1. In the <u>W</u>eb Page Title text box, type **Welcome to The Fictitious Company!**. Press TAB to move to the next text box.

2. In the Na<u>m</u>e text box, type **T. Oddler**—The Fictitious Company's webmaster. Press TAB to move to the next text box.

3. In the <u>E</u>-mail Address text box, type T. Oddler's e-mail address: **toddler@fictitious.com**

4. Choose <u>N</u>ext or press ENTER to move to the next window.

Building a Basic Structure

You're now ready to build the basic structure of your web site. Corel WordPerfect will have already created three general topics for you. While these topics are okay for a personal home page, for a company home page—especially for the Fictitious Company sample—they won't do.

To build the basic structure:

1. In the Table Of <u>C</u>ontents box, uncheck the boxes next to all three default pages (My Hobbies and Interests, My Personal Background, and My Professional Information).

2. Choose <u>A</u>dd. Corel WordPerfect will display the Add A Page dialog box.

3. In the Page <u>N</u>ame text box, type **News** and press ENTER or choose OK.

4. Choose <u>A</u>dd. In the Page <u>N</u>ame text box, type **Products and Services** and press ENTER or choose OK.

5. Choose <u>A</u>dd. In the Page <u>N</u>ame text box, type **Special Offers** and press ENTER or choose OK.

6. Choose <u>A</u>dd. In the Page <u>N</u>ame text box, type **How to Contact Us** and press ENTER or choose OK.

NOTE: *The Web Page Expert will place "How to Contact Us" at the top of your list because it creates the main Table of Contents alphabetically. Don't worry—you can always change the order later.*

7. Choose <u>N</u>ext or press ENTER to move on.

Breezing Through the Rest of the Web Page Expert

The Web Page Expert can then help you choose a color scheme for your pages. If you want to set the design of your pages now, go ahead and fill in these options (for complete directions, see Chapter 4). However, you may want to determine these items later.

For The Fictitious Company example, you will want to leave the colors and background with their default settings. To do so just choose <u>N</u>ext or press ENTER to move on. The Web Page Expert will then tell you it's finished—so just agree with it so it'll get to work by choosing <u>F</u>inished or pressing ENTER.

Once you've completed this series of dialog boxes, the Web Page Expert will work for a while, then deliver you a set of web pages in Corel WordPerfect format. You'll have a home page that contains a table of contents linked to a set of pages—each with the titles you created in the Web Page Expert (see Figures 5-6 and 5-7). From here you can tailor the pages as you like.

Building a Home Page and Site Structure from Scratch

While the Web Page Expert builds you a basic set of pages with very little effort, the pages it builds fit a predefined structure. With only a pinch of daring and a little more effort, you can build your own web site structure.

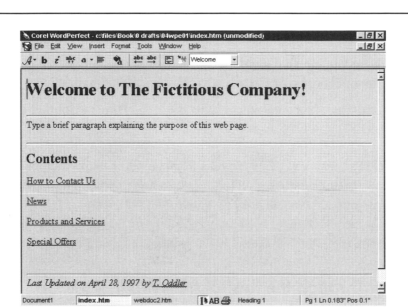

FIGURE 5-6 The home page the Web Page Expert creates using your information

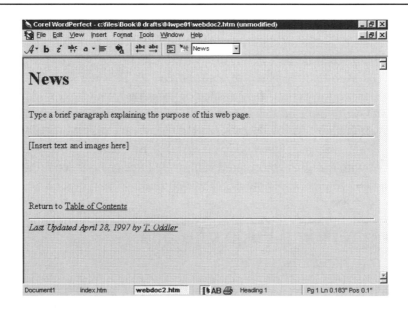

FIGURE 5-7 A sample secondary page the Web Page Expert creates using your information

When you build your own web site structure, you have control over every piece of the layout. You control what each page is named, what each link looks like, and the order of the links. With Corel WordPerfect's Web Editor, it's easy to build your pages the way you want them, complete with links and design elements. If you prefer, you can also use these steps after you've made a basic template, but only if you know the structure in advance.

As you did when you created a web site structure using the Web Page Expert, you can try creating a sample web site structure for The Fictitious Company. You can modify these steps to fit the site you want to create. Once you've sketched a site structure, you'll need two kinds of pages: a *home* page (that is, *index.htm*) and *secondary* pages.

NOTE: *In web parlance, "home page" is often used interchangeably with "web page" to mean the main page at your site. In this book, "home page" refers only to the main page—usually named* index.htm *so web browsers know it's the right one. "Web page," as used in this book, means any page in HTML or other format readable by a web browser such as Netscape Navigator.*

Creating a Home Page

This section goes hand in hand with "Creating Secondary Pages" next. You may choose to skip ahead and read that first to get an idea of the possible components your web pages can include. In this section, you'll create the sample The Fictitious Company home page and specify each of the secondary pages. You can try more fancy tricks as you read further in this chapter.

You'll need to start with a blank document and the Web Editor loaded. To tell Corel WordPerfect you're going to create a web document so it can load the Web Editor:

1. Choose File | Internet Publisher.

2. From the Internet Publisher dialog box, choose New Web Document.

3. From the Select New Web Document dialog box, choose Create A Blank Web Document from the Select Template list and press ENTER (or choose Select).

You'll then see a blank document screen with the Web Editor loaded (see Figure 5-3 to refresh your memory).

> **REMEMBER:** *When you create a home page from scratch, Corel WordPerfect doesn't automatically include the whole site when you publish it to HTML. If you want to have Corel WordPerfect* automatically *include all the main pages, you can create your pages using the Web Page Expert and then modify them later.*

You will create a home page like the one shown in Figure 5-8.

To create the home page's title section:

1. On the Internet Publisher toolbar, click the Horizontal Line button. Corel WordPerfect will insert a line and move the cursor to the next line.

2. Type **Welcome to The Fictitious Company!**

3. Press ENTER.

4. Highlight the line you just typed.

5. On the Text Formatting property bar, select Font/Size and choose Heading 1.

6. Press CTRL-END to move the cursor to the next line.

7. On the toolbar, click the Horizontal Line button.

The page's title will now have a horizontal line above and below it—and appear in HTML's standard Heading 1 format—the largest standard HTML style available.

You can now create the main table of contents for this home page. Since the Web Page Expert simply titles the table of contents "Contents," you may want to try something different. To create the main table of contents:

1. Type the following paragraph, or something close, and then press ENTER:

   Thanks for visiting! We've designed our Web site so you can find the information you need quickly and easily. Just click one of the links below:

2. Click the Insert Bullet button on the toolbar.

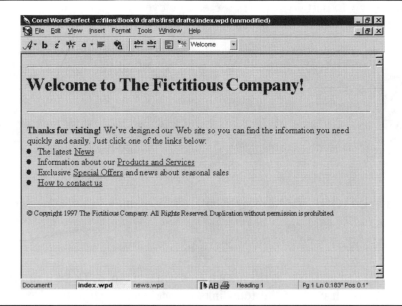

FIGURE 5-8 The sample home page for The Fictitious Company, created from scratch

You've now begun a bulleted list (wasn't that easy?). Next you'll enter the four main subject areas for The Fictitious Company's web site.

3. Type the following text, pressing ENTER after each line:

The latest News
Information about our Products and Services
Exclusive Special Offers and news about seasonal sales
How to contact us

4. When you press ENTER after the last line, you're left with an extra bullet. Just press BACKSPACE to delete it.

Now here's the fun part: creating links to the secondary pages. Since you're not using the Web Page Expert, you can name your secondary pages anything you want.

The Web Page Expert gives pages it creates clever names like *webdoc1.htm.* You may prefer to use more descriptive names, as shown here:

Secondary Page	Suggested Filename
News	news.htm
Products and Services	products.htm
Special Offers	offers.htm
How to Contact Us	contact.htm

 CAUTION: *Be sure to type your filenames exactly as they appear, including* case. *Many elements of the World Wide Web are case sensitive—so to be safe, keep everything in* lowercase.

Now you can add links to the main topics you just typed. These instructions will walk you through each of the four links—since each is slightly different. You'll create the link in exactly the same way each time, however. To add links:

1. Highlight the word "News" on the first bulleted line.

2. On the toolbar, from the Hyperlink button's pop-up menu, choose Create Link. You'll then see the Hyperlink Properties dialog box, shown here:

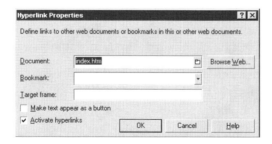

3. In the Document text box, type **news.htm** and choose OK. The word "News" will now appear in Corel WordPerfect as a blue, underlined link.

4. Highlight the words "Products and Services" in the second bulleted line.

5. On the toolbar, from the Hyperlink button's pop-up menu, choose Create Link.

6. In the Document text box, type **products.htm** and choose OK.

7. Highlight the words "Special Offers" in the third, bulleted line.

8. On the toolbar, from the Hyperlink button's pop-up menu, choose Create Link.

9. In the Document text box, type **offers.htm** and choose OK.

10. Highlight the text in the final bulleted line.

11. On the toolbar, from the Hyperlink button's pop-up menu, choose Create Link.

12. In the Document text box, type **contact.htm** and choose OK.

Each of the words or phrases you highlighted now appears as a blue, underlined link.

 TIP: *You might want to save your work at this stage. Choose File | Save and name the file* **index.wpd***. Save it in Corel WordPerfect format for now, but remember to choose Publish To HTML before you place it on your web site.*

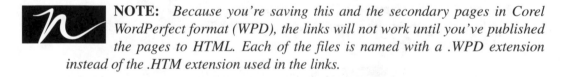 **NOTE:** *Because you're saving this and the secondary pages in Corel WordPerfect format (WPD), the links will not work until you've published the pages to HTML. Each of the files is named with a .WPD extension instead of the .HTM extension used in the links.*

Now you can add the last two elements to finish the page:

1. Press CTRL-END to move the insertion point to the last line.

2. Click the Horizontal Line button on the toolbar.

3. Type the following text—or something similar:

© **Copyright 1997 The Fictitious Company. All Rights Reserved. Duplication without permission is prohibited.**

4. Highlight the line of text you just typed.

5. On the property bar, from the Font Attributes drop-down menu, choose Small.

That's it! Save your page (in Corel WordPerfect format as **index.wpd**) so you can create some secondary pages. If you want to see what the page would look like viewed from the Web, click the View In Web Browser button on the toolbar.

 REMEMBER: *Before you can copy these pages to your web site, you will need to publish them to HTML (File | Internet Publisher | Publish To HTML).*

Creating Secondary Pages

To produce secondary pages, begin as you did when you created your home page. Start with a blank document and the Web Editor loaded. To tell Corel WordPerfect to load the Web Editor:

1. Choose File | Internet Publisher.

2. From the Internet Publisher dialog box, choose New Web Document.

3. From the Select New Web Document dialog box, choose Create A Blank Web Document from the Select Template list and press ENTER (or choose Select).

You'll then see a blank document screen with the Web Editor loaded (Figure 5-3).

To continue your practice pages for The Fictitious Company, follow these directions to create the first secondary page—the News page (see Figure 5-9). The sample page you create will include only placeholder text instead of real information. But this placeholder text will suffice for you to practice creating the pages.

To create a secondary page:

1. On the toolbar, click the Horizontal Line button.

2. Type **The Fictitious Company**; press ENTER.

3. Type **News**; press ENTER.

4. Highlight the first line you typed.

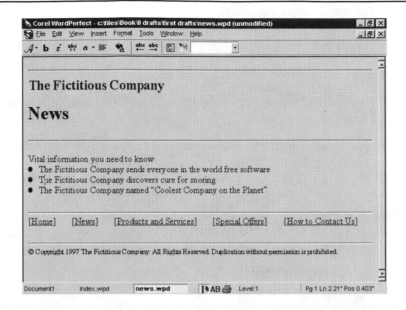

FIGURE 5-9   A sample secondary page, part of The Fictitious Company's web site

5. On the property bar, select Font/Size and choose Heading 3.

6. Highlight the second line you typed ("News").

7. On the property bar, select Font/Size and choose Heading 1.

8. Press CTRL-END to move the cursor to the next line.

9. On the toolbar, click the Horizontal Line button.

The page title will have a horizontal line above and below it. When you create other secondary pages, just replace the word "News" with the title of each page.

Now you can create some placeholder text to represent the page's contents. On a real secondary page, you might have more than just text—you might instead include a series of links to other documents. For example, see the four types of documents listed in Table 5-3 under the "News" heading. This secondary page could branch to third-level pages that include links to these documents—press releases, company news—as well as to third-level pages that include information—web site news and job listings.

To create some placeholder or "dummy" content:

1. Type **Vital information you need to know:** and press ENTER.

2. Click the Insert Bullet button on the toolbar.

3. Type the following text (or whatever you want), pressing ENTER after each line:

   The Fictitious Company sends everyone in the world free software
   The Fictitious Company discovers cure for snoring
   The Fictitious Company named "Coolest Company on the Planet"

4. Press BACKSPACE to delete the extra bullet, and then click the Horizontal Line button on the toolbar to finish off the content section of the page.

Now comes a little more linking. As you can see in Figure 5-9, the model for The Fictitious Company's secondary web pages includes a list of links at the bottom to enable quick access to other main areas—or back to the home page.

Insider Tip

Most well-designed sites include text-based links at the bottom or top of the page to enable quick access without having to wait for graphic images to load. Even Corel's graphically rich site includes text-based links (and a low-graphics version of the site)!

To create the line of links:

1. Type each of these main headings:

   [Home]
   [News]
   [Products and Services]
   [Special Offers]
   [How to Contact Us]

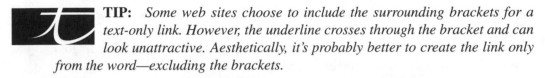

TIP: *Some web sites choose to include the surrounding brackets for a text-only link. However, the underline crosses through the bracket and can look unattractive. Aesthetically, it's probably better to create the link only from the word—excluding the brackets.*

2. Highlight the word "Home." *Don't* highlight the surrounding brackets.

3. On the toolbar, from the Hyperlink button's pop-up menu, choose Create Link.

4. In the <u>D</u>ocument text box, type **index.htm** and choose OK.

5. Highlight the word "News." *Don't* highlight the surrounding brackets.

6. On the toolbar, from the Hyperlink button's pop-up menu, choose Create Link.

7. In the <u>D</u>ocument text box, type **news.htm** and choose OK.

8. Highlight "Products and Services." *Don't* highlight the surrounding brackets.

9. On the toolbar, from the Hyperlink button's pop-up menu, choose Create Link.

10. In the <u>D</u>ocument text box, type **products.htm** and choose OK.

11. Highlight "Special Offers." *Don't* highlight the surrounding brackets.

12. On the toolbar, from the Hyperlink button's pop-up menu, choose Create Link.

13. In the <u>D</u>ocument text box, type **offers.htm** and choose OK.

14. Highlight "How to Contact Us." *Don't* highlight the surrounding brackets.

15. On the toolbar, from the Hyperlink button's pop-up menu, choose Create Link.

16. In the <u>D</u>ocument text box, type **contact.htm** and choose OK.

NOTE: *You don't really need all five links on each of the five pages you would create. For example, there's no need to have a link to "News" on the News page. But if you are creating this as a template page for all four secondary pages—or as a template for all of the site's pages—you might want to create all five links and then delete as appropriate.*

Now you can add the last two elements to finish the page:

1. Press CTRL-END, ENTER, and then click the Horizontal Line button on the toolbar.

2. Type the following text:

   © Copyright 1997 The Fictitious Company. All Rights Reserved. Duplication without permission is prohibited.

3. Highlight the text you just typed.

4. On the property bar, from the Font Attributes button's drop-down menu menu, choose Small.

Now you can save this secondary page (in Corel WordPerfect format) as **news.wpd**. If you want to see what the page would look like viewed from the Web, click the View In Web Browser button from the toolbar.

If you choose, you can create similar pages for the other three secondary pages—*products.htm, offers.htm,* and *contact.htm.* You can follow the above directions to re-create each page, or simply choose File | Save As three times and name each file as the three additional pages you need. You can then modify each file appropriately by changing the title and any placeholder content you want to add.

REMEMBER: *Before you can copy these pages to your web site, you will need to publish them to HTML (File | Internet Publisher | Publish To HTML).*

Now you've learned the ins and outs of Corel WordPerfect's special web document editing environment. You've also learned how to use the Web Page Expert to get a jump start on building a web site structure—as well as how to build one from scratch. Next you'll delve deeper into the web page formatting features Corel WordPerfect offers. In the following chapters, you'll learn about formatting text, adding graphics, using hyperlinks, using tables and columns, creating web forms, and more. The next chapter begins by showing you how to format text.

Formatting Text on Your Web Pages

Since most web pages contain mainly text, it's fortunate that Corel WordPerfect's word processing tools can be used to create web pages in the Web Editor environment. For example, you can find and replace, check spelling (including Spell-As-You-Go), and more.

Corel WordPerfect makes it easy to format text on any HTML document. But HTML is limited to its predefined styles—and to only a couple of fonts. (If you want more font control, try using Envoy, discussed in Chapter 19, and Corel Barista, discussed in Chapter 18.)

From the Web Editor's Text Formatting Property bar, you can quickly access two HTML formatting features: Font/Size (using HTML's standard styles) and Font Attributes. The property bar provides quick, access to both (see Figures 6-1 and 6-2).

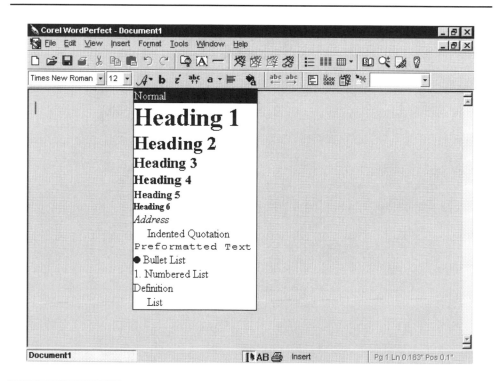

FIGURE 6-1   The Font/Size pull-down menu on the Text Formatting Property bar lists HTML paragraph styles

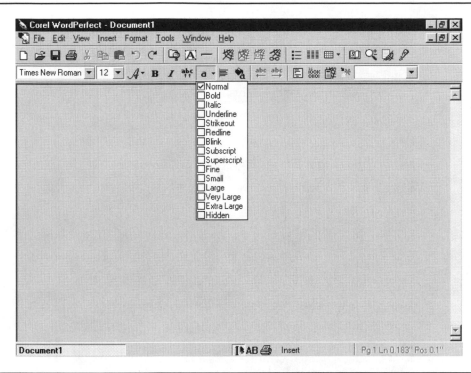

FIGURE 6-2 The Font Attributes pull-down menu on the Text Formatting Property bar lists character-level HTML formatting

Font/Size: HTML's Predefined Styles

HTML predefined styles work much like Corel WordPerfect styles. In fact, the Web Editor includes Corel WordPerfect styles that emulate HTML styles. HTML styles are all *paragraph based*. This means that you can only apply them to a paragraph—a block of text separated by a hard return (represented by the code [HRt], visible in Corel WordPerfect's Reveal Codes window). You can't apply these styles to only a character, word, or sentence unless they are paragraphs on their own. (Corel WordPerfect enables you to create styles that can be applied to any character, word, or sentence.)

HTML's predefined styles can't be changed—they're part of the generally accepted way of expressing layout elements that can be read by any browser. And although the most widely used browsers (Netscape Navigator and Microsoft Internet Explorer) display these predefined styles similarly, other browsers may not. Figure 6-3 shows these predefined styles in Netscape Navigator.

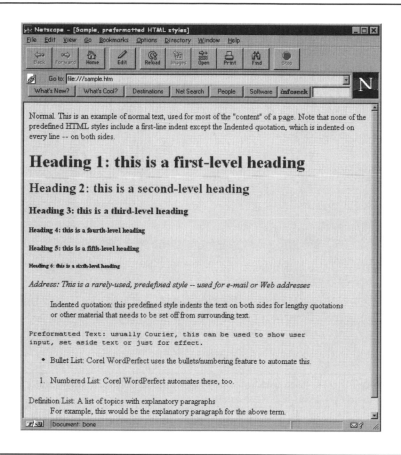

FIGURE 6-3   Predefined HTML styles shown in Netscape Navigator

REMEMBER: *Most web browsers like Netscape Navigator allow users to specify the fonts they want to use. For example, although a variety of Times Roman is the default normal text, a user might specify Helvetica, Arial, or any other commonly used font. So unless you use a product like Envoy or Corel Barista, you can't guarantee that those who read your web page will see your pages in the same font they were created in. That said, most people* don't *bother to change the fonts in their web browser.*

Corel WordPerfect makes it easy to remember what each of these predefined styles looks like—the Font/Size pull-down menu is WYSIWYG (what you see is what you get).

Applying Text Paragraph Styles

Most of these paragraph styles apply to formatting text. (See the next section, "Creating Lists," for information on creating bullet, numbered, and definition lists.) There are two ways to access any of these predefined paragraph text styles:

- Choose Format | Font, select the paragraph style you want and choose OK.

- Select the paragraph style you want from the Font/Size pull-down menu on the Text Formatting Property bar.

These predefined paragraph styles include several styles of text:

- *Normal*   This is regular text. In most browsers, this is Times New Roman in a 12-point size.

- *Headings 1-6*   These are heading levels. They are bolded normal text in progressively smaller sizes. For the most part, you'll probably use only the first three or maybe four levels of headings. Heading 5 and Heading 6 are even smaller than normal text—so they're not that useful as headings, though they make nice footers or navigation tools. You might want to use them if you're designing a layout that uses smaller body text (the default text typeface).

- *Address*   This is rarely used. You can use it to set apart an e-mail or web address—but for the most part, you'll create links to those instead of just listing them.

- *Indented quotation*   This is a long block of text that's indented from the right and left. The web browser will automatically indent on both sides for you, so the line length may vary based on the browser and its window size. This predefined style is also known as "blockquote"—"indented quotation" is Corel WordPerfect's name for it.

- *Preformatted text*   This paragraph style uses a monospaced font (usually Courier) to keep all formatting—including indents and tabular columns—intact. It's similar to the Monospaced font attribute you can set using the Font dialog box (see "Other Font Attributes" later in this chapter for details). But unlike the Monospaced font text attribute, it keeps spacing and line breaks intact when published to HTML and viewed in a web browser. Use it to preserve tabular information when you're not sure everyone viewing your document would be able to view the information if it were presented by use of an HTML table.

Creating Lists

HTML's paragraph styles also include three kinds of lists. Corel WordPerfect makes it easy to create these because you can use its automated list tools (see Figure 6-4 to see these list types in action). The three HTML list types are

- *Bullet list* Much like Corel WordPerfect's bullet lists, this is a list of items separated by a line break (no extra space between paragraphs). Each item is marked with a bullet.

- *Numbered list* This is similar to a bullet list, except the items are sequentially numbered.

- *Definition list* This is best used for a glossary or list of terms; items in this kind of list consist of two parts: a *term* and a *definition*.

To create a bullet or numbered list, either:

1. In the Web Editor, choose Insert | Bullets & Numbering.

2. Select a list type (either Bullet or Numbered); choose OK.

3. Type the list items, pressing ENTER after each.

Or:

1. From the property bar's Font/Size pull-down menu, choose either Bullet List or Numbered List.

2. Type the list items, pressing ENTER after each.

CAUTION: *If you create a bullet or numbered list using Corel WordPerfect's QuickBullets feature, the list will* not *translate correctly to HTML. You must use either Insert | Bullets & Numbering or the Font/Size feature on the Web Editor's Text Formatting Property bar.*

Definition lists are a little different from bullet or numbered lists. Each item in the list consists of the term and the definition.

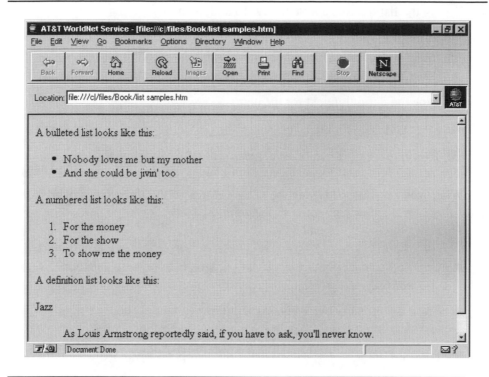

FIGURE 6-4 Samples of the three main list types: bullet, numbered, and definition

To create a definition list, either:

1. In the Web Editor, click Insert | Bullets & Numbering.

2. Select Definition List, then choose OK.

Or:

1. From the property bar, choose Font/Size.

2. Select Definition List from the pull-down menu.

Typing the list items is a little tricky. To add list items:

1. Type the term for the item; press ENTER.

2. Press TAB to indent the item's definition.

3. Type the definition text for the item.

4. Press ENTER.

5. To create the next item's term, press SHIFT-TAB and type the term.

When you've finished typing the items for any of the three types of lists, you must then select a new paragraph style to end the list.

There are three ways to end a list:

■ Choose Format | Font, select a text paragraph style, such as Normal, then choose OK.

■ From the property bar's Font/Size pull-down menu, choose a new text-paragraph style.

■ Press ENTER after the last list item and then press BACKSPACE.

For a handy reference to each predefined HTML style, see Table 6-1. The styles are listed in the order they appear on the Font/Size pull-down menu from the property bar. Note that the appearance of each style can change based on the settings of each individual browser—most web browsers enable the user to change the default fonts. Note also that many of these styles are ready to take advantage of Corel WordPerfect's ability to automatically generate tables of contents. The third column in Table 6-1 notes whether each style is premarked to help you quicky generate a table of contents. (Tables of contents are covered further in Chapter 9.)

Applying Font Attributes

Unlike HTML paragraph styles, font attributes can be applied to a text selection as small as a character. Font attributes include formatting characteristics such as bold, italic, underline, and blink. They also include size specifications like small and large.

Font attributes aren't as easy to figure out as preformatted HTML styles. Corel WordPerfect's Web Editor allows you to specify some font attributes that are

Style Name	Description	Marked for TOC?
Normal	12-point Times New Roman	No
Heading 1	Bold, 26-point Times New Roman	No
Heading 2	Bold, 20-point Times New Roman	Yes
Heading 3	Bold, 16-point Times New Roman	Yes
Heading 4	Bold, 14-point Times New Roman	Yes
Heading 5	Bold, 11-point Times New Roman	Yes
Heading 6	Bold, 9-point Times New Roman	Yes
Address	Italic, normal text	No
Indented Quotation	Normal text indented on both left and right margins	No
Preformatted Text	11-point Courier New, special tab settings approximately every $\frac{3}{4}$ inch	No
Bullet List	Uses bullet outline feature, normal text	No
Numbered List	Uses numbered outline feature, normal text	No
Definition List	Uses definition outline feature, normal text	No

Predefined HTML Styles Accessed from the Font/Size Pull-Down Menu

TABLE 6-1

changed when a document is published or converted to HTML (see "Other Font Attributes" later in this chapter for a list). However, these attributes are understandably changed: hidden, for example, is used principally to retain text that

isn't seen in a document when printed or distributed—so it wouldn't follow to bring hidden text to an HTML-formatted document.

Basic Font Attributes

Three basic font attributes are accessible directly from the Text Formatting Property bar:

- Bold
- Italic
- Monospaced

Each of these attributes is pretty much self-explanatory and they are the same whether they are applied from the buttons on the property bar or from the check boxes in the Font dialog box (see the next section, "Other Font Attributes," for more information).

It's important to note, however, how Corel WordPerfect behaves when you set font attributes. The easiest way to set them is to *select the text to which you want the attribute applied* before you apply it. If you do so, the attribute will be applied to only the selected text.

However, you can also set the attribute as you're typing. To do so, just turn the attribute on (or set a new font color), type the text to which you want the attribute applied, then turn the attribute off (or restore the font color to its previous hue).

Other Font Attributes

A handful of other font attributes are only a few clicks away, either in the Font dialog box or on the Font Attributes drop-down menu.

The Font Dialog Box

From the Font dialog box, you can apply the Bold, Italic, Monospaced, and Blink attributes. The first three options are the same as the corresponding buttons on the property bar.

The Monospaced attribute uses the default monospaced font, usually Courier, instead of the proportionally spaced default normal font, usually Times Roman. While the monospaced font is used in the Preformatted Text paragraph style, selecting only the Monospaced font attribute from the Font dialog box (or the property bar) does *not* preserve spacing or line breaks when the document is published to HTML. Use the Preformatted Text paragraph style (explained earlier) if you want to preserve that kind of formatting.

Blinking text, obviously, blinks when the page is published to HTML, but the Blink attribute doesn't really blink when you view it in Corel WordPerfect—it appears as shadow text. However, in browsers that support it, it will blink when you publish the document to HTML. Some web experts consider the blink attribute outdated, kind of like the HTML equivalent of a hot pink "I'm with Stupid" T-shirt.

To apply these font attributes:

1. Choose Format | Font. You'll see the Font dialog box (see Figure 6-5).

2. Choose any paragraph style you want to apply.

3. From the Appearance group box, check the box that applies to the attribute you want to select (Bold, Italic, Monospaced, or Blink). You can select multiple attributes.

4. Choose OK.

The Font Attributes Drop-Down Menu

In addition to the three fundamental font attributes—Bold, Italic, and Mono-spaced—available on the property bar, Corel WordPerfect Web Editor makes others available from the drop-down menu that appears when you choose the Font Attributes button, as was shown in Figure 6-2.

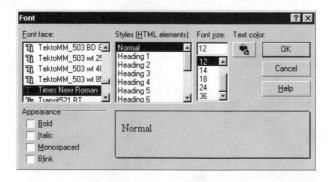

FIGURE 6-5   You can choose paragraph styles and basic font attributes from the Font dialog box

You'll learn about the attributes that specify *size* in the next section, so ignore those for now. Of the remaining attributes, not all are particularly useful—some don't convert to HTML; others *do* convert but are not supported by all browsers. Table 6-2 lists how each font attribute is converted.

To apply any of these other font attributes:

1. Select the text to which you want to apply the attributes.

2. From the property bar, choose Font Attributes.

3. Select the attribute you want to add from the pull-down menu.

4. To turn off any attribute, follow steps 2 and 3 above to deselect the attribute.

 REMEMBER: *To add multiple attributes, choose Font Attributes from the property bar again, and then select the next attribute you want from the pull-down menu.*

All font attributes, whether basic, "other," or size-related, display slightly differently from browser to browser. See Figure 6-6 to understand how the attributes listed in the property bar appear in Netscape Navigator.

Converted Exactly	Converted, But Not Necessarily Supported By All Browsers	Changed	Deleted
Bold	Redline	Shadow	Hidden
Italic	Strikeout	(inaccessible under	Double
Underline		Web Editor menus)	underline
Subscript		is converted to Blink.	
Superscript		Internal hypertext	
Font color		links' color is	
Font size		changed to blue (or	
		the custom color you	
		specified for links)	
		from green.	

How Corel WordPerfect Converts Key Font Attributes When a Document Is Published to HTML

TABLE 6-2

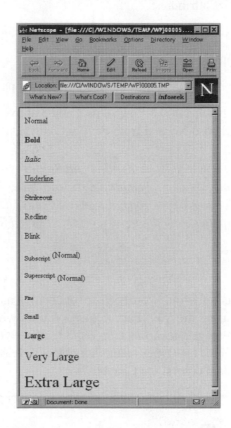

FIGURE 6-6   Font attributes listed in the property bar as they appear in Netscape
Navigator

Size Attributes

In addition to the basic and additional attributes, you can specify a relative size for text.
The text's size is relative because it is based on the size of the default or normal font.

REMEMBER: *Most browsers' default normal font is 12-point Times
Roman. However, most browsers allow individual users to change this font
to whatever they choose.*

You can specify five relative size attributes: Fine, Small, Large, Very Large, and
Extra Large. To see how each of these appears in a web browser, see Figure 6-6.

To specify font size attributes:

1. Select the text to which you want to apply the attributes.

2. From the property bar, choose Font Attributes.

3. Select the size attribute you want to add from the pull-down menu.

4. To turn off any attribute, follow steps 2 and 3 above to deselect the attribute, or choose Normal from the Font Attributes pull-down menu.

CAUTION: *Whereas with other attributes you can apply multiple attributes, you cannot apply multiple size attributes. Corel WordPerfect and HTML don't allow oxymorons in size attributes (like "jumbo shrimp"), so Corel WordPerfect applies only the most recently selected font size attribute to the text you've selected.*

Font Color

You can apply any color Corel WordPerfect supports to any block of text. If you created your pages using the Web Page Expert, you may have already selected a special color for your page's text, links, or visited links. Even if you have, you can change any of those three text types to another color. To learn more about changing the document's standard colors, see Chapter 7.

Insider Tip

Although you can choose any of the 256 colors offered in the color palette, don't. If you can restrain your design desires, try to stick with the basic 16 colors listed across the top of the color palette (the first 16 squares). These 16 colors will appear on just about any system under just about any browser. It's the closest thing to a guarantee you'll get out of standard HTML that a color will appear as you've intended it. Of course, many people use systems that support more than 16 colors, so if you need to use another shade, do so—but realize the potential problems it might cause. For example, since each operating system (Windows 95, Macintosh OS, etc.) uses a different, 256-color palette, the color you choose may be changed to a different hue when it's viewed.

To change the font color of a block of text:

1. Select a block of text.

2. From the property bar, choose Font Color.

3. Choose a color from the pop-up palette, as shown here:

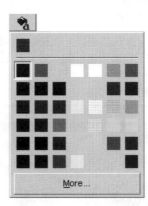

Changing Paragraph Justification

Corel WordPerfect supports HTML's paragraph justification, too. Unlike Corel WordPerfect, HTML does not support multiple justification attributes on the same line (like placing the filename flush left and the page number flush right in a document footer).

Insider Tip

If you want to simulate a combination of flush left, centered, and flush right text on the same line, it's possible with HTML. Just lay out your lines using the Preformatted Text paragraph style, separating the text with spaces or using custom tab settings. Another option is to use a three-cell table.

If you're unfamiliar with the three types of justification—left, right, and centered—take a look at Figure 6-7 to see each type viewed in Netscape Navigator.

You can apply these justification attributes to any paragraph. To set a paragraph's justification:

1. Select a paragraph or place the insertion point anywhere in the paragraph.

2. Choose Format | Justification, then either <u>L</u>eft, <u>R</u>ight, or C<u>e</u>nter.

Or, from the Web Editor property bar, click on the Justification button, then choose either Center, Left, or Right from the pop-up menu.

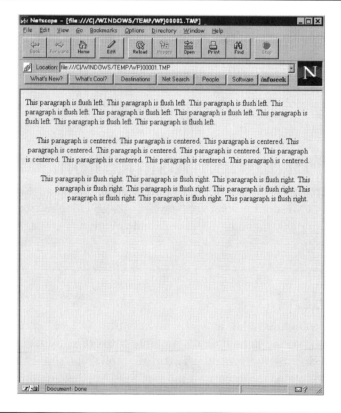

FIGURE 6-7   The three justification types as viewed in Netscape Navigator

You can also use the Corel WordPerfect keyboard shortcuts, listed here, to quickly justify text.

Justification Setting	Keyboard Shortcut
Left	CTRL-L
Right	CTRL-R
Center	CTRL-E

REMEMBER: *Justification settings remain in place even after you've pressed ENTER. To change to a different justification setting, select a new one from the property bar or menus.*

Line Breaks Versus Paragraph Breaks

HTML automatically adds a little extra space (called a *paragraph break*) between paragraphs. When you press ENTER to create a hard return, or [HRt] code in Corel WordPerfect, you're creating a <P> tag when the document is translated to HTML.

However, if you only want to end one line and begin another, you can insert a line break that will translate to an HTML tag of <BR>. A *line break* moves text to the next line without adding the extra space that a paragraph break provides.

To create a paragraph break, simply press ENTER. To create a line break, choose Insert | Line Break in the Web Editor. See Figure 6-8 to compare paragraph breaks with line breaks as they appear in a web browser.

NOTE: *A line break is not the same as inserting a Corel WordPerfect soft return [SRt] code. If you know what that is, don't use them instead of line breaks. If you don't know what a soft return is, don't worry about it.*

TIP: *To quickly insert a line break, press CTRL-SHIFT-L.*

In this chapter, you've learned how Corel WordPerfect makes it simple to use all of HTML's predefined font attributes, styles, and formatting. Because Corel

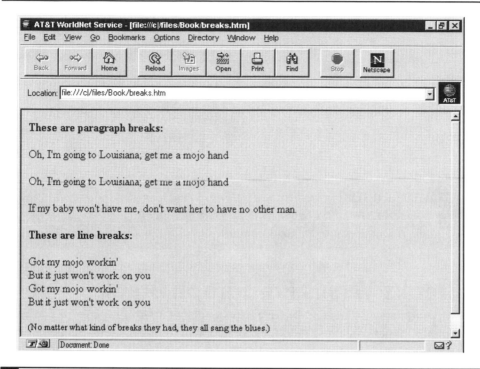

FIGURE 6-8   Paragraph breaks versus line breaks as seen in Netscape Navigator

WordPerfect's Web Editor environment is so easy to use, HTML documents are easy to create and modify. In the next chapter you'll move beyond just words to learn how Corel WordPerfect provides a wealth of graphic tools to help you add pizzazz to your web documents.

Working with Graphics: Lines, Colors, Backgrounds, and Images

7

HTML's ability to work across operating systems, computers, and configurations is fantastic. Unfortunately, this compatibility introduces some limitations. But even within these limitations, you can achieve attractive, compelling online designs.

HTML provides support for a variety of graphics, from lines to images. And since there are no limits on *what* you place as an image, whether it be text or fancy graphics, you have a lot of flexibility for your web creations. In fact, whenever you see a web page that looks too attractive to be HTML, there's a good chance it uses graphics well. Corel WordPerfect makes the most of HTML's limited graphic abilities. In this chapter, you'll learn about adding lines, colors, background images, and graphics to your web documents.

Adding Horizontal Lines

One of the basic graphic elements is the line. In fact, if you look at your favorite web pages, it's a safe bet that they're rife with horizontal lines. Your pages can use them, too: it's simple to add horizontal lines to any web document. Suppose you want to add horizontal lines to divide sections of a web page. For example, you might place a line between the page heading and the body text. You might also place a line before recurring footer information like copyright or "last modified" statements.

Insider Tip

HTML supports only horizontal lines. If you want to add vertical lines, or even fancier horizontal lines than the standard HTML types, you can do so by inserting lines as graphics.

Once you've created a horizontal line, you can change its position (right, left, center, or full), its length, and its thickness.

Creating Horizontal Lines

You can change some things about a horizontal line—but you have to make one before you can modify it. There are three ways you can create a horizontal line in a web document:

- In the Web Editor, click <u>I</u>nsert | <u>H</u>orizontal Line.

- Press CTRL-F11.
- Click the Horizontal Line button on the toolbar.

Corel WordPerfect will insert a horizontal line that stretches from the left margin to the right margin. You can start typing text on the next line after the horizontal line.

Modifying Horizontal Lines

You can change the length, position, or thickness of a horizontal line. For example, you may choose to place a thicker, 2-inch, left-justified horizontal line above headings as a recurring design element (see Figure 7-1).

To change the length, position, and/or thickness of any line:

1. Select the line you want to edit. When you've selected the line, it appears with square *handles,* like this:

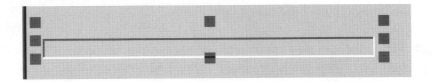

   Note that when you move the cursor over the selected line, it changes to the four-arrow cursor. When the cursor appears this way, you can click and drag the line to a new location.

2. With the line selected, right-click on the line. You'll see a pop-up menu that provides a few things you can do with the line: find out what kind of line it is, cut, copy, delete, or edit it.

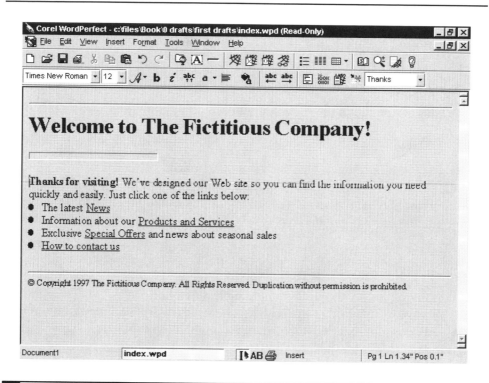

FIGURE 7-1 Lines used as design elements

3. From this pop-up menu, choose Edit Horizontal Line. You will then see the Edit Graphics Line dialog box (Figure 7-2).

 TIP: *You can also edit horizontal lines using the menus. Choose Edit | Edit Line. If no line is selected, Corel WordPerfect will edit the next line found in the document.*

4. To change the position of the line, select the option you want from the Horizontal drop-down list in the Position/Length group box: Left, Right, Centered, or Full.

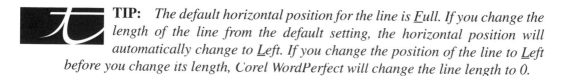 **TIP:** *The default horizontal position for the line is Full. If you change the length of the line from the default setting, the horizontal position will automatically change to Left. If you change the position of the line to Left before you change its length, Corel WordPerfect will change the line length to 0.*

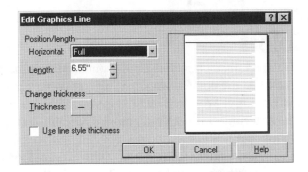

FIGURE 7-2   When you edit a horizontal line, you'll use the Edit Graphics Line dialog box

5. To change the line's length, type the length you want in the Length box in the Position/Length group box. You can also use the Length box's arrow buttons to select the length you want.

6. To change the line width, choose the Thickness button in the Change Thickness group box. From the pop-up palette, choose the line width you want.

TIP: *If you decide to use the default line width (the standard HTML style), check the Use Line Style Thickness check box. This check box is then automatically unchecked when you change the thickness from its default setting.*

7. When you're finished making changes to the line, choose OK to close the dialog box.

Corel WordPerfect makes it easy to change horizontal lines in just about any way. Don't forget to preview your pages in a web browser like Netscape Navigator to see exactly what your lines and layout will look like on the Web.

REMEMBER: *You can instantly view your pages as they'll look in a web browser. Just choose File | Internet Publisher | View in Web Browser.*

Adding Pizzazz by Changing Document Colors

Another great way to add distinction and zip to your web documents is to change their default colors. While the default black text on a gray background is pleasant, it's not very distinctive. Corel WordPerfect allows you to change the colors of five elements in your web documents: page background, default text, hypertext links, active links, and visited links.

Both *page background* and *default text* are self-explanatory terms. But the differences among the three types of links are a bit more slippery. Here's how to tell the difference: a *hypertext link* is simply a link that takes you to a bookmark within the web document or to a different web location. The color of a hypertext link changes briefly to the *active link* color when it's clicked. Once a link has been clicked, the location it's linked to has been visited, and you've returned to the previous site, the hypertext link color changes to that of a *visited link.*

Any of these colors you set can be overridden by browser settings. Some web browsers don't support active and visited text link colors. And each browser can be set to have visited links expire after a certain period. Thus, as with many of your HTML formatting settings, any changes you make can be ignored by settings defined by browser users.

To change the colors of your page elements:

1. Choose Format | Text/Background Colors. You'll then see the Text/Background Colors section of the HTML Document Properties dialog box (Figure 7-3).

NOTE: *While you can apply colors to selected text (as you learned in Chapter 6), the settings described here apply to the entire document.*

2. To change the color of regular text, choose Regular Text from the Text Color group box, and select the color you want from the pop-up palette.

3. To change hypertext colors, move to the Hypertext Color group box. Choose Hypertext Link, Visited Hypertext Link, or Active Hypertext Link, and select the color you want from the pop-up palette (it's the same palette for each choice).

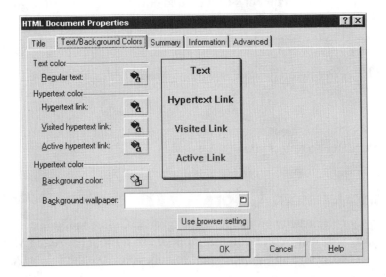

FIGURE 7-3   Use the Text/Background Colors area to change colors of key web page elements

Insider Tip

Here's how you can use the color preview panel in the Text/Background Colors tab of the HTML Document Properties dialog box to your advantage—it shows you a thumbnail sketch of the settings you've made. Remember: no matter what color combination you choose, it's important to maintain *contrast* between your text and background color choices. Greater contrast means it's easier to read. And you'll also want to make sure there's a noticeable difference between the color of regular text, hypertext links, and visited hypertext links (active links aren't nearly as important). Your readers will need to be able to easily pick out links to determine the ones they've visited from the ones they haven't.

4. To change the document's background color, choose the <u>B</u>ackground Color option toward the bottom of the dialog box and select the color you want from the pop-up palette.

 TIP: *To reset all the colors to their default shades, choose the Use <u>B</u>rowser setting button.*

5. When you finish changing colors, choose OK. The document colors will be updated to reflect your choices.

Creating Custom Colors

In any pop-up color palette on the Text/Background Colors tab, you can customize the palette to choose any color you can think of. To do so, choose the More button at the bottom of any pop-up palette. When you do, you'll see the Select Color dialog box (see Figure 7-4).

Using this tool is somewhat like giving a pressurized can of whipped cream to a five-year-old. While the results may be spectacular, the child wielding the can may be the only one who appreciates them. It's the same with using custom colors or lots of colors on your web pages. While you can specify any color or palette you choose, for HTML and web work it's best to stick with the basic 16 colors, or, at most, 256

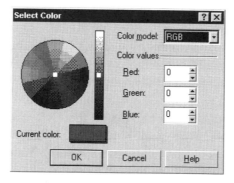

FIGURE 7-4   Use the Select Color dialog box to load or create special colors

colors. In most cases, there's no guarantee that those reading your web pages will have more than 256 colors available.

Describing Colors Using Color Models

There are three ways of defining the color you want. These ways are called *color models.* To select the model you want, click the Color Model drop-down list and choose the one you like. The controls in the dialog box change to match the color model you choose. The default model, *RGB,* defines colors much like you learned to do as a child—as a mix of the primary colors (red, green, and blue) found in light. You can define a color in the Color Model group box by entering a value between 0 and 255 for each color.

You may prefer to use the model designed for use on computer monitors—*HLS,* for hue, lightness, and saturation. Similar to the controls on your television set, you can set each of these (again in the Color Model group box). *Hue* defines the general color in a full circle from red to red: 0 = red, 120 = green, 240 = blue, then back to 360 = red. *Lightness* (sometimes called Luminosity), similar to a contrast control, adjusts how much white and black the color contains. *Saturation* adjusts the intensity or brightness of the color.

NOTE: *While color palettes are not included by default when you install Corel WordPerfect 8, color models are.*

If you're familiar with printed materials—or if you're attempting to approximate a printed color—you may prefer to use the *CMYK* color model. CMYK uses the four colors used on a printing press: cyan, magenta, yellow, and black ("K" is used for black since "B" might be confused with blue). You can adjust each value in the Color Model group box from 0 (lightest) to 255 (darkest). When each value is 0, the resulting color is white; when each is 255, the color is black.

Whether you use custom colors or the default colors, changing your document's colors is a great way to add a distinctive look to your pages. Even subtle modifications like changing link colors can show that you've paid attention to the smallest details of your site. Don't agonize over it, though: remember that Netscape Navigator and other web browsers allow users to override a document's (or web page's) custom colors with those the users set themselves (although most people don't bother to customize those settings).

Creating a Unique Look with Background Images

You can customize more than the colors of your web pages. You can also choose a background image or pattern for each page you create. (Corel WordPerfect sometimes refers to page backgrounds as *wallpaper*—like the wallpaper you can customize on your Windows desktop.) Figure 7-5 shows a web page with a background.

You can choose your own background image—in pretty much any graphics format (BMP, GIF, JPEG, and so on)—or choose one of the many images Corel WordPerfect Suite includes. In fact, Corel WordPerfect Suite has images specially designed for use as backgrounds. You can use any of the images the Web Page Expert

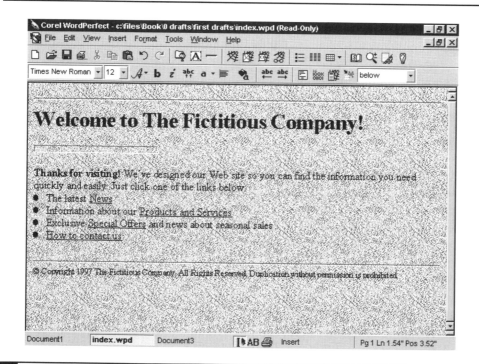

FIGURE 7-5   A web page created with one of Corel WordPerfect's texture images (sandstone.bmp) as a background

provides (see Chapter 4 for details). If you've installed your files using the default location, these GIF format files are in a \Corel\Suite8\Template folder on your hard drive. Since these files are in GIF format, they cannot be scaled or resized. They are, however, custom-designed for use on web pages.

Corel WordPerfect Suite also provides a wide variety of textures as part of its clipart collection. If you installed these when you installed the program, they should be on your hard drive in the \Corel\Suite8\Graphics\Textures folder. If you didn't install them, you can access them on the Corel WordPerfect Suite CD-ROM in the \Corel\Suite8\Graphics\Textures folder. These textures are in Windows bitmap (BMP) format, but are automatically converted to either GIF or JPEG format when you publish your page to HTML. Textures are grouped into ten folders: wood, objects, food, paper, fabrics, nature, organic, oil, stone, and design.

Insider Tip

Just about any of the textures that ship with Corel WordPerfect Suite could be used as web page backgrounds. Avoid those with many colors or lines—it's hard to read text placed on these backgrounds. Since they're a bit busier, you may want to avoid images in these folders: objects, food, and design. And no matter what the original format of your background image is, as a general rule of thumb, smaller is better. A smaller image downloads faster—so people viewing your pages don't have to wait as long.

Because you're in Web page view (meaning, you're working in Web Editor mode), once you've specified a background image, it will appear as you edit your web document in Corel WordPerfect. The background image will tile to fit the width of your editing window, just as it will when the document is viewed in a web browser.

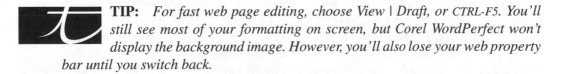

TIP: *For fast web page editing, choose View | Draft, or CTRL-F5. You'll still see most of your formatting on screen, but Corel WordPerfect won't display the background image. However, you'll also lose your web property bar until you switch back.*

To add a background image to your document:

1. Choose Format | HTML Document Properties, and select the Text/Background Colors tab to bring up the HTML Document Properties dialog box (see Figure 7-3).

2. In the Background Wallpaper text box, type the name of the file you want to use, or choose the small file-folder icon to browse for the file.

3. When you've selected the image you want, choose OK.

 **NOTE:**   *When you change the zoom percentage of your document editing window in Corel WordPerfect, the background image will not scale. Since bitmapped images do not scale, it will tile to fit the width of the screen.*

More Than Text: Adding Graphics

Shuffling through electronic pages filled with text can be as engaging as reading the phone book's white pages. If you're looking for a particular tidbit of information, fine, but there's nothing else on the pages to hold your attention. Web pages are a lot like that; a well-designed web page gets its appeal from the judicious use of graphics.

Corel WordPerfect makes it easy to use any kind of image in your web documents. You can insert graphics in any format Corel WordPerfect supports—from Corel DRAW (CDR) format to Computer Graphics Metafile (CGM). When you publish your document, Corel WordPerfect will automatically convert your graphics to either a GIF- or a JPEG-format file. GIF and JPEG are the standards for graphics on the Web. JPEG, the newer format, is a little faster and is great at delivering near-photo quality in a small size. GIF is best at compressing and displaying images with large areas of one color—like logos or line art.

CAUTION: *Before you add an image to your web document, check that the original artist or vendor you got the image from will allow you to redistribute the image (unless you personally created the images you plan to use). Many clipart collections—like that included with Corel WordPerfect Suite—have license agreements that specifically prohibit you from distributing their images "as computer images." However, these agreements might change as the Web becomes more widely used—and more people publish their documents electronically.*

To add a graphic to your web document:

1. Place the insertion point where you want to place the graphic.

2. Choose Insert | Graphics | From File. You'll then see the Insert Image dialog box (see Figure 7-6). (If you were inserting a clipart image from the Corel WordPerfect Suite, you could choose Insert | Graphics | Clipart. You'd then be able to use Corel WordPerfect Suite's scrapbook features to browse for the image you want to use.)

3. Use the Insert Image dialog box—similar to the File Open dialog box—to find the graphic you need. Select the image and choose Insert.

TIP: *Use the preview features of the File Open dialog box to view an image before you select it. If you've installed QuickView Plus, a bonus application with the suite, you can also use that for an instant preview of any graphic.*

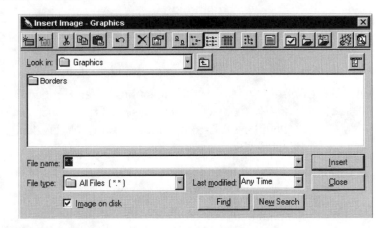

FIGURE 7-6   The Insert Image dialog box—use this to add any graphic to your web document

Insider Tip

To keep your web document small as you're working with it in Corel WordPerfect format, here's a trick. When you insert an image—and you know the image will remain in the same place in the future (say, a directory on your hard drive)—check the Image On Disk check box at the bottom of the Insert Image dialog box. This will tell Corel WordPerfect to read the image from its original file instead of saving a copy of the image as part of the Corel WordPerfect file. Just don't remove the image from its original location!

When you insert an image, it's not placed on the page as it would be as if you placed a rubber stamp imprint on a piece of paper. Instead, it's placed in a "box," or frame, that you can reposition (like a yellow sticky note) anywhere you like. Table 7-1 lists the predefined graphics box styles.

Style	Explanation
Image	Used with graphics, especially those on disk. No borders.
Figure	Also used with graphics. Hairline border.
OLE 2.0 Box	Used with object linking and embedding (OLE) objects—those inserted from other, OLE-compliant programs. No borders.
Watermark	Used to create a page background. No borders.
Text Box	Used to set text aside from the main body text. Thick top and bottom borders.
Table	Used for tables, spreadsheets, and so on. Thick top and bottom borders.
Equation	Used for scientific or mathematical equations or formulas. Box fills page or column width. No borders.

Predefined Graphics Box Styles

TABLE 7-1

Style	Explanation
Inline Equation	Used for equations inserted into a line of text (character anchor). No borders.
Inline Text	Used to set aside text in a line of text (character anchor). No borders.
Button	Used to create a graphics box that looks like a raised button, usually for hypertext links (character anchor).
User	Used for graphics or any other image. No borders.

Predefined Graphics Box Styles (*continued*)

TABLE 7-1

Once you've added the image, you can change any of several properties: position, size, caption, and HTML properties. You can select the property you want to change in three ways:

■ Select the image you want to change (a selected image has handles, or black squares, at each corner and in the center of each side), then right-click the image and choose the property you want to change from the QuickMenu (see Figure 7-7).

■ With the image unselected, choose Graphics | Edit Box (SHIFT-F11).

■ Click the image, then use the tools on the Graphics property bar, shown here, which appears when you select a graphic:

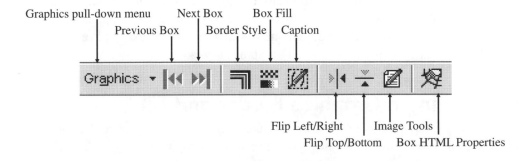

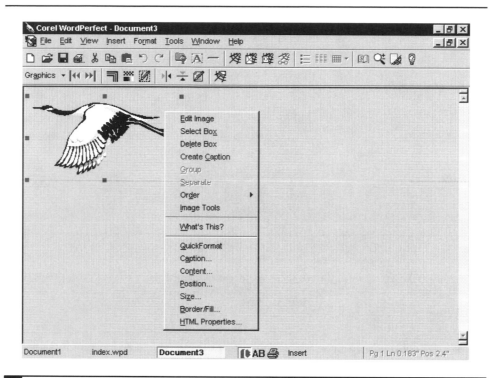

FIGURE 7-7 The graphics QuickMenu provides many ways for you to customize your selected images

Out of these three techniques for changing image properties, it's easiest and quickest to use the Graphics property bar, and the directions here will focus on that method. The Graphics property bar is also the best way to edit more than one image property—it stays on the screen until you select something other than the graphic. You can also use it to edit more than one box at a time—just use the Previous Box and Next Box buttons to move among graphics boxes.

Changing a Graphic's Border and Fill

You can use all of Corel WordPerfect's standard graphics box border and fill abilities in web documents. That sounds straightforward enough—until you discover the power Corel WordPerfect has under the surface in these features.

To select a standard border or fill for your graphic:

■   In the Graphics property bar, choose the border you want from the Border Style pop-up palette.

■   In the Graphics property bar, choose the fill you want from the Box Fill pop-up palette.

If you're not satisfied with the standard borders or fill patterns, right-click the image and choose <u>B</u>order/Fill from the QuickMenu. You'll then see the Box Border/Fill dialog box.

Under the Border tab (see Figure 7-8), you can choose from more border styles using the predefined styles shown in the A<u>v</u>ailable Border Styles box. Or you can create your own style by using the tools under <u>C</u>olor, <u>L</u>ine Style, <u>D</u>rop Shadow, and <u>R</u>ounded Corners. Experiment a little—it's fun!—and use the preview area to see your custom border style as you adjust the options. (Don't forget to use the online <u>H</u>elp when you need it).

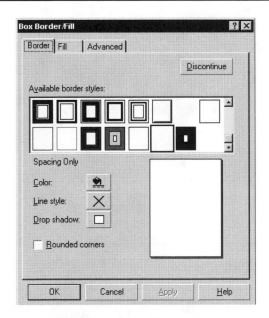

FIGURE 7-8   The Border tab's custom border options

Under the Fill tab (see Figure 7-9), you can choose from a wide variety of fill styles in the Available Fill Styles box. Or you can create your own style by specifying the Foreground and Background colors you want, as well as the fill Pattern. (If you've selected a gradient fill from the Available Fill Styles box, you adjust the Start color and End color instead of Foreground and Background colors. See the following section, "Creating Gradient Fills.")

 NOTE: *A gradient fill is one that progresses from dark to light—like a horizon, light falling on a ball, and so on.*

Under the Advanced tab (see Figure 7-10), you can make a wide variety of adjustments, including the drop shadow's color and width, the sharpness of the curve on rounded corners, and spacing inside and outside a border. But the most fun tool set adjusts a gradient fill.

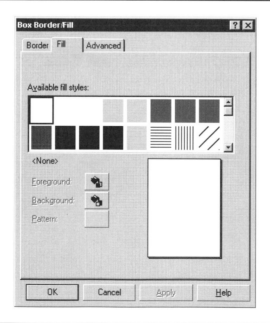

FIGURE 7-9   The Fill tab's custom image-fill options

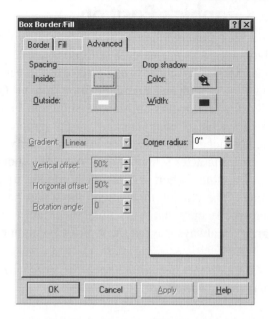

■ **FIGURE 7-10**   The Advanced tab's industrial-strength border and fill options

Creating Gradient Fills

To create a custom gradient fill:

1. Choose a gradient fill under the Fill tab (gradient fills move from one color to another). Note that you can change the start and end colors to your liking.

2. Then, under the Advanced tab, use the tools in the Gradient group box to fine-tune your gradient fill. You can choose a Linear, Circular, or Rectangular gradient. You can also adjust where the gradient starts on the page with the Vertical Offset and Horizontal Offset settings. You can adjust the angle of the gradient with the Rotation Angle setting.

TIP: *As you're playing with cool tools like the custom gradient fill, don't forget that the main purpose of your web page is to be legible and to communicate. If your gradient fill looks neat but renders the page unreadable, perhaps it's time to reconsider using it.*

Changing a Graphic's Position

The tools on the Graphics property bar also give you great flexibility in where you place a graphic—both what it's attached to and its position.

First, you can attach a graphic either to a character or to a paragraph. Right-click the graphic you want to work with and choose Position from the QuickMenu (Figure 7-7) and the Box Position dialog box appears, as shown in Figure 7-11. From the Attach Box To drop-down list, choose Character or Paragraph.

When a graphic is attached to a *character,* you can specify its position relative to the baseline for that character's line of text. You can choose Top, Centered, Bottom, or Content Baseline. When you attach a graphic to a *paragraph,* your control is more limited. The graphic moves with the whole paragraph—not just a line of text. You can specify only that it remain at the left or right margin, or in the center of the paragraph (it always stays at the top of a paragraph).

 NOTE: *Corel WordPerfect will attach the graphic to the character or paragraph nearest your cursor.*

Adding a Title to an Image

In exploring the Web, you've probably noticed how placeholder boxes appear before graphics load onto web pages. And you've probably noticed the Web's ability to show a brief, descriptive text phrase inside the graphics box before the image loads. Corel WordPerfect makes it easy to add these descriptions, which Corel WordPerfect calls *titles,* to images in your web documents.

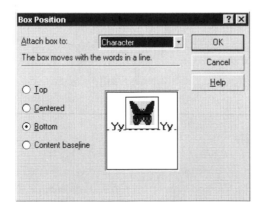

FIGURE 7-11   Fine-tune your image's position with the Box Position dialog box

Insider Tip

It's not just a good idea to use image titles—it's *essential*. You never know if people reading your pages may have graphics turned off or aren't patient enough to wait for them to load. That's why they're sometimes called *alternate text*—they act as an alternative to the graphic.

The best graphics titles are more than descriptive: they describe what happens when you click on the graphic—if the graphic is a link. For example, as an image of a music CD is loading, the alternate text—the title—would tell page readers what will happen if they click there. (To learn how to create a link, see Chapter 9.)

To add a graphics title:

1. From the Graphics property bar, choose Box HTML Properties. You'll then see the HTML Properties dialog box (see Figure 7-12) with the Image tab automatically selected.

2. In the Alternate Text box, type the descriptive title you want to add.

3. Choose OK.

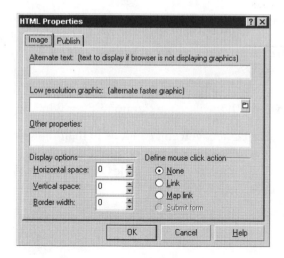

FIGURE 7-12   The HTML Properties dialog box

You may notice other options and tabs in the Box HTML Properties dialog box—you'll learn how to use those later in the book.

Adding a Caption

In some cases, you may want to add a caption to your images. For example, you might use captions on your images if you're publishing something technical—like this book or an academic publication. You can use all the power of Corel WordPerfect's caption feature to specify caption position, to change caption rotation, and even to automatically number them.

 NOTE: *When you publish your page to HTML, the captions are not converted as text. Instead, they're converted as part of the graphic.*

To create an image caption:

1. Right-click the image, then select Caption from the QuickMenu. You'll see the Box Caption dialog box (Figure 7-13).

2. Change any settings you wish to change in the Caption Position, Caption Width, Caption Numbering Method And Style, and Rotate Caption group boxes.

 TIP: *If you want to return the caption settings to their factory preset condition, choose Reset. This will delete any caption text you've typed, but will restore the settings to their original condition.*

3. When you have the settings as you like them, choose Edit to edit the caption text. You'll then see the Caption Editor window.

   Corel WordPerfect lets you edit captions in their own window—away from the distractions of the main document window. In a web document, you can use any of the predefined styles or attributes to change the caption's appearance.

4. When you've finished editing the caption, choose Close. Your caption will appear by the graphics box.

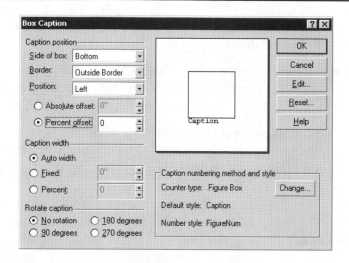

FIGURE 7-13   Use the Box Caption dialog box to specify details about an image caption

Changing the Contents of a Graphics Box

If you've changed your mind about the image in the graphics box—or if the original image has changed—you can update the contents, as well as change the position of the image within the box.

To change the contents of a graphics box, right-click the image, then choose Content from the QuickMenu. You'll see the Box Content dialog box, shown here, where you can choose the following options:

■ If you want to change the image—the file—the graphics box contains, type the new name in the Filename box, or click the file folder icon to browse to find the image you want.

■ If you want to change the type of the graphics box contents from an Image to Text, an Equation, an Image On Disk, or even an Empty Box, select the type you want from the Content Type drop-down list.

■ To change the position of the box contents within the graphics box, select the settings you want from the Content Position group box (both Horizontal Position and Vertical Position).

 TIP: *If you're editing a text box, you can also adjust the text rotation within the box by using the settings in the Rotate Text Counterclockwise group box.*

■ To avoid image distortion and preserve the ratio between the image's horizontal and vertical measurements, check the Preserve Image Width/Height Ratio check box.

■ To edit the image, choose Edit. (See "Changing an Image's Appearance Using Image Tools" later in this chapter.)

When you're finished changing the contents, click elsewhere in the document to return to the Web Editor.

REMEMBER: *Looking to cut the size of your Corel WordPerfect file? Even if you created a graphics box without checking the Image On Disk check box, you can still change the box contents to Image On Disk. As long as you expect your graphic to remain in the same place, this can keep your file size manageable.*

Changing the Size of a Graphics Box

You may want to adjust the size of a box once you've created it. The easiest way to change the size of a graphics box is to select the box, click one of the black handles, and drag the image to the size you want. The handles on the corners of the image will resize both horizontally and vertically; those on the sides will resize the image only on that side.

TIP: *Hold down the CTRL key while clicking and dragging an image handle to preserve the image's proportions while resizing it.*

You can also change the box size using precise tools. To do so, right-click the image, then choose Si**ze** from the QuickMenu. You'll see the Box Size dialog box, shown here:

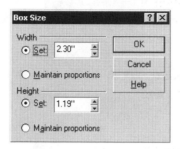

- You can **S**et the Width or S**e**t the Height of the box using the measurement boxes.

- To restore the image's proportions, choose **M**aintain Proportions (Width) and/or M**a**intain Proportions (Height).

When you're through adjusting the size, choose OK.

 TIP: *In web documents, the images you'll be using are bitmapped images. Bitmapped images don't look very good when you enlarge them. Since they're created dot by dot, when you enlarge them, the dots get bigger and the image becomes less sharp. As a general rule of thumb, you can make a bitmapped image smaller* without distortion, *but if you enlarge it, expect the image quality to suffer.*

Changing an Image's Appearance Using Image Tools

If the image you chose needs a little fine-tuning or even a major overhaul, Corel WordPerfect provides a full complement of image-editing tools.

To edit an image, right-click the image, then choose **I**mage Tools from the QuickMenu. You'll then see the Image Tools palette, shown here:

Once you've displayed the Image Tools palette, you can use its tools to adjust the image to your liking. You can make adjustments using these buttons and tools on the main Image Tools palette (to further refine the image, use the E̲dit Attributes feature):

- *Rotate*   Rotates the image freehand (just click and drag to rotate)

- *Move*   Moves the image by dragging

- *Flip*   Mirrors the image vertically (the button with the vertical axis) or horizontally (the button with the horizontal axis)

- *Zoom*   Enlarges or reduces the image in increments, or returns image to normal size

- *BW Threshold*   Sets the black and white threshold—the level at which a shade of gray is converted to white or black

- *Contrast*   Adjusts the image contrast

- *Brightness*   Adjusts the image's brightness

- *Fill*   Adjusts the fill of vector-based images—changes the hue of solid color areas

- *Invert Colors*   Inverts the image's colors—changes white to black, red to green, and so on

- *Edit Contents*   Edits the image using Corel Presentations

- *Edit Attributes*   Fine-tunes the image's attributes

- *Reset Attributes*   Returns the image to its original appearance

Editing an Image

With Corel WordPerfect Suite, you can also edit any image by using all the tools that Corel Presentations provides.

To edit an image, select the image you want to edit. Right-click the image and choose <u>E</u>dit Image from the pop-up menu.

Corel WordPerfect will load the tools for Corel Presentations. Leaving the document in place, the menus and toolbar will change to reflect the drawing tools you now have available (see Figure 7-14). Don't underestimate the power of this feature—these tools include professional-strength abilities and all of Corel Presentations' drawing power.

NOTE: *You don't need to know this to take advantage of the technology, but editing an image from within Corel WordPerfect using Corel Presentations tools is called editing in place. It uses Windows' object linking and embedding (OLE) technology to save you the effort of jumping among applications to edit objects.*

When you're finished editing the image, click the Close button to return to Corel WordPerfect's regular Web Editor screen.

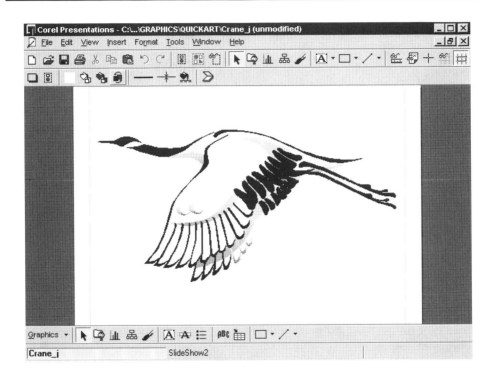

FIGURE 7-14   Editing an image using Corel Presentations tools—while still in Corel WordPerfect

Creating and Inserting Your Own Graphics

Besides boxes that contain images, Corel WordPerfect allows you to create your own images—from scientific equations to your own art. In fact, you can use Corel WordPerfect's Draw, Chart, and TextArt abilities to make your own graphics. (You can choose each from the Graphics option on the Insert menu.) See Table 7-2 for an explanation of each type of graphic you can create for your web documents.

Type	Explanation
Clipart	A Corel clipart image stored on disk or CD-ROM. Note that you can use Corel's scrapbook to browse for the exact image you want, then just drag and drop it into your document.
From file	Insert a graphics file from any disk using a dialog box similar to the File Open dialog box. Corel WordPerfect will automatically convert it for use in your document.
TextArt	Use Corel WordPerfect's TextArt module to create custom text—warped and twisted any way you like, in any font—and insert it into your document.
Draw Picture	Use Corel WordPerfect Presentations to create your own drawing and insert it into the document.
Chart	Use Corel WordPerfect Chart to create a chart and insert it into the document.
Acquire Image	Scan an image from a TWAIN-compliant scanner or other image source attached to your computer.
Select Image Source	If you have multiple scanners or other image sources, you can select among them with this option.
Custom Box	Use one of Corel WordPerfect's predefined graphics styles (see Table 7-1).

Types of
Graphics
You Can
Add to Web
Documents

TABLE 7-2

While you can use any of these predefined graphics box styles, you may want to experiment to see which fits your needs best. To see the standard graphics box styles as they appear when published to HTML, see Figure 7-15.

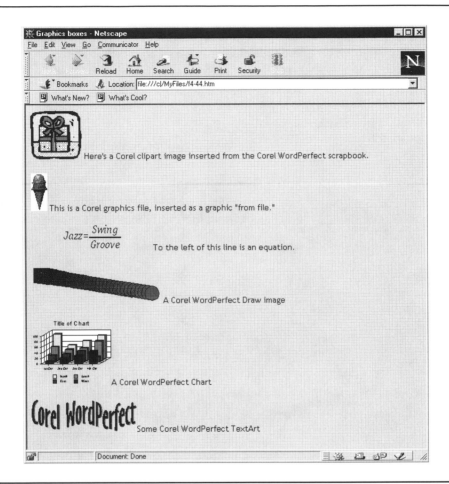

FIGURE 7-15   Corel WordPerfect's standard graphics box styles as seen when published to HTML

In this chapter, you've learned the basics of placing graphics in your HTML documents using Corel WordPerfect. In the next chapter, you'll learn about some fancier graphics tricks that add professional polish and visual zip to your pages.

Amazing Pages with
Advanced Graphic Tricks

8

So far, you've learned the basics of the Web and of web publishing. In the last few chapters, you learned the basic tools Corel WordPerfect provides for placing text and images on a page that's bound for the Internet. In this chapter, you'll learn some advanced techniques that will help you add professional polish to your pages.

These tips and techniques won't be what you'd expect to learn as a beginner. However, they're not difficult to learn, and you'll find that they add a spark to your web designs that will get them noticed. You'll first learn a trick to use on every page you produce.

Essential Elements: Creating Alternate Text and Images

Have you ever loaded a web page that showed text within an outlined box in place of an image while the image loaded (see Figure 8-1)? The text that appears inside the box is called *alternate text*. It's placed there to give web visitors an idea of what a graphic contains before the graphic loads—or if they have told their web browser not to load graphics automatically. This alternate text is all but essential for good web page design.

TIP: *If your graphic image is a link to another page, be sure to include the alternate text. People will be able to view the graphic link's alternate text—and the link will still work as it should without them having to wait for the whole page to load.*

Good alternate text, most importantly, actually fits within the outlined "placeholder" box for the graphic. It also describes the image and the action that will transpire if the graphic is a link. For example, an advertisement's alternate text might read, "Click here for free kazoo lessons." Or, a site's link to another page might read, "Products" or "Contact Us!"

NOTE: *In some web browsers, the alternate text will also appear as a special help box as users allow their pointer to linger over the image. This help box is displayed just as are those that appear when you move your pointer over buttons on Corel WordPerfect's property bars.*

If you're really interested in making the graphic image available to all visitors, and the graphic image is particularly large, you can specify an alternate image to be loaded. For example, you might have a lovely, 200K, 256-color GIF file, but you can specify a lower-resolution, 16-color JPEG file as an alternate image.

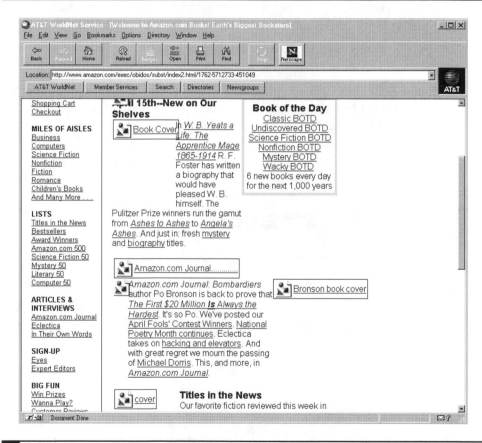

FIGURE 8-1   The alternate text inside the outlined graphics boxes loads before the image is downloaded to a web browser

With Corel WordPerfect 8, it's amazingly easy to add alternate text to your graphic images. To do so, first create or load a web page with a graphic in it, then:

1. Right-click the image and choose <u>H</u>TML Properties from the QuickMenu. The HTML Properties dialog box will appear, with the Image tab selected (Figure 8-2).

2. In the <u>A</u>lternate Text box, type the alternate text you want to use.

3. If you want to specify an alternate image, in the Low <u>R</u>esolution Graphic text box, type the name of the alternate image you want to use. You can also click the small file-folder icon at the right side of the text box to browse for the image file you want.

4. Choose OK to close the HTML Properties dialog box.

Not only is alternate text easy to create, but it's the polite thing to do. Not everyone has his or her browser set to automatically load graphics, so the better your alternate text, the more likely people will be to enjoy your site. And while you're at it, if you're creating complex, high-resolution color graphics, you may find it worthwhile to specify an alternate *image* as well. Now that you've become

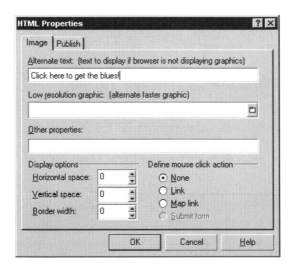

FIGURE 8-2   The HTML Properties dialog box—type the alternate text you want in the first text box

acquainted with the advanced features of the HTML Properties dialog box for graphics, it's time to learn more about its powers.

Advanced Graphics Tricks

An image's HTML Properties dialog box settings are your best friends when it comes to publishing pages that contain graphics. This dialog box gives you total control over how your image appears, how it loads, and how it's stored on the web server.

Let's first look at the other options under the first tab in the dialog box—the Image tab shown in Figure 8-2. You already learned about the first two options. Remember to always add alternate text to your images and an alternate, low-resolution graphic in place of particularly large, high-resolution ones. You'll probably never use the Other Properties text box, but if you wanted to add HTML tags to the graphic image, you could do so here.

You can also change the borders and margins around a graphic image. To change either the space on the left and right, or top and bottom of the image:

■   In the Display Options group box's Horizontal Space text box, type the number of pixels you want as the horizontal space between the graphic and the edges of its box.

■   Adjust the Vertical Space in the same way using the corresponding box.

You can also adjust the size of the graphic's border from here. Type the number of pixels you want as a border in the Border Width box. Choose OK when you're all done adjusting the settings.

Creating Links from Graphics

It's just about as easy to turn a graphic into a link, as long as you're already in the HTML Properties dialog box. But on the Image tab, the settings you'll use in the Define Mouse Click Action group box can be a little tricky.

The Define Mouse Click Action group box (Figure 8-2) contains four options: None (the default selection), Link, Map Link, and Submit Form. Unless you're editing the properties of a graphic in a web form, the final option will be grayed out and inaccessible.

The thing that makes this group box particularly tricky is what happens when you select either the Link or Map Link radio button: an additional tab—Link or Map

Link, respectively—appears in the dialog box. Since these options actually create new tabs in the dialog box you'll complete, they'll be discussed a bit more shortly. Of course, the <u>N</u>one option—the first one listed—means that if someone clicks on the graphic in the web browser, nothing happens. But when someone clicks on a graphic marked with a <u>L</u>ink or <u>M</u>ap Link attribute, something *does* happen—and you can decide exactly what that is.

If you want to create a link from a graphic, choose the <u>L</u>ink radio button in the Define Mouse Click Action group box of the graphic's HTML Properties dialog box. A new Link tab will appear in the dialog box. Click on the Link tab to see a new batch of options, as shown in Figure 8-3.

Under the Link tab, you can define the link's destination in three ways—you can have the graphic link to a specific URL (or web document), a bookmark within the current document or within the document at the specified URL, or within the target frame, if your page uses HTML frames.

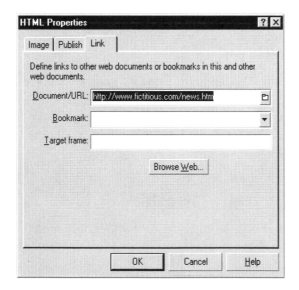

FIGURE 8-3 The options under the Link tab—use them to define your graphic's link destination

- To link the graphic to a specific URL (or web document), type that URL in the Document/URL text box. For example, to create a link to Corel's web site, you would type **www.corel.com**. If you want to specify a location—a *bookmark*—in the *current* document, don't type anything in the Document/URL text box (the default is the current document).

TIP: *If you don't know the URL off the top of your head—most URLs aren't as easy to remember as Corel's—just choose the Browse Web button. This button will launch your web browser and allow you to find the page you want to link to. When you return to Corel WordPerfect, the URL of the current page in the browser will appear in the dialog box. Of course, if your browser's already running, you can just copy the URL from the Location line in the browser and paste it into Corel WordPerfect.*

- To link the graphic to a particular predefined bookmark in either the current document or a document you specified in the Document/URL text box, type the name of the bookmark in the Bookmark text box. If you're choosing a bookmark in the current document, you can choose the bookmark from the drop-down list.

TIP: *If you're trying to figure out the bookmark that you're linking to, in most URLs, a bookmark is at the end of the URL with a number sign (#). For example,* **www.fictitious.com/docs/sample.htm#products** *designates "products" as the target bookmark.*

- To link the graphic to a particular target frame in the document, you can type the name of that frame in the Target Frame text box. You should be able to determine the frame name by investigating the URL closely—or by using Netscape's Copy Link Location right-click option. If you created the framed page, you will probably know the frame name; if not, you can also check with the page's creator.

Choose OK to close the text box and create your graphic link.

The Link option is pretty straightforward. But images can also be image maps, and that's what the Map Link option is all about.

Linking Graphics to Image Maps

Image maps are incredibly useful for web page design. They allow you to build sophisticated menus and button bars that don't rely on simple text. Or, you can take a map and specify different links for different locations on the map. Or, you can take a group picture and specify a different link for each person in the picture. Or...well, you get the idea.

Image maps are simply graphic images—usually GIFs—which have been designated as a hyperlink. With a normal graphic hyperlink, anywhere you click on the image takes you to the same destination or URL. With an image map, however, the graphic has been divided up and, depending upon where in the image you click, you'll be taken to a different URL. This is done by creating a list of coordinates defining specific areas within the graphic, and specifying a hyperlink for each area. As you'll see in a bit, this list is stored either in a separate file on your server or included in the HTML source of your document.

As you may be aware, web images—both GIFs and JPGs—are *bitmapped* images. This means they're made up of a collection of tiny dots called *pixels*. A typical 320x240 image is 320 pixels wide and 240 pixels high. Think of that image as a grid, with the source position (0,0) in the upper-left corner.

You can now find any point in the graphic by specifying the number of pixels over and down from the upper-left corner—for example, position (160,120) would be a point in the center of the 320x240 image mentioned earlier. Let's take this one step further. Using these coordinates, you can specify any rectangular area. For example, the pair of coordinates (160,120) and (170,130) define a rectangle 10 pixels wide and 10 pixels high, with the upper-left corner at the position (160,120).

This is a simplified explanation of a complex system, but you get the idea. Shapes other than rectangles can be used in image maps as well. Circles and wildly shaped polygons are possible, but difficult to create. There are several tools on the market that can be used to create image map listings. However, Corel Presentations 8 can create image maps as well.

Installing the Corel Presentations Image Map Macro

In Corel WordPerfect Suite 8, Corel Presentations includes a handy macro for creating image maps (bitmapped images with special link areas defined). But this macro probably wasn't installed into your system by default. To install it:

1. Run the Corel WordPerfect Suite setup program. The setup program's probably accessible from Windows 95 Start menu. Choose Corel WordPerfect Suite 8 | Setup & Notes | Corel WordPerfect Suite Setup.

2. When prompted, choose Custom Setup.

3. When you see the list of components, click on Corel Presentations, then choose Components.

4. You'll see another list; click on Presentations Macros, then choose Components again.

5. Check the box next to the Image Mapping macro, then choose OK twice to return to the main list.

6. Deselect any components you don't want to reinstall; then choose Install to add that macro.

Creating an Image Map

Once you've added the macro, to create an image map from a bitmapped image you've already saved in GIF or JPEG format:

1. Launch Corel Presentations.

2. Choose Tools | Macro | Play.

3. In the Play Macro dialog box, you will see a list of macros. Choose imgemap.wcm, then choose Play. You'll then see the Create HTML Image Map Code dialog box:

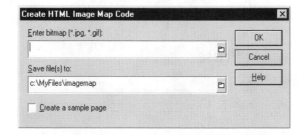

4. In the Enter Bitmap text box, type the name of the image you want to use (or use the small file folder button at the end of the text box to browse for the image). You must use either a JPEG or GIF file.

5. In the Save File(s) To text box, type the destination folder for the files.

6. If you want Corel Presentations to build a sample web page so that you can test the image map you create, check the Create A Sample Page check box. Choose OK to continue.

7. Follow the rest of the prompts to build your image map. Corel Presentations will walk you through each step.

Now, follow these directions to add your new image map to your Corel WordPerfect web document. In the HTML Properties dialog box for a graphic image, you can specify that you want your graphic to serve as an image map.

To create an image map link from a graphic, choose the Map Link radio button in the Define Mouse Click Action group box of the graphic's HTML Properties dialog box. A new Map Link tab will appear—click on it to see a new batch of options (see Figure 8-4).

HTML Properties

Image | Publish | Map Link

Server side map information

CGI script:

Client side map information

File: <current document>

Name:

OK   Cancel   Help

FIGURE 8-4   The options under the Map Link tab—use these to specify details about your graphic's image map abilities

The options under the Map Link tab fall in two groups: Server Side Map Information and Client Side Map Information. The major difference between client- and server-side image maps is where the link information gets processed.

SERVER SIDE MAP INFORMATION   As you might suspect, server-side image map links get processed on the web server. This is the traditional method and is supported by all web browsers. In effect, when a reader clicks on a server-side image map, the coordinates for the location where the reader clicked are sent to the server. There, a program—usually a common gateway interface (CGI) script—takes the coordinates, compares them with a *map list* (containing a cross-reference between image coordinates and links) also stored on the server, and creates a hypertext link to whatever URL is specified in the list.

While you may have some creative ideas as to what you'd like to place in the Server Side blank, there's very little you have to say about it in most cases. You need to check with your web administrator to find out what program is installed on your server to process image maps. Also, you need to send your image map list file to the administrator so it can be stored in the right place on the server.

To complete your image map, type the name of the CGI script your webmaster has in place for you in the CGI Script text box. If you've specified all the HTML Properties you want to specify, you can choose OK and return to editing your document. If you want to change how the image will be published to the Web, see "Changing How a Graphic Is Published to the Web" later in the chapter.

CLIENT SIDE MAP INFORMATION   *Client*-side image maps, on the other hand, are processed by the user's machine instead of the web server. First of all, the CGI program is actually part of the reader's browser software, such as Netscape 3.0. Also, the coordinate list is usually contained in the HTML file itself, rather than stored on the server. While this is more efficient, all browsers do not support it, and you should be careful about using it.

To specify the client-side map information, you need to complete the two fields in the Client Side Map Information group box. First, you can specify the image map list in the File text box. Since the client-side image maps usually include the list in the source HTML, the default value here is to use the current document. However, you could use a separate image map list file. This is helpful if you want to use the same image map in several different documents.

In the Name text box, enter the bookmark name that specifies the location within the HTML source of the map coordinate information—either within the current document or in the separate document you specified in the File text box.

Once you've specified all the link or image map link information you want, you can also change options about how the graphic will be published to the Web. That's what you'll learn about next.

Changing How a Graphic Is Published to the Web

The last tab you'll look at in the HTML Properties dialog box provides the final piece in the complete control over web graphics. Under the Publish tab, shown in Figure 8-5, you'll find a group of controls that help you when your graphics are published to the Web.

The first thing you'll notice under the Publish tab is something you can't change...in the dialog box, anyway. The Local Location label shows the directory on your system in which the original graphic file is stored.

But if the graphic is stored on your web server, you can specify that location here, too. You may want to store graphics that are used in several documents in only one location on your web server. If they're only stored in one place, it'll save space

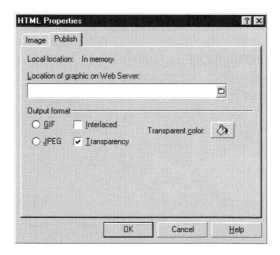

FIGURE 8-5 The graphic HTML Properties dialog box Publish tab options—use these to control how your image is converted and published to the Web

and time keeping all of the files updated. To specify where you've stored the file on your web server, type the graphic's location in the Location Of Graphic On Web Server text box. Here you won't change the name of the graphic. Instead, you'll use the Select Folder dialog box (see Figure 8-6) to specify where the graphic's stored, *not* its name.

Once you've specified your image location on the web server—if you wanted to—you can also tell Corel WordPerfect exactly how you want your graphic converted when it publishes the document to HTML. Regardless of its original format, you can change any graphic to either GIF or JPEG formats. Plus, you can specify additional GIF settings if you choose.

Converting Images to GIF Format When Published

To tell Corel WordPerfect to convert the image to GIF format—best for line art or graphics with large, solid areas—choose the GIF radio button in the Output Format group box on the Publish tab. (A JPEG file, on the other hand, creates smaller file sizes and is Corel WordPerfect's default format.) Once you've chosen the GIF button, you can specify two more settings. First, you can have Corel WordPerfect

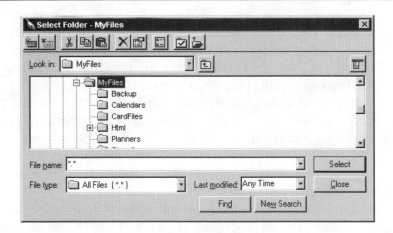

FIGURE 8-6   Use the Select Folder dialog box to specify exactly where your graphic image file is stored on your web server

automatically create an *interlaced* GIF image. An interlaced image doesn't display simply top to bottom as it loads. Instead, it loads, say, every tenth line first, then fills in the intermediate lines. This technique helps the graphic take shape more quickly on the page. To specify an interlaced GIF, check the Interlaced check box.

If you selected a GIF image, you can also have it automatically created as *transparent*. A transparent GIF image has one color—usually white or the image's predominant background color—specified as transparent. When the image is placed on a web page, you won't see the specified transparent color. Instead, any color or image behind the graphic—such as the web page's background image—will show through.

To create a transparent GIF image, check the Transparency check box. Then use the Transparent Color drop-down palette to choose the color in the GIF image you want to designate as transparent.

Once you've changed any of these options as desired, you can close the HTML Properties dialog box and apply your changes by choosing OK.

Now that you've learned all about these advanced formatting options for graphics in HTML documents, it's time to learn something no other word processor does like Corel WordPerfect.

Preserving Text Formatting with Text Boxes

Corel WordPerfect 8 includes a cool new trick that no other program has yet tried—sneaking your hard-won text formatting into HTML documents by converting it to bitmapped, perfectly sized graphic images. Of course, you probably won't want to try this with every piece of text in a page, but for small areas of text like logos, letterhead, and the like, this is a technique you can't do without.

Here's the basic idea: first, you'll create what Corel WordPerfect calls a *text box*. A text box is basically a graphic box that contains text or any other Corel WordPerfect formatting you desire. When you close the box, you'll be returned to the Web Editor—with only the web tools handy. But when the document is published to HTML, the formatting inside the text box will be converted to a graphic image—and thereby preserved perfectly.

To create a text box, choose Insert | Text Box. Corel WordPerfect will clear the document window and let you work on the text box by itself—with a full complement of Corel WordPerfect's formatting tools. Add whatever text, formatting, and so on, you want; then choose the Close button to return to the web document and the Web Editor. You can then position the box just as you would any other graphic image. A sample text box is shown in Figure 8-7.

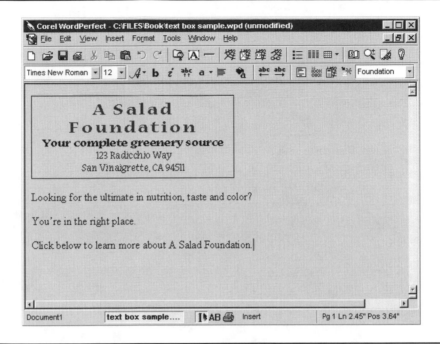

FIGURE 8-7   A sample text box in the Web Editor

You might use a text box to create a company logo, like the one in Figure 8-7, special link graphics, advertising banners, or special text-based icons and buttons. While you don't want to overdo text boxes, they're a great way to preserve some document formatting and to create web graphics quickly (Corel WordPerfect automatically converts them to JPEG).

In this chapter, you've learned some advanced tricks to use on the graphics in your web-bound documents. Now that you've mastered web graphics in your Corel WordPerfect documents, it's time to learn about creating links in your documents—even creating links from your graphics!

Hyperlinks

9

S ince the World Wide Web consists of interlinked documents, what's a web document without some links? Corel WordPerfect makes it easy to create links in your web documents. You create links just as you would in a regular Corel WordPerfect document—and they can point to bookmarks within the document, other web documents, or other files. Links are truly the key to the World Wide Web—they make it easy to jump from one piece of information to another, respond to questions, download files, and more.

In this chapter, you'll learn how to link your web documents to almost anywhere. You can link text or graphics to other web documents, files, e-mail addresses, ftp sites—just about any Internet resource. You'll also learn how Corel WordPerfect can automatically generate a hypertext table of contents for your web documents.

Text Hyperlinks

When you're editing a web document using Corel WordPerfect's Web Editor, you're just a click away from creating a text hyperlink.

Any word, phrase, sentence, or block of text can become a hyperlink. You'll probably want to keep the link itself down to a word or two for the sake of readability. For example, instead of creating a link of the whole sentence "Click here for more information about our products," you might create the link only on the word "here."

In fact, once you've created a hyperlink, Corel's hyperlink features are only a click away. While the insertion point rests within any hyperlinked text, you'll see the Hyperlink property bar. It's a great feature to use if you're planning to work exclusively on links for a while:

 **TIP:** *You can also access the Hyperlink property bar by choosing Tools |*
Hyperlink.

The buttons on the Hyperlink property bar provide quick-click access to
commonly used hyperlink features. You'll appreciate them especially when you're
changing and tracking several hyperlinks at a time. Table 9-1 offers a description of
each of the tools on the Hyperlink property bar.

Tool	Name	Description
	Hyperlink Perform	Jump to the link's destination—a web document, network document, or bookmark—just as if you had clicked the link in your web document.
	Hyperlink Previous	Move back to the preceding hyperlink in the document.
	Hyperlink Next	Move ahead to the next hyperlink in the document.
	Hyperlink Remove	Change the current hyperlink to plain text.
	Hyperlink Edit	Change the current hyperlink using the Hyperlink Properties dialog box tools.
	Hyperlink Toggle	An especially useful tool: activates/deactivates (turns on or off) all hyperlinks in the document. Often, it's much easier to edit a document when the links are deactivated—no chance of inadvertently clicking a hyperlink.
	Hyperlink Style Edit	Edit the Hyperlink Style (usually grayed out).

The
Hyperlink
Property Bar

TABLE 9-1

Creating a Text Hyperlink

Since the easiest type of link to create is based in text, you will learn to create those first. A text-based hyperlink is simply a highlighted word that, when clicked, jumps to a separate document (located anywhere on the Web or a network) or to a bookmark within the current document. To create a text-based hyperlink:

1. Type the text for the link, then select it.

2. From the Internet Publisher toolbar, choose the Hyperlink button, then choose Create Link from the pop-up menu that appears. You'll see the Hyperlink Properties dialog box (Figure 9-1). From this dialog box, you can choose options for what kind of link to create and how and where it will appear.

Once you're in the Hyperlink Properties dialog box, you can choose any of several options:

■ To link to a document or location on the Web, in the Document text box, type that location *exactly* as it would appear if you were using a web browser. To link to a document stored on a local network, type the folder and filename in the Document text box.

 TIP: *It's safest to create your links using the* http:// *prefix (***http://** *www.corel.com*).

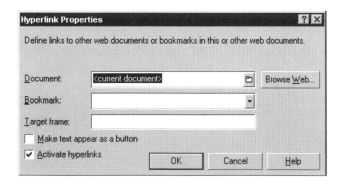

FIGURE 9-1 The Hyperlink Properties dialog box. Deselect the Activate Hyperlinks check box to avoid inadvertently clicking hyperlinks.

- To link to a bookmark you've already placed in the document, enter the name of the bookmark you want in the Bookmark text box.

Insider Tip

Use the Browse Web button to launch your web browser to find the link you want. When you return to Corel WordPerfect, the URL of the last location you visited will appear in the Document box. If you type the URL in the Document box and then click Browse Web, your web browser will attempt to load that web document for you.

CAUTION: *You must create a bookmark before you attempt to link to it. Once you've created bookmarks, you can use the drop-down menu in the Bookmark box to choose the bookmark you want.*

- To link to a bookmark within the web document you've linked to from the Document text box, type the bookmark name in the Bookmark text box. You can find the bookmark name by viewing the document source in your web browser.

Once you've specified the destination for the link, you can choose three additional options:

- If you want your link to connect to a particular target frame in the document, type the frame name in the Target Frame text box. If you created the destination document, you'll probably have a good idea of the frame's name; if not, you can check the URL or check with the page's creator.

- To make your link appear as a button, as shown in the following illustration, check the Make Text Appear As A Button check box.

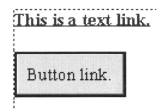

- If you want to disable the document's hyperlinks while you're editing the document, uncheck the Activate Hyperlinks check box. Hyperlinks will still appear as hyperlinks, but you won't be able to click on them to jump to their destinations. Instead, when you click on a hyperlink, you'll see the Hyperlink property bar and can choose the Hyperlink Perform button to jump to the link's destination (or right-click the link and choose Open Hyperlink from the QuickMenu). Why would you want to disable the links? It's very easy to inadvertently click on a hyperlink while editing a document, and this is an easy way to avoid frustration.

When you're finished selecting your options in this dialog box, choose OK to create the text hyperlink in your document.

Graphics Hyperlinks

You've probably seen web pages that include a series of custom-designed, graphic buttons that link to other pages. These graphics are hyperlinks, just like the text-based links you already know how to create. In fact, it's just as easy to create a hyperlink to a graphics image as it is to link to text.

 TIP: *It's sometimes fastest to create and place all the graphics you want* before *you make links out of them.*

Creating a Graphics Hyperlink

To make a graphic image into a hyperlink:

> **1.** Select the graphics image you want to change to a hyperlink.

2. On the Internet Publisher toolbar, choose the Hyperlink button, then choose Create Link from the pop-up menu that appears. You'll then see the Hyperlink Properties dialog box (Figure 9-1).

3. In the Document text box, type the address of the link you want to create (for example, **http://www.corel.com**) and choose OK.

TIP: *If you've added alternate text (a title) to your graphic image, it will appear as an underlined text hyperlink in the web browser once you've added the hyperlink to your graphic.*

Advanced Hyperlink Tricks

Because you're using Corel WordPerfect, it's easy to use the full range of HTML's hyperlink abilities. You can use some special HTML tricks to make creating links inside your document easier. You can also create links that do more than just link to other HTML web pages.

The World Wide Web and web browsers such as Netscape Navigator provide access to more than just HTML pages. While HTML is the standard, browsers provide you access to most of the Web's resources, including ftp, gopher, Usenet newsgroups, and more.

A Quick Internet Resource Primer

Because the Web is where most of us spend our time on the Internet, it's easy to forget that the Internet contains more than HTML documents. The Internet was around long before the Web became as ubiquitous as it is today. So, there are a lot of ways to access information other than through HTML.

While the Web was the first widely used graphical interface to Internet resources, these resources were already organized. Most of the files and documents contained on the Internet were and still are contained on servers that use the file transfer protocol (ftp). FTP sites contain folders and subfolders of documents. Figure 9-2 shows a sample ftp directory as viewed in Netscape Navigator. FTP sites can contain documents of any type—from word processing documents to graphics, from compressed files to huge animations. These documents can also be for just about any platform—not just Windows 95 or NT, but for Macintosh, UNIX, or DOS.

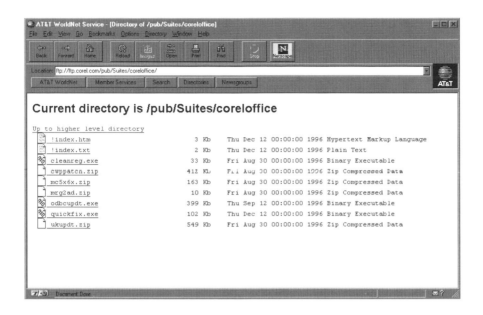

FIGURE 9-2 A directory on Corel's ftp site

 CAUTION: *Before you download a file from an ftp site, be sure it's for your platform—Windows 95 or NT. Check the file's size before you download so you won't be surprised by the download's duration.*

NOTE: *Most well-managed ftp sites contain a* readme *file in each folder to help you decipher the sometimes-cryptic document names and to help you find the document you're looking for. Some of the newer ftp sites have created hyperlinked HTML readme documents. These allow you to click on the document you want and download it directly from that link, rather than after returning to the main directory.*

Another convenient Internet resource was once the most common way of finding information on the Internet: gopher. A gopher provides a set of menus that link to other Internet resources. Like the other Internet resources, gopher is a good, text-based interface. But HTML's attractiveness and link abilities have largely superseded gopher menus. Some useful gophers still exist, however. See Figure 9-3 for a sample gopher menu.

Pundits, industry observers, and web gadflies say the key to the Web becoming as common as television—or at least as common as cable television—is the idea of *community.* By "community," they mean the Internet's ability to bring people together to talk, and to share information and ideas. This community exists on several levels: from the Net equivalent of a barely controlled, populist afternoon talk show to useful exchanges of ideas, technical information, and practical advice on life, parenting, and careers.

On the Internet, people exchange ideas in two main ways: through *e-mail* and through *Usenet newsgroups.* The origins of each aren't important to this discussion, but their implications are. Since people share information in these two ways, HTML-based web documents can take advantage of both. You're probably familiar with e-mail—exchanges among specific recipients that aren't necessarily meant for just anyone to read.

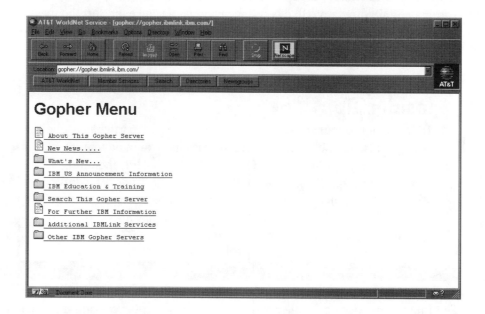

FIGURE 9-3   A gopher menu—Internet gophers provide a text-based way to look for Internet information

Insider Tip

A hybrid of a newsgroup and e-mail is a *mailing list.* Mailing lists provide a way for an individual or company to communicate information via e-mail to a select group. Some mailing lists allow any member of the list to send messages to the group; others allow only the list's owner or moderator to do so. These mailing lists aren't accessible from the Internet unless the owner has made mailing list archives available somewhere.

If you're not familiar with a Usenet newsgroup, here's a quick look at the basics. A newsgroup is similar to a bulletin board, where people can "post" notes to each other or to everyone. Like a physical bulletin board, everyone can read everyone else's messages. Each newsgroup is designed to focus on one topic. Within each newsgroup, certain programs (like Netscape Navigator) can even sort the messages by subject—an original posting followed by any replies. To see a newsgroup in Netscape Navigator, take a look at Figure 9-4.

Insider Tip

To learn more about any of these Internet resources, particularly about newsgroups and their different classifications, you may want to look for other books published by Osborne/McGraw-Hill, including *The Internet for Busy People, Second Edition* (1997) and *The Internet Complete Reference, Second Edition* (1996). For a convenient way to browse the Internet's resources by subject, you may also want to pick up Harley Hahn's *Internet & Web Yellow Pages, 1997 Edition.*

The Internet provides one other resource type or way of accessing information or Internet servers—*telnet.* This is seldom used, but is a way of remotely logging into a network or server connected to the Internet. Once you've logged on, you can

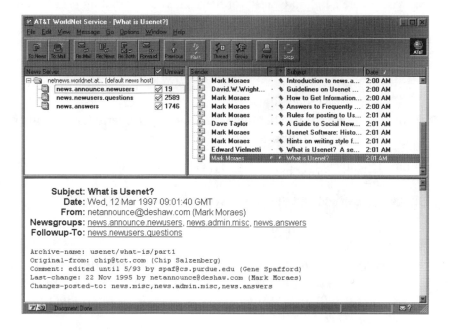

FIGURE 9-4   A sample Usenet newsgroup

use UNIX commands to wander around that server or network as much as you like. The bottom line: you'll probably never have to use it, but it's there.

Creating Links to Other Internet Resources

You learned earlier in this chapter about creating a link in Corel WordPerfect's Web Editor using the Hyperlink Properties dialog box. Although you've so far learned how to link only to other web documents, linking to other Internet resources is just as easy.

CAUTION: *Unless you're creating an intranet where you know exactly what access and browser each user has, you can't guarantee that everyone who views your page will be able to take advantage of all the non-HTML links you create. While HTTP, e-mail, and ftp links are widely supported, gopher, newsgroup, and telnet links may not be.*

When you create a link in Corel WordPerfect, you're creating HTML that tells the reader's web browser to search for a specific *type* of Internet resource. You can create links to any of the Internet's resources as follows:

1. While in Corel WordPerfect's Web Editor, highlight the text or image you want to create as the link.

2. From the Internet Publisher toolbar, choose the Hyperlink button, then Create Link from the pop-up menu that appears.

3. In the <u>D</u>ocument text box of the Hyperlink Properties dialog box (Figure 9-1), type the link you want to add. See Table 9-2 for a list of the types of links you can add and the proper syntax to use.

4. Choose OK to close the dialog box and create the hypertext link.

REMEMBER: *If desired, you can usually omit the* http:// *prefix before a web address. But to be safe, type the extra seven characters. You can even use Corel WordPerfect's AutoCorrect feature or customizable keyboard to create a keyboard shortcut.*

Internet Resource	Link Syntax	Example
HTTP (Web)	http://www.*sitename.com*	http://www.corel.com
ftp	ftp://ftp.*sitename.com/ directory/file*	ftp://ftp.corel.com/wordperfect
E-mail	mailto:*user@company.com*	mailto:toddler@fictitious.com
gopher	gopher://*sitename/filename*	gopher://gopher.well.sf.ca.us
Usenet newsgroups	news:*groupname*	news://rec.music.bluenote
telnet	telnet://*sitename*	telnet://spacelink.msfc.nasa.gov

Syntax and Examples of Links to Each Type of Internet Resource

TABLE 9-2

Probably the most widely used aspect of the Internet is so obvious that it's easily overlooked: e-mail. If those reading your web page have browsers that support e-mail or that can link to an e-mail program (and all but the most archaic browsers do), you have an easy way to get instant feedback from any page. In fact, when you create a page using the Web Page Expert, Corel WordPerfect places an e-mail link on the bottom of the page (see Chapter 4).

You can place an e-mail link anywhere you want to give web visitors the chance to respond to you or your company. Besides reporting problems with the web site, you might allow people to contact regional sales managers directly or even contact product managers. Or you could create special e-mail boxes to receive requests for information, contest entries, or survey results.

Besides web pages (HTTP or HTML) and e-mail, ftp is probably the most commonly used Internet resource. It's a way to organize files and documents into usable folders. Even if you don't have an ftp server of your own, you can still link to ftp resources. For example, you might want to allow your web page visitors to download the latest version of certain Corel WordPerfect printer drivers for Corel WordPerfect for DOS. You can create a link that connects directly to Corel's ftp site. (Don't forget to get permission first from the webmaster or other person in charge of any web or ftp site to which you want to link.) Once you've linked to an external ftp site, you don't have to worry about keeping a file updated on your server—you can link directly to the source so your link will always point to the latest versions.

Linking to Other Document Types

Not only can you link to other Internet resources, but you can also link your web pages to other document types. Later in this book (in Chapter 19) you'll learn about creating Envoy documents—documents created in a special format that preserve most of a document's formatting, type, and layout. But Envoy documents are similar to most non-HTML documents. Therefore, unless your web visitors have configured their web browsers to know how to handle non-HTML documents, things can get a bit tricky.

When most web browsers encounter a file of a breed they don't recognize, they offer to let you either save the file to disk, or specify an external application in which to view the file. An *external application* simply means any program that isn't the browser. Browsers like Netscape Navigator can automatically launch other programs to read non-HTML documents. For example, if you created a link to a Corel WordPerfect file, your web visitors could either download that file or tell Netscape Navigator to download the file, and then launch and load the file into Corel WordPerfect. Some programs, like Corel WordPerfect Suite, tell Netscape Navigator when they're installed about the types of files they can read. When Navigator encounters a known, or "registered," file type and application—called a *helper app*—it shows a warning window (see Figure 9-5). If you choose Continue, it will load the helper app with the file. If you choose Cancel, it will display a Save As dialog box to give you the opportunity to save the file.

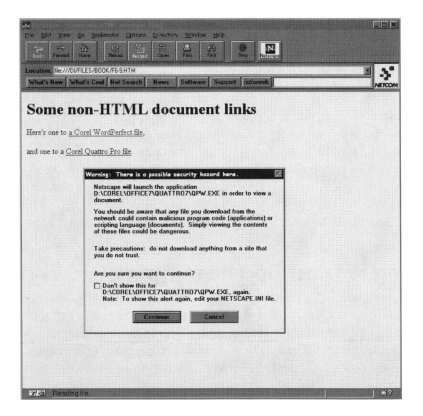

FIGURE 9-5 Netscape Navigator's warning window when you launch an external application to read a file

More commonly, you may choose to add links to multimedia elements such as sounds, graphics, or even movies. Netscape Navigator will automatically load files it already knows how to view, such as JPEG and GIF graphics. Sometimes you may want to make only a small version of a graphic available on your main web pages but allow visitors to click on the small graphics to load a larger version (your graphic file). Or you may want to link to sounds—Windows WAV files.

It's easy to create a link to an external file. To do so:

1. While in Corel WordPerfect's Web Editor, highlight the text or image you want to create as the link.

2. From the Internet Publisher toolbar, click the Hyperlink button, then choose Create Link from the pop-up menu.

3. In the Document text box of the Hyperlink Properties dialog box, type the filename you want to link to.

4. Choose OK to close the dialog box and create the hypertext link.

Insider Tip

Since you'll probably want to keep the files in a certain folder or the same folder as the HTML document, you probably won't want to use the Browse Web button of the Hyperlink Properties dialog box. Instead, type just the filename or the *relative* path and filename in the Document text box. A relative path and filename means the path *relative* to where the HTML document will be stored. For example, if you place all the sound files in a folder called *sounds,* you would type **/sounds/sound.wav**.

When your web page visitors click on a link to a sound file for the first time, they may not have configured their web browser to automatically launch the right application (helper app). If they're using Netscape Navigator, they'll see the following dialog box:

From the Unknown File Type dialog box they can choose More Info to learn more about helper applications and plug-ins. This option will connect them to Netscape's web site, which contains details about both topics.

TIP: *If you want to learn more about helper apps and plug-ins, Netscape's site has a wealth of information as well as full instructions for using Navigator. (Visit Netscape at* **www.netscape.com.***)*

Smart web visitors, however, will probably click Pick App, which will display the Configure External Viewer dialog box shown here:

Navigator will list a MIME type. While you may feel that the only good type of mime is one you can't see, *this* type of mime doesn't involve face paint or being trapped in an imaginary box. A MIME—multipurpose Internet mail extension—is simply a label for a standard file format. Web browsers and servers use these labels to correctly transfer and then display different file types. For example, the MIME type for the Windows WAV file is audio/x-wav.

Now that you understand what a MIME type is, forget it. From now on, all you or your web page visitors need to do is specify which application you want to use to open this type of file. Use the Browse button in the Configure External Viewer dialog box to hunt for an application you want to use. For example, you might choose

c:\windows\sndrec32.exe for WAV format files. Once you've finished typing or choosing the application you want, choose OK. Navigator will download the file and launch the helper application.

If your web page visitors choose Save File from the Unknown File Type dialog box, they'll be prompted to save the file using the standard Save As dialog box. Of course, clicking Cancel will abort the whole link.

Internal Links: Instant Table of Contents

At least the medieval town crier could tell by the heft of a scroll how long it would take to holler a proclamation. But when you scroll through a web document, sometimes there's no telling how long it's going to be. You may have to scroll until your index finger is sore just to find the information you want in a long HTML document.

Corel WordPerfect alleviates this pain with a nifty trick. Of course, it's long offered an automatic table of contents feature. And you can use this feature to mark any piece of text for inclusion in a table of contents. But when you're using Corel WordPerfect's Web Editor, it automatically includes table of contents markings in all heading levels past H1 (that is, H2 through H6). (See also "Applying Text Paragraph Styles" in Chapter 6 and Table 6-1 for more information.)

This feature makes it simple to generate a table of contents for any document—if you've used any heading styles at all. You can create a special area for the table of contents by setting it off with horizontal lines and a heading (but don't use a heading style unless you want the table of contents to refer to itself). See the sample in Figure 9-6.

If you have a long Corel WordPerfect document, take a moment now to load it, convert it to a web document (File, | Internet Publisher | Format as Web Document), and save it with a new name. Now, try these directions to make an automatically generated table of contents in a web document.

 REMEMBER: *You must have a document that already has some headings created by use of any of the HTML styles Heading 2 through Heading 6—or you'll end up with an empty table of contents.*

1. Place the insertion point where you want the table of contents.

2. Choose Tools | Reference | Table of Contents. You'll see the Table of Contents property bar:

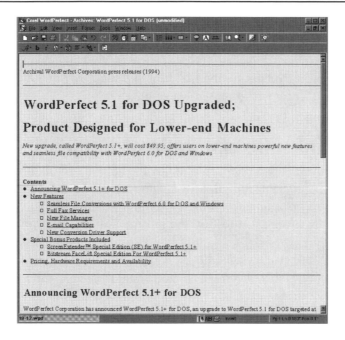

FIGURE 9-6   A sample document that includes a table of contents. You may want to set off your document's table of contents with horizontal lines, a special heading, or other graphic devices.

3. To specify the place for your table of contents, choose <u>D</u>efine. Corel WordPerfect will insert a line of placeholder text to show you where your table of contents will appear, like this:

```
<< Table of Contents will generate here >>
```

Your document is now ready to have its table of contents generated. To generate a table of contents:

1. If the Table of Contents property bar is still displayed, choose <u>G</u>enerate. Or you can choose <u>T</u>ools | Referen<u>c</u>e | Ge<u>n</u>erate. You'll see the Generate dialog box:

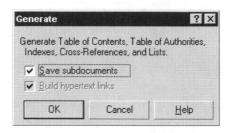

NOTE: *If you have created the document as a* master *document, meaning a document comprised of other documents, you can automatically save those other documents, called* subdocuments. *Just check the* Save *Subdocuments check box. The* Build Hypertext Links *check box is already checked for you because you're creating a web document when you generate a Table of Contents in a standard Corel WordPerfect document, you can choose not to create hyperlinks.*

2. Choose OK to generate the table of contents.

Corel WordPerfect will work for a while, then insert a table of contents *complete with hyperlinks* right into your document. When your document is published to HTML, this table of contents will provide a handy, hypertext guide to your document.

Easy Linking: Specifying a Base URL

No matter how well planned your web site, chances are you'll need to change some documents around. But when you've created links within a web page that point to other documents—documents that were located and linked relative to the page's original location—what do you do? You can spend your time changing all those links…or you can specify a *base URL.*

REMEMBER: *Corel WordPerfect creates a complementary HTG folder to accompany any document you publish to HTML. This folder contains graphics and other related files. If you move the document from its original location without moving the HTG folder as well, these files will no longer be accessible—unless you use the Base URL feature.*

Although "base URL" sounds like a nickname for a baseball player, it's really just an element inside your web document's header (the <head> section). No matter where you move your web document, if the base URL points to its original location—or at least to the location from which all the document's links will be valid—you'll be in good shape.

To create a base URL in Corel WordPerfect's Web Editor:

1. Choose Format | HTML Document Properties. The HTML Document Properties dialog box will appear.

2. Choose the Advanced tab.

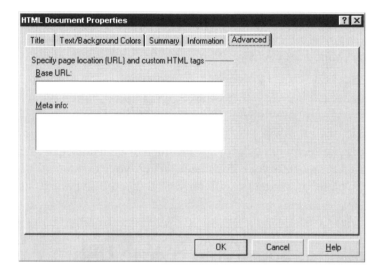

3. In the Base URL text box, type the URL you want to use.

4. Choose OK.

Instant Links with QuickLinks

Corel WordPerfect 8 makes it amazingly easy to create links in your documents—whether they're destined for the Web or not. Whenever you type the address of an Internet resource, such as a URL (*http://...* or *www...*), Corel WordPerfect will automatically recognize that as something it can create a hyperlink from. Other word processors can do similar things—but Corel WordPerfect is smart enough to create hyperlinks from common words or phrases you've defined as well. For example, let's say every time you use the word "order" on your Fictitious web site you want to create a link to your product order page. Every time you type the word "order," Corel WordPerfect will turn that word into a hyperlink to the ordering page—exactly as you've defined it. Here's the trick, though—you need to precede the word or phrase with the at symbol (@)—so in this example, you'd type **@order**.

Take a look at how it works. First, let's make sure QuickLinks is turned on. To change QuickLinks options and turn them on or off:

1. Choose Tools | QuickCorrect.

2. Choose the QuickLinks tab from the top of the window (see Figure 9-7).

3. To turn QuickLinks on or off, check the Format Words As Hyperlinks When You Type Them check box, then choose OK.

TIP: *You can also insert QuickLinks entries in a flash from the QuickCorrect dialog box. Just highlight the entry on the QuickLinks tab that you want to insert in your document and choose Insert Entry.*

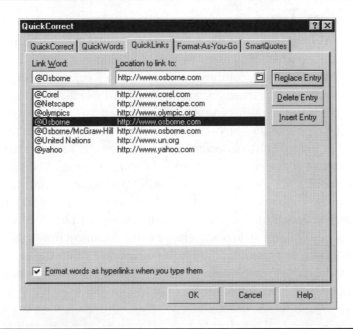

FIGURE 9-7   Use the QuickLinks options to tell Corel WordPerfect to convert certain words to web hyperlinks

As you can see in Figure 9-7, Corel WordPerfect comes preloaded with a few of these key words/links. As with all of Corel WordPerfect, you can tailor this list to fit your needs. It's easy to add and delete any word or phrase you like. Here's how you add and delete phrases from the QuickLinks list:

- To delete a QuickLinks entry, highlight the entry and choose <u>D</u>elete Entry. Corel WordPerfect will display a message box asking if you want to delete the entry. Choose <u>Y</u>es.

- To add a QuickLinks entry, type the key phrase you want to use in the Link <u>W</u>ord text box. Then type the URL of the Internet resource you want to use in the <u>L</u>ocation To Link To text box.

 NOTE: *If you didn't already type an at symbol (@) before your link word or phrase, Corel WordPerfect will add one automatically.*

When you're finished adding and deleting QuickLinks entries, choose OK to close the dialog box.

Insider Tip

In most cases, you will want to type the full URL of the page or resource to which you want to link. For example, you might type **http://www.fictitious.com/orders/orders.htm**. Remember that you can link to any type of Internet resource as listed in Table 9-1. In some cases, however, if you know that you may be changing the location of your files, you can type a *relative* link. These links don't include Internet resource info, but instead link to a document in a location that's relative to where the original document was read from. Sound confusing? It's really not: if you access *fictitious.htm* from **www.fictitious.com**, a relative link to the orders document mentioned before would read simply **/orders/orders.htm**. The advantage to this is that all the links you create in this way will remain in placc rclative to the document from which they were linked. The disadvantage is that you cannot change the location of any of these documents without updating the links. But in some cases, using relative links can save you time and hassle.

When you're creating web documents, QuickLinks can save you a lot of clicking and typing—and that's what Corel WordPerfect is best at. Be sure to take advantage of the automation this new tool provides. QuickLinks will even automatically convert e-mail addresses (such as toddler@fictitious.com) to mail to: links. (You don't need to type an @ first.)

In this chapter, you've learned about the basics of hyperlinks—what they are, the types of links you can create, and how Corel WordPerfect helps you create them. You've learned that links mean more than jumping to and from web documents scattered across the globe. Instead, links mean you can organize and offer information in usable, attractive ways. In the next chapter, you'll learn more ways to present information on the Web by use of Corel WordPerfect's comprehensive tables features.

Cool Page Design Using Tables

10

Since the early days of WordPerfect for DOS, tables have been a mainstay for millions of people. Tables are an effective way to present numbers, lists, and information. With the latest version of Corel WordPerfect, the Tables feature includes abilities that equal those of many spreadsheets. But tables are also effective ways to design pages destined for the Web.

In fact, many pages you see on the Web are designed by use of tables—they're one of the few ways you can (almost) guarantee that the document layout you've created will be preserved on your readers' browsers.

NOTE: *Most people are using web browsers that support tables. However, a few may be using older browsers that don't. While this is rare, it's still a possibility that a web page you create that uses tables may not look right when it's viewed in certain older browsers such as early versions of Mosaic or America Online's initial browsers.*

Corel WordPerfect provides a wealth of table tools to make it easy to work with these powerful layout grids. In this chapter, you'll look first at the basics of creating a table in Corel WordPerfect. Next you'll learn a little about some of the table features Corel WordPerfect provides. Then you'll learn about specific table-formatting features that are important when you publish your documents to HTML.

Creating Tables in Corel WordPerfect

Tables are a vital part of creating your web pages. First, they are a great way to present all kinds of information to your reader. Tables keep information organized and are easy to read. For example, instead of writing a paragraph comparing two similar products, try putting the same information into a table. People who visit your web site may not want to spend a lot of time reading long paragraphs filled with tons of information. But if the same information is presented through a table format and is well designed, they're more likely to read it.

Also, a Corel WordPerfect table works as a spreadsheet. You can calculate numbers, find percentages, and more. This feature can be very helpful when you're presenting numbers on product sales, statistics on equipment—the possibilities are endless!

Creating a table is simple. In fact, the new Tables feature allows formatting with a simple click of your mouse. To create a web table:

1. From the Web Editor menus, choose Insert | Table. You'll then see the HTML Table Format dialog box (Figure 10-1).

2. Change the Table Appearance, Table Size, and alignment settings according to what you want your table to look like. You'll learn more about individual settings in this dialog box later in the chapter.

3. Choose OK and the table will appear on the screen.

As with many other features in Corel WordPerfect, table settings also can be adjusted by means of a right-click anywhere on the table. As with the menu options, select any cells, rows, or columns you want to modify first.

To access the HTML Table Properties dialog box in a flash using the QuickMenu:

1. Right-click the table.

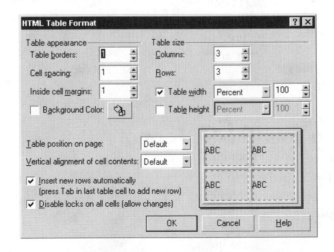

FIGURE 10-1   The HTML Table Format dialog box has all the components for beginning your table

2. Choose Format from the QuickMenu, shown here:

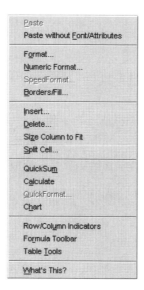

Because the Web Editor places all Corel WordPerfect's table tools at your disposal, working with tables in the Web Editor is as easy as if you were working in Corel WordPerfect. For example, placing information inside a web page table is just like doing so in a table in a regular document. You just place the cursor inside the cell and type in the information. To go to the next cell, press the TAB key or click in the desired cell.

Changing Your Table's Format

Creating web tables in Corel WordPerfect isn't like pouring concrete—you can change the layout anytime you like. In fact, you can even change the fundamental structure—the settings you specified when the table was created. (If only it were that easy to move a sidewalk.)

If you want to change the format of your table:

1. Right-click the table and choose F̲ormat from the QuickMenu. You will be taken to the HTML Table Properties dialog box (see Figure 10-2).

2. Choose the Table tab and make the changes you want, then choose OK. You'll learn more about the settings next.

The HTML Table Properties dialog box is important for formatting your table at any time throughout the table creation process. There are four sections that make up this dialog box. The Table tab is very similar to the HTML Table Format dialog box (Figure 10-1)—it contains all of the same formatting components. The Row and Column tabs enable you to adjust the justification, appearance, and size of the row or column your cursor is in. The Cell tab lets you change the appearance and certain attributes of a particular cell.

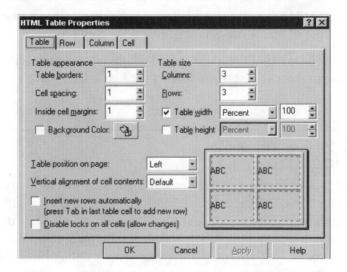

FIGURE 10-2   The HTML Table Properties dialog box enables you to change your table's format and specific settings. The first tab for table settings is shown here.

Adjusting Table Settings

Under the Table tab (Figure 10-2), you can adjust settings that control aspects of the entire table—appearance, size, and alignment.

TABLE APPEARANCE   The settings that adjust your table's appearance, including margins around, inside, and outside the table, are contained in the Table Appearance group box. Each of these measurements is in pixels—individual dots on the computer screen—except, obviously, the table background color setting. To adjust these settings:

■   If you want to adjust the border around the outside of the entire table, choose or type the number of pixels you want in the Table <u>B</u>orders box.

 TIP: *HTML's default table border is 0. You may want to choose a table border of 2 or more just to give your table a bit more breathing space.*

■   If you want to adjust the space between individual cells, choose or type the number of pixels you want in the Cell S<u>p</u>acing box.

■   If you want to adjust the space around the text inside each cell, choose or type the number of pixels you want in the Inside Cell <u>M</u>argins box.

Insider Tip

HTML calls cell margins "cell padding" (in fact, part of the HTML code for the <TABLE> tag is CELLPADDING=#). This setting is the space in pixels around the text inside each cell. HTML's default setting is 1—that's not nearly enough. Corel WordPerfect's default used to be 5—but you may be happier with a setting of at least 6. Remember to preview your pages in your web browser to get a true idea of how they'll appear. Table border and cell margin settings are particularly hard to get a feel for without a browser preview.

To see what a sample table might look like as you adjust the three border settings, watch the preview illustration in the lower right of the dialog box:

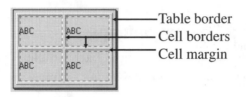

The table border will appear as the outside border of the preview table. The cell border settings will be reflected in the horizontal and vertical lines separating the four cells. The cell margins are displayed as dotted lines within each preview cell. This preview table reflects settings of 5 pixels for each setting.

The final setting in the Table Appearance group box allows you to specify a Background Color for your table. To specify a background color, check the Background Color check box and choose the color you want from the pop-up palette.

TABLE SIZE   You can also adjust the size of the table using the settings in the Table Size group box. To change the number of rows and columns in your table, choose or type the settings you want in the Columns and Rows boxes. You can also specify the table's size in both a percentage of the browser window and in specific pixels. (See "Column and Table Sizing" later in this chapter for more details on these settings.) If you want to specify the Table Width and Table Height, check the appropriate check boxes, select either Percent or Pixels from the drop-down list, and choose or type the setting you want in the corresponding boxes.

TABLE POSITION AND ALIGNMENT   You can also specify table position and alignment settings in the group of options at the lower left of the dialog box. First, to specify the *entire table's* position on the web page, choose the position from the Table Position On Page drop-down list: Default (usually left), Left, or Right. Then, to specify how you want text aligned *within each cell,* choose the alignment you want from the Vertical Alignment Of Cell Contents drop-down list: Default (usually center), Top, Center, or Bottom.

Finally, you can set two more items—but you probably won't use either of them much. First, you can allow Corel WordPerfect to automatically insert new rows as you enter data in your table by checking the Insert New Rows Automatically check box. Also, in Corel WordPerfect tables, you can lock specific cells so you don't accidentally modify them. You can disable this setting by checking the Disable

Locks On All Cells (Allow Changes) check box. The default setting is unchecked, thereby allowing cell locking. When you're finished with all these settings, you can choose a different tab in the dialog box or choose OK.

Adjusting Row and Column Settings

The Row and Column tabs are virtually identical. Each tab allows you to change the settings of the current row or column. (The Row tab is shown here.)

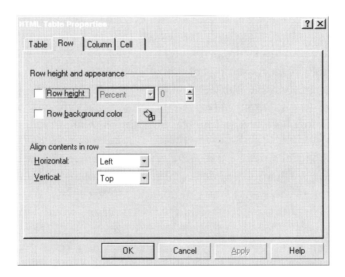

TIP: *The HTML Table Properties dialog box will format only the row, cell, or column your cursor appears in. If you want to change the properties of more than one row, cell, or column, select the desired area, then right-click on the highlighted area and choose Format.*

ROW/COLUMN SIZE AND APPEARANCE   You can adjust the appearance and size of the row or column using the first group of settings (Row Height And Appearance and Column Width And Appearance) on each of the Row and Column tabs. You'll learn more about this under "Column and Table Sizing" later in this chapter, but in the meantime, you'll need to know how. You can specify the height of a row or the width of a column in either a percentage of the browser window or in a specific number of pixels. To do so, choose either Row He̲ight (on the Row tab) or Column W̲idth (on the Column tab) and type the setting you want in the box.

And, as you can with the entire table, you can specify a specific background color for a row, column, or group of either. To do so, choose the B̲ackground Color check box and select the color you want from the pop-up palette (shown here under the Column tab):

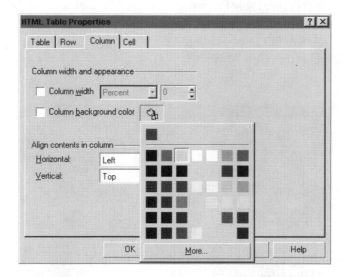

ROW/COLUMN ALIGNMENT   The settings in the Align Contents group boxes on each tab allow you to change the position of text within the cells in each row or column. To adjust the H̲orizontal alignment—like Corel WordPerfect's standard justification settings—choose the justification you want from the H̲orizontal drop-down list: D̲efault (usually left), L̲eft, C̲enter, or R̲ight. (M̲ixed only appears when you've selected cells that already have different alignment settings.)

Then you can adjust the vertical alignment of text within the row or column. To do so, choose the alignment you want from the V̲ertical drop-down list: D̲efault (usually center), T̲op, C̲enter, B̲aseline, or B̲ottom. Top and Bottom align text within the cells with the top and bottom of text, including ascenders (like the top of an "h") and descenders (like the bottom of a "p"). Baseline aligns text relative to the typographic baseline—the bottom of letters without descenders, like "a" or "o."

Now that you've adjusted any row or column settings you wanted to under the Row and Column tabs, you can either close the dialog box by choosing OK or adjust cell settings, as discussed next.

Adjusting Cell Settings

The Cell tab in the HTML Table Properties dialog box enables you to change settings for individual cells—not necessarily a whole row, column, or table at a time. The settings under this tab fall in two categories and are grouped into two group boxes: Align Cell Contents and Cell Attributes:

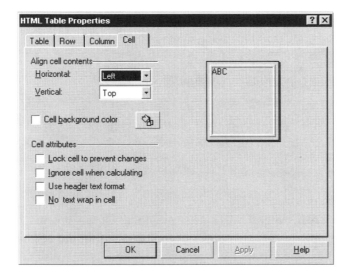

CELL ALIGNMENT You can adjust alignment settings much as you did for rows and columns. Horizontal justification is similar to the paragraph justification settings you're probably familiar with in Corel WordPerfect already. To set it, choose the justification you want from the Horizontal drop-down list: Default, Left, Center, or Right. (Mixed only appears when you've selected cells that already have different justification settings.) You can also adjust where text is placed vertically in the cell. Just choose the placement you want from the Vertical drop-down list: Default, Top, Center, Baseline, or Bottom. (For an explanation of each setting, see "Adjusting Row and Column Settings" earlier.) As you can with an entire table, row, or column, you can adjust an individual cell's background colors. Check the Cell Background Color check box, and choose the color you want from the pop-up palette.

CELL ATTRIBUTES   You can also change various cell attributes. Check the Lock Cell To Prevent Changes check box if you want to prevent the cell's contents from being accidentally overwritten. Of course, when you publish the document to HTML, the document's contents will be editable with any HTML editor. This setting is for your convenience while you're editing the document. Next, if you have a cell that includes some explanatory text, contains a subtotal, or the like, you can exclude it from calculations performed on the table or on a group of cells. To do so, check the Ignore Cell When Calculating check box.

You can adjust a few more settings in this group box. If you have a cell or group of cells you want to appear on every page of a table (if the table spans multiple pages), check the Use Header Text Format check box. Since HTML documents don't comprise multiple pages, this setting won't have any effect on your final web document unless you publish it to Corel Barista or Envoy. Finally, you can also disallow text wrapping to another line within a cell by checking the No Text Wrap In Cell check box.

Now that you've adjusted your table, row, column, and cell settings to your liking, choose OK to close the dialog box. Next, you'll learn more about particular table customization options.

Changes with the Table Property Bar and QuickMenu

In Corel WordPerfect 8, there's a new Table property bar that appears automatically when you are in tables:

This property bar contains some of the same formatting functions the HTML Table Properties dialog box does, but it also contains some different ones. From here you can change font attributes, insert rows or columns, and more, just by clicking the corresponding button. Table 10-1 describes each button on the Table property bar.

Now that you've learned about tables, you can spend a few minutes learning about Corel WordPerfect's support for columns in HTML-bound documents.

Tool	Name	Description
Table ▾	Table pull-down menu	Provides quick access to table, cell, row, and column formatting tools
General ▾	Numeric format	Quickly adjust the numeric format of selected cells: general, decimal, currency, and more
	QuickJoin	Combine selected cells into one or drag a range of cells to combine them together
	QuickSplit: Rows	Create new rows by clicking and dragging
	QuickSplit: Columns	Create new columns by clicking and dragging
	Insert Row	Insert a new row before (above) the current one
	Select Table	Select the entire table—all cells
	Select Table Row	Select the entire row in which the insertion point currently rests
	Select Table Column	Select the entire column in which the insertion point currently rests

The Table
Property Bar

TABLE 10-1

Using Web Columns

Corel WordPerfect also allows you to create columns in your documents. While HTML doesn't really support columns, Corel WordPerfect automatically converts columns in your documents to HTML tables.

TIP: *If you want to format existing text in columns, you can place the cursor at the beginning of the text you want to place in columns. All the text following that point will be placed in columns. Or, to format a specific block of text in columns, just select the text before you click the Columns toolbar button or before you create columns from the menus.*

It's just as easy to insert columns into your document—the quick way to create columns is only a click away. Just click the Columns button on the toolbar. When you click the button, you'll see six options in a drop-down menu:

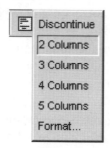

You can skip the Discontinue option for now—but remember it when you want to turn off the columns later. To create columns by use of the default settings or the most recently used column settings, just choose the number of columns you want from the drop-down menu; you can choose two, three, four, or five columns. You can also change the columns' format by choosing the Format option.

NOTE: *You can create more than five columns, but generally, you won't want to—they'll make the lines of text so narrow that they will be virtually unusable.*

Customizing Web Columns

If you want to start your columns with a greater degree of control and specify any settings up front (rather than relying on the default settings available on the toolbar), you can try a slightly different approach. Choose Format | Columns | Format. You'll then see the Web Columns dialog box:

In the Web Columns dialog box, you can specify key column settings. First, to set the number of columns you want, choose or type them in the Columns box in the Number Of Columns group box.

To specify the amount of room the columns will take on the page, choose the Total Width In check box in the Column Attributes group box. Then choose either Percent or Pixels from the pop-up menu:

- If you want the columns to take up a certain percentage of the web browser window, regardless of its size, type that percentage in the Total Width In text box (the default is 100).

- If you want the columns to take up a specific amount of room on the screen regardless of the browser's window size, type that number in pixels in the text box instead.

Later in this chapter in the "Column and Table Sizing" section, you'll learn advantages and disadvantages of choosing percentages or pixels.

Finally, you can adjust the space between columns as well. This setting controls the space between *all* columns—you cannot adjust space between individual pairs of columns. To adjust the space between columns, choose or type the number of pixels you want in the Spacing Between Columns text box (in the Column Attributes group box).

NOTE: *The preview window on the right side of the dialog box will change to reflect the settings you've specified.*

When you've finished specifying the settings you want, choose OK to dismiss the dialog box and begin typing text in columns. When you're finished with columns, choose the Columns button on the toolbar, and then select Discontinue or choose Format | Columns | Discontinue.

Now that you've learned about columns, it's time to learn more about tables. Columns are basically HTML tables that are formatted and displayed differently in Corel WordPerfect—but they still end up as HTML tables. Even if you're planning to work exclusively with columns, the rest of this chapter will help you understand how to take advantage of HTML tables' formatting abilities.

Visual Appeal with Shading

Shading can add really great effects to your tables. In Corel WordPerfect 8, you can use not just shades of gray, but any hue you like. Figure 10-3 shows a table that has the left column shaded to separate its information from the rest of the table. Some things you may want to put in a similar, left-hand column are navigational information, illustrations, relevant links, or even subheadings—you decide!

To shade one column of your table:

1. Create a new table similar to the one in Figure 10-3 using the steps outlined earlier in the chapter.

2. Highlight the column you wish to shade by placing the cursor in the column and clicking the Select Table Column button on the Table property bar.

3. Right-click the highlighted column and choose Format from the QuickMenu. Or, click the Table button from the toolbar, then choose Format.

4. In the HTML Table Properties dialog box, choose the Column tab.

5. Check the Column Background Color check box.

6. Click the adjacent pop-up menu (it looks like a paint can pouring into a square).

7. Choose the desired color from the pop-up menu for your column, and then choose OK.

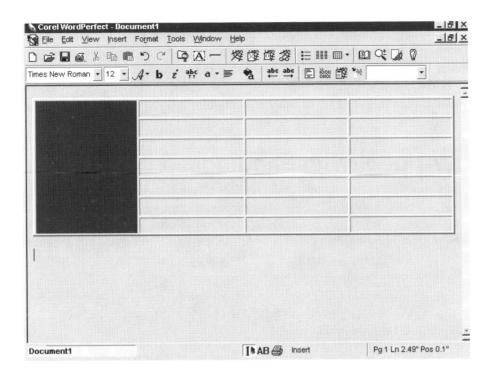

FIGURE 10-3 This is an example of a table with the left column shaded and joined. Formatting a column this way can even double as a left margin to your web page.

Joining Shaded Cells

If you're planning on creating a list of text within a table column, there's an easy way to make the column more unified and easier to work with. Corel WordPerfect's Join Cells feature makes it simple to create one cell from many. Here's how:

1. Highlight the column.

2. Right-click the selection.

3. Choose Join Cells from the QuickMenu (it only appears when you have selected more than one cell).

The individual cells in the column have now been united into one, tall cell. You'll probably find it easier to work with text in a left-hand column that's been joined into one cell—especially if you're creating a list of links, news items, or even headings.

Making Text Readable in Shaded Cells

If you are going to put text inside your newly shaded column, you will want to adjust the font color to assure it's readable. To adjust the font color:

1. Select the shaded cells, then click the Font Color button on the property bar.

2. Choose the desired color from the color palette that pops up.

TIP: *To shade a row, one particular cell, or even the entire table, just highlight the area you want to shade and follow the same instructions as for shading a column.*

Don't forget: you may want to click the View in Web Browser button on the toolbar to check for legibility once you've played around with both shading and font color settings.

Column and Table Sizing

With Corel WordPerfect you can size your tables in two ways: pixels or percentages of the window. In general, you're better off using percentages because you can never be sure how wide your readers' browser window will be. When you set a table to a specific size using pixels, the table will remain the same size regardless of the size of the browser window. In a way, these two ways of measuring your table size are similar to using bitmapped versus vector images. A bitmapped image—specified in pixels—must remain the same size to maintain its resolution. A vector image—specified in general descriptions like percentages—can be resized and still retain the proper proportions and resolution.

In the example mentioned earlier, you might have created a table that has a smaller left-hand column used as a navigational and orientation aid. If you created this kind of table layout with three columns for the content of a page, you might end up with something like Figure 10-3, which shows columns in proportions specified in percentages, not pixels—so they'll look reasonably good at most browser window sizes.

To customize a column's size using percentages:

1. Select the column.

2. Right-click the column and choose Format.

3. Choose the Column tab in the HTML Table Properties dialog box.

4. Check Column Width, and make sure Percent is selected from the drop-down list.

5. Type the percentage in the Percent text box and choose OK.

To specify a column width in pixels, although it's not recommended, follow the same process—only choose Pixels from the Column Width drop-down list and type the number of pixels in the text box instead.

Insider Tip

If you are creating a page layout that is precisely specified, you can specify the table's size and column widths in pixels. You will be able to maintain some control over your layout, but your pages will not be able to dynamically resize themselves based on the web site visitor's browser window size.

Ideas for Table Formatting

You know that tables are good for practical reasons, but they are also great for making your page look really up to date and modern. Making your web pages look cool is rather easy when you use tables. All you need is Corel WordPerfect's Tables feature and a little creativity.

Experiment with cell lines, colors, and fill patterns (see the upcoming bulleted list for examples). Also, change the size of the cell widths and heights. You can easily change the row, column, or cell heights by clicking on a cell's border and dragging it to the desired size. Or, you can right-click the table and choose Format. Then, from the HTML Table Properties dialog box, you can customize the sizes.

Make your tables look distinctive, especially if you're using them to format your entire web page. The more extraordinary your pages look, the more likely people are to notice them.

> **NOTE:** *Custom borders are converted to standard borders when printed from Corel WordPerfect to HTML. So, if you've labored over a custom border in a document, it will look great if you're printing to paper from a standard Corel WordPerfect document but it won't come across on the Web.*

Here are some other ideas to get you started on your own, attention-getting, table-based layouts:

- Use Corel WordPerfect's hypertext abilities to link a cell value to a URL.

- Use a single-cell table to insert a pull quote—text taken from the main content of a page and set apart from the regular text.

- Don't stick with strict column sizes—join, split, or resize as needed.

- Create perfectly aligned lists with custom bullets.

- Place graphics exactly within the text by placing the graphic within a table cell—or a specially sized cell created by joining other cells.

- Use tables to control your page's white space. White space is important to avoid a cluttered page.

- Use tables to design attractive HTML forms. You can use a table as a layout grid to perfectly align fields.

As you can see, tables are an important element when creating web pages. They are an essential feature for producing well-balanced, unified-looking pages. Aside from making your pages organized, it's a simple way to speed up your web creating process. Don't waste time by formatting each section of your page and attempting to align your text—just place it in a table and formatting becomes a snap.

Not only do tables speed up formatting, but they're also important to attract a reader's attention. Many web site visitors are just "browsing through." So, if important information is placed within a nicely designed table, the reader is more likely to pay attention to it. Do yourself and your readers a favor by using tables in your web pages.

Web Page Design Essentials

11

arlier in this book, you learned the basics of using Corel WordPerfect's Web Page Expert and of creating, converting, and publishing web documents. In this chapter, you'll learn some ways to make your pages look polished and professional. On the Web, image is everything. You'll start by learning how to create document titles and how to make your documents more easily indexed by popular web search engines. You'll then learn some keys to making your web site a worthwhile place to visit.

Document Titles, and Head and Meta Elements

Corel WordPerfect automates web page creation so much that you don't have to know even the slightest bit of HTML. That's a *good* thing—because generally, you don't need to get your hands dirty with the exact HTML that makes your documents look good on the Web.

However, Corel WordPerfect makes it easy for you to add HTML if you want. In fact, it supports HTML like nobody's business. But before you investigate some of the HTML, you'll need to learn a bit about how a web page is structured in HTML.

Compare the two screens (a and b) shown in Figure 11-1. Figure 11-1a shows a simple web document, created in Corel WordPerfect, that contains only a heading and a line of body text. Figure 11-1b shows the HTML for that web document, displayed by choosing View | Document Source in Netscape Navigator. (You could see this same HTML by opening the HTML document as an ASCII text document in Corel WordPerfect.)

(a)

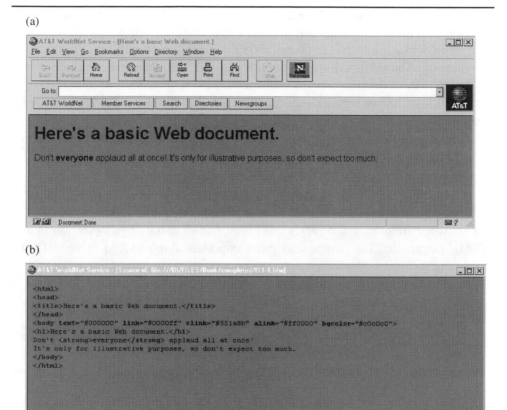

(b)

FIGURE 11-1 (a)A basic web document shown in the browser window and (b)the same web document shown as its HTML source

Any HTML document contains some basic elements—three sets of paired tags, in this order:

```
<html>
<head>
</head>
<body>
</body>
</html>
```

These paired tags provide the basic structure for an HTML document. As you can see in Figure 11-1b, certain elements appear in the <head> portion of the document, while the document content is in the <body> section. Corel WordPerfect provides some powerful tools to automate the stuff that appears in the <head> section of the HTML document. This is information *about* the document, rather than information contained within the document. (The document content falls within the <html> and </html> tags.)

You can add special information in this <head> section using Corel WordPerfect's special web features.

Adding Document Titles

Corel WordPerfect makes it easy to add information to the <head> section in any HTML document. The easiest and most important thing to add to any HTML document's <head> information is the document title. A *document title* is the title or description that appears in the title bar of your web browser when the document is loaded. For example, in Figure 11-1a, the title of the web document is "Here's a basic Web document."

Corel WordPerfect will automatically create a document title—contained within a pair of <title> tags—for your web documents if you have any headings defined. In other words, Corel WordPerfect will use the first instance of any HTML heading style as the title for your web document unless you tell it otherwise.

NOTE: *Corel WordPerfect will use headings in descending order. It will first look for an instance of the Heading 1 style. If it doesn't find any, it will look for the first instance of a Heading 2 style, and so on, through the Heading 6 style.*

You can, however, name a document anything you want. The best document titles describe the contents of the page instead of providing a generic heading. They're also not too long and not too short. For example, these would be poor web page titles:

- The Fictitious Company's Web Site (on all pages in the site)
- My Page
- Information

- Home Page

- News

- Reasons why you may want to consider the Fictitious Company as your employer, including our comprehensive benefit plan, great corporate culture, and amazing cafeteria

Examples of better titles might include these:

- Fictitious Jobs

- How to Contact Fictitious

- Fictitious News and Happenings

- Today's Special Offers and Prices

- Working for Fictitious

To change a web document's title:

1. Choose Format | HTML Document Properties. You'll see the HTML Document Properties dialog box, open to the Title tab (Figure 11-2).

2. Type the document title you want in the Custom Title text box.

3. Choose OK.

Once you've created a new document title, the document title information will appear in the <head> of the HTML document. Note that you can use only plain text in the document title. Bold, italic, and other special text formatting aren't allowed.

Insider Tip

Corel WordPerfect automatically creates a title for your document because each HTML document must have one (and only one). If you don't specify a title—and the document doesn't have any headings—Corel WordPerfect will create an empty or blank title.

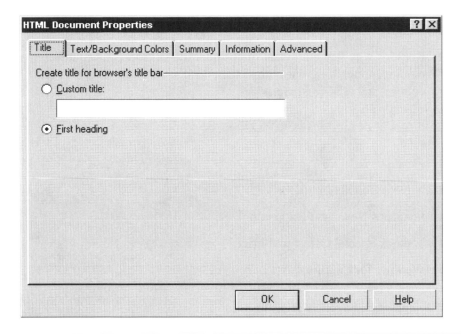

FIGURE 11-2   The Title tab of the HTML Document Properties dialog box—if you don't want to use the first heading, type a new document title in the box

Specifying Additional Information for Search Engines

You're probably familiar with web search engines. *Search engines* use both human and automated processing to sort and categorize web pages by the information they contain. Corel WordPerfect makes it easy to add special information to your web pages that helps them get categorized correctly. This special information is contained in a part of the <head> section of your HTML document. Information about your web document is called *meta* information and is contained in codes inside a special <meta> tag.

Insider Tip

Since the Web is a sprawling network, most web users rely on search engines to find the information they need, rather than hoping to stumble across the right stuff. Commonly used search engines include

Infoseek	**www.infoseek.com**
Excite	**www.excite.com**
HotBot	**www.hotbot.com**
Search.Com	**www.search.com**
Yahoo	**www.yahoo.com**
AltaVista	**www.altavista.com**

These meta tags can sound confusing. But you don't need to know how they work to use this special way of helping web search engines correctly categorize your web documents. Just fill in the blanks discussed next.

Use this technique to add a description and special keywords to your document that may not appear in the document itself. Instead, like creating an index for a book, you can specify the most important concepts or *keywords* that appear in the document. A search engine will look at these keywords and consider them as more reliable ways to describe what your document contains than its automated analysis of the document's contents. For example, if your document features information about your company's search for local distributors, you might choose keywords like "home business," "business opportunities," and so forth.

To add a description and keywords to your document:

1. Choose Format | HTML Document Properties.

2. From the HTML Document Properties dialog box, choose the Advanced tab (see Figure 11-3).

3. In the <u>M</u>eta Info box, type the following, replacing the sample text shown in italics with a list of words that apply to your document:

<META NAME="Description" CONTENT="*Insert your document description here.*"><META NAME="Keywords" CONTENT= "*Replace, these, with, words and phrases, separated by commas*">

 NOTE: *Although in normal HTML you would separate the two META lines with a line break, Corel WordPerfect doesn't allow that within the dialog box. It doesn't matter to the web browser, however.*

4. Choose OK to close the dialog box.

When you publish your document to HTML, this information will automatically be added to the document's <head> section. When automated search software

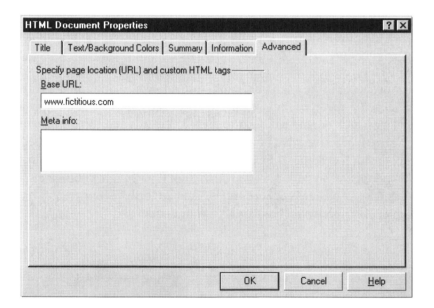

FIGURE 11-3   The advanced options in the HTML Document Properties dialog box. Use the Meta Info box to add special information to your document's <head> section.

examines your document, it will most likely look at the description and keyword information to correctly describe and categorize your pages.

Adding Other <head> Information

While the meta information is probably the most useful, you can also add other information to the <head> section of your documents. For example, you might want to add information about the document's author (you!). You can do this a few different ways.

First, you can manually add a comment to the header information. When you create a comment in Corel WordPerfect using the Web Editor, it's automatically converted to an HTML comment. An HTML comment looks like this:

```
<!—Here's a comment. July 21, 1997 5:22:00 PM—>
```

Web page creators commonly add to the <head> of a document comments that list the author name and the revision date. To add this type of comment to the <head> information:

1. Choose Fo<u>r</u>mat | <u>H</u>TML Document Properties.

2. From the HTML Document Properties dialog box, choose the Advanced tab (Figure 11-3).

3. In the <u>M</u>eta Info box, type the following, replacing the sample text shown in italics with your own information:

   <!—Author: T. Oddler, Revised: July 1, 1997—>

 NOTE: *If you've already added some meta information, just type this text before or after the existing text.*

4. Choose OK to close the dialog box.

Another way to identify a web document's author is by adding a special <link> tag to the document's <head> info. To add this kind of tag:

1. Choose Format | HTML Document Properties.

2. From the HTML Document Properties dialog box, choose the Advanced tab (Figure 11-3).

3. In the Meta Info box, type the following, replacing the sample text shown in italics, with your own information:

<LINK HREF="*mailto:toddler@fictitious.com*" REV="author">

4. Choose OK to close the dialog box.

If your web server supports it, you can also use a special <head> tag to create a web page as a front-end to a server-based search engine. If you don't know what that means, check with your MIS manager or your Internet service provider. If your web server has this capability, they will know—and there's nothing you can do on your side to change that. To create this special kind of web page, sometimes called an "index page," you need to put only one special tag in the <head> section. You don't need to add anything to the page's contents.

To create an index page:

1. Choose Format | HTML Document Properties.

2. From the HTML Document Properties dialog box, choose the Advanced tab (see Figure 11-3).

3. In the Meta Info box, type **<ISINDEX>**.

4. Choose OK to close the dialog box.

A web page that contains only this tag in the <head> section will look like the one shown in Figure 11-4.

FIGURE 11-4 A web page that provides access to a web server's keyword search engine, created with the <ISINDEX> tag

Designing Easy-to-Use Web Pages

Designing web pages gives you a special responsibility. It's a responsibility to your readers that you'll make your pages easy to read, use, navigate, and find. You've learned elsewhere in the book about making pages easy to read (see Chapter 6). But some other elements of good page design are equally important.

Of course, designing attractive, engaging web pages is as simple yet complex as designing attractive, engaging printed pages. In other words, there is a good reason professional graphic designers are paid for their skills and knowledge. While the average person can produce good-looking pages, professionals can often give them an extra touch that sets them apart from the crowd. Here, you'll learn a few points to remember when designing web pages. But don't substitute this brief section for a good understanding of graphic design principles or for consulting with a graphic design professional. As the Web is used more and more, most designers have come in contact with projects for the Web. If you don't have a graphic designer at your business, be sure to consult one who has experience designing pages that are viewed on a computer screen or on the Web.

Because the Web is a network of interconnected pages, it's important to make it easy to move among them. Your web page readers will want navigation to be easy—or they might just click somewhere else. And they'll want to be able to contact you and know essential facts about the page in a matter of seconds. Here's a checklist of some key elements you should consider for each of your web pages. These

elements represent not just courtesy to your page readers, but an increased chance that your pages will be read and remembered.

PROVIDE A WAY BACK   Although most browsers, such as Netscape Navigator, have a "back" button to return you to the previous page, you may still want to provide a link back. For example, you may have created a web site that includes several levels. The first level, the home page, is the first page you'll want to provide a link to from any document or page on your site. You can do that as easily as creating a text hyperlink that reads "back to home page" or "top." In most sites, pages on the second level are similar to the home page: they're usually lists of links and act more as tables of contents than as pages full of information. You will want to provide links back to these secondary pages from third-level pages, and so on. For example, a press release may include a link at the bottom of the page that reads "back to press release main page." Again, it's just as easy to link back to these pages as it is to other hyperlinks.

PROVIDE A TEXT MENU OF LINKS   Although you may have poured your heart, soul, and a few sleepless nights into a beautiful graphic menu, you'll still want to include a text-based equivalent on each page. (Some people actually build a text-based "mirror" of their site structure.) Why? Several reasons. Some people, to increase the speed with which web pages load, turn their graphic images *off*—they only load a page's images when they want them, not as the default. Other people, especially those using a dial-up, modem-based connection to the Web, don't want to wait for a page's graphics to load when they know they want information that's contained on a page below the one they're loading. A text-based menu to your site can appear on every page—at least as far down as the secondary level. Some web experts recommend that you place the text-based menu at the top of the page with the graphic menu at the bottom, so that the text-based menu appears first. Whatever you choose, you will want to make sure your text-based menu includes links to each of the major areas on your site. You may even want to ensure that each secondary page is listed—about eight at the most.

MAKE YOUR PAGES APPEAR FRESH   Does it really matter if you drink your Pepsi by the date on the bottom of the can? That's debatable, but in the Web world, timeliness is everything. Almost nothing makes a page less appealing than stale information. At least every week, if not more frequently, add new information or links to your site. Start with your home page, since that's where the most people visit. Along with adding new information, take a cue from Corel WordPerfect's Web Page Expert: include an "Updated on" line at the bottom of your page. If you keep your master home page in Corel WordPerfect, you can insert a date code (CTRL-SHIFT-D) so that each time you publish the page to HTML, the date will reflect that day's date. But by providing an "updated on" message, remember that you're committing to keep the page current. As with a stale can of Pepsi, nobody wants to read a page that's long past its updated expiration date.

DON'T BE A STRANGER   If you're on the Web, you have a responsibility to keep your pages updated and to fix any problems they contain. On at least the home page, provide a way for web readers to contact you. If you have different departments or groups people may want to contact, include a link to a page of contacts. Besides the address of the webmaster (you?), you may want to include e-mail addresses for customer service, product orders, and requests for information.

BREAK IT UP   HTML may not provide very thrilling typographic capabilities, but they're enough to make pages readable. Take advantage of headings to provide visual cues to the organization of your documents. Don't let paragraphs drag on for more than four or five sentences. And don't let your web pages get much past four or five screens. Like any design rules, these are meant to be broken—but understand that doing so makes your pages harder to read and less inviting.

LET PEOPLE KNOW WHAT THEY'RE IN FOR   This applies in two ways. For links to other documents, be sure you're providing enough of a description of the link's destination that people have a good idea of where they'll end up. And if you're linking to a file for downloading, be sure to include key information such as file size (usually in kilobytes), system requirements, and complete file description.

TEST YOUR SITE   Recruit representative customers, users, and even your family to try out your site. Watch them to see what they have a hard time with. Are they having a difficult time finding your special offers or web-only sales? Fix it. Do they get lost in your link menus? Reduce the number of main areas.

Of course, these tips could go on and on. But the preceding tips are just enough to get you started on designing engaging, easy-to-use web pages. Beware, however—using too many design methods can make your page cluttered and hard to read.

 NOTE: *See Appendix A for links to web sites with other page design tips.*

Advanced Tips and Techniques

12

Corel WordPerfect Suite 8 is a bit like those late-night infomercials. Just when you think you know exactly what you're getting, you hear, "but wait—that's not all." This chapter is the "but wait—that's not all" part of what Corel WordPerfect has to offer. While you've already learned a lot in this part of the book, here you'll find a compendium of powerful features that don't necessarily fit with the basics discussed elsewhere. In any case, they're features you can use to create dynamic web pages. You'll start by learning how to insert some cool things and rapidly progress to font specifications and Java applets.

> **NOTE:** *If you can't immediately think of a good use for all the features listed in this chapter, read it anyway. Why? If you are at least familiar with Corel WordPerfect's web capabilities, you'll be surprised how many ways there are to take advantage of these advanced abilities.*

Using Special Characters in Your Web Pages

As in other Corel WordPerfect documents, you can use symbols in your web pages that you can't access directly from the keyboard. These symbols range from bullets to international characters (like the ones you'll want to use to spell "résumé" correctly).

If you've spent much time working with your PC typefaces, you've probably noticed that they contain many more characters than you might type from the keyboard. But because Corel WordPerfect makes inserting symbols so easy, you don't normally realize which symbols or special characters are contained in a given font and which are created by use of Corel WordPerfect's extensive set of symbol and international fonts.

Odds are you've noticed some strange typefaces when scrolling through the list of fonts on your system. These typefaces—all beginning with the letters "WP"—are the fonts Corel WordPerfect installs in order to access this wide set of symbols and international characters. Here's the rub: any symbol that's contained in one of Corel WordPerfect's special fonts, not in the default typeface (usually either Times Roman or Courier), will likely not appear on your web page.

Even though Corel WordPerfect can assign a specific font on a web page (you'll learn how later in the chapter in "Fancy Web Typography"), there's no guarantee that the person viewing the page will have the correct fonts needed to view the page properly. So it's safest to stick with the default fonts (unless you're planning to publish to Corel Barista or Envoy—this is covered more in Chapters 18 and 19).

Characters contained in standard fonts are surprisingly easy to access. A Windows font includes a set of characters that goes beyond those shown on the keyboard, and most fonts include the same set of characters (they're shown in Table 12-1 if you're just dying to see them). Before you look at those characters, however, here's the secret to using characters that will actually appear on your web pages.

When you insert a special character or symbol in your document, you can't choose just any of the characters in the set of symbols Corel WordPerfect provides (again, unless you're publishing your page using Corel Barista or Envoy). And you don't need to be in the Web Editor (Web Page view)—these characters will translate just fine back and forth between regular documents and Web-bound ones. Here's how to do it:

1. Choose Insert | Symbol, or choose the Insert Symbol button from the property bar:

   You'll then see the Symbols dialog box. This dialog box provides a quick route to view all of Corel WordPerfect's character sets and to choose a symbol or character from any of them just by pointing and clicking. However, in this case, you'll want to ignore all of the character sets except one.

2. From the Set pop-up menu, choose the User-Defined character set (see Figure 12-1).

TIP: *If you're familiar with the old* CTRL-W *shortcut from previous versions of Corel WordPerfect, that's another quick way to insert a symbol.*

Here's where it gets tricky. Although this font set includes all the characters you can access in Windows (and that will display on the Web), you can't see them in the

FIGURE 12-1   The Symbols dialog box—choose the User-Defined set to access the full range of Windows font characters

preview window. That's where Table 12-1 comes in handy; use this cross-reference, adapted from the old character set reference sheet that used to ship with WordPerfect 5.1, to find the character you want. To obtain the number for the symbol, add the number shown at the top of its column to the number shown in the leftmost column of its row. For example, the number for "¢" is 162. Once you've found the character you want:

3. In the <u>N</u>umber box, type **12,#**, where # stands for the character number you want to use.

NOTE: *In this example, "12" stands for the character set number—the User-Defined character set is character set number 12.*

4. If you're finished inserting special characters, choose Insert <u>A</u>nd Close. If you want to insert more than one character, choose <u>I</u>nsert and repeat step 3 as many times as you wish.

Insider Tip

Windows has long had a secret technique for inserting these same characters that will work in any Windows application. If you want to insert these characters without using Corel WordPerfect's Symbols dialog box, hold down the ALT key while typing *###* on the numeric keypad where *###* stands for the symbol number listed in Table 12-1. If the symbol number has fewer than three digits, add a 0 to the beginning (0##).

	0	1	2	3	4	5	6	7	8	9
000- 120	(Characters 000 through 120 aren't used for text and do not appear on screen)									
130	,	ƒ	„	…	†	‡	^	‰	Š	<
140	Œ					'	'	"	"	•
150	—	—	~	™	š	>	œ			Ÿ
160		¡	¢	£	¤	¥	¦	§	..	©
170	ª	«	¬	-	®	-	°	±	²	³
180	´	µ	¶	·	¸	¹	º	»	¼	½
190	¾	¿	À	Á	Â	Ã	Ä	Å	Æ	Ç
200	È	É	Ê	Ë	Ì	Í	Î	Ï	Ð	Ñ
210	Ò	Ó	Ô	Õ	Ö	×	Ø	Ù	Ú	Û
220	Ü	Ý	Þ	ß	à	á	â	ã	ä	å
230	æ	ç	è	é	ê	ë	ì	í	î	ï
240	ð	ñ	ò	ó	ô	õ	ö	÷	ø	ù
250	ú	û	ü	ý	þ					

TABLE 12-1   Characters in Corel WordPerfect's Special Character Set 12

Odds are, you'll find uses for several of these characters even if you don't use non-English words. For example, symbols such as ™, ©, and ® are used a lot—and they're natively supported by HTML. But there's no reason to learn the HTML when you can insert symbols so easily with Corel WordPerfect.

Inserting Other Cool Stuff

As this chapter promised, that's not all. You can also insert a host of other useful document codes into your Corel WordPerfect documents to easily update your web pages.

Inserting an Automatically Updated Date

First, Corel WordPerfect features the ability to insert the current date as well as the current time into your documents. Just choose Insert | Date/Time. You'll see the dialog box shown in Figure 12-2. Of course, it's nice not to have to type the current

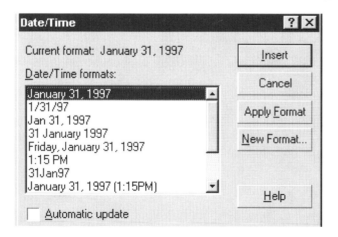

FIGURE 12-2   Corel WordPerfect's Date/Time dialog box—to have the date or time automatically updated in your documents, be sure to check the Automatic Update check box

date, but the real power of this feature is hiding at the bottom of the dialog box: it's the Automatic Update option.

You've probably seen "last updated on" messages on web pages you've visited. Here's the easy way to add a special code that automatically updates the date and time to your Corel WordPerfect documents you'll publish to the Web.

1. Place the cursor where you want the current date and time to appear.

2. Choose Insert | Date/Time.

3. Select the Date/Time format you like best—one that includes the time, or perhaps one that follows the international style with the day of the month listed first.

4. Check the Automatic Update check box.

5. Choose Insert. The dialog box disappears and the current date and time (if you selected both) appears in your document.

This is a real time-saver.

Adding Sounds to Your Web Pages

If you're reasonably sure that your web site visitors' web browsers will support it, you can add sound to your web pages. Sound is particularly attention getting. While most people are becoming used to visual niceties on a web site—from animation to elaborate slide shows—sound is a pleasant surprise (assuming you're inserting *pleasant* sounds). It's amazingly simple to insert a sound into your Corel WordPerfect–created web page. You may want to be in Web Page view before you begin this process, but it will work regardless.

To add a sound to your document:

1. Choose Insert | Sound. You'll see the Sound Clips dialog box (Figure 12-3).

   If you have any other sounds in your document, they'll be listed in this dialog box. You'll explore the other options in this dialog box in a moment. First, continue with placing your first sound into the document.

2. Choose <u>I</u>nsert. You'll then see the Insert Sound Clip Into Document dialog box, shown here:

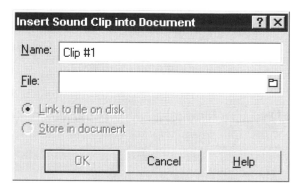

FIGURE 12-3   The Sound Clips dialog box—choose Insert to select the sound you want to add to your web page

3. In the <u>N</u>ame box, type a descriptive name for the sound, such as "Fictitious company sound."

4. In the <u>F</u>ile box, type the folder and name of the sound file you want to use, or click the small folder icon at the end of the box to find the file by browsing.

Insider Tip

You can use any sound format Corel WordPerfect supports, but for the most part, you'll probably stick with Windows wave-format (WAV) files. Of course, these files can be long—and therefore tedious to download if you don't keep them small. If you're using the files for music clips only, you may want to consider using MIDI-format files instead.

Once you've specified the sound file you want to insert, you can choose either to refer to the sound file while it remains on your hard drive (or wherever) or to place it inside your document. Like choosing to keep a graphic image on disk instead of embedding it in the document, each choice has its advantages and disadvantages. If you keep a sound file on disk, your Corel WordPerfect file size will be smaller—and in some cases, you may be using a sound in more than one place on your web site, so you may want to store the sound only once. On the other hand, if you embed the sound file in your Corel WordPerfect document, the document will be self-contained. If you move the file to a different computer or location where you don't have access to the original sound file, no worries: it's all part of the document.

 NOTE: *Regardless of whether you save the sound clip with your Corel WordPerfect document, when you publish the document to HTML, the sound file will be stored separately.*

■ To keep the file separate from the document, choose the <u>L</u>ink To File On Disk radio button.

■ To make the sound file part of your document, choose the <u>S</u>tore In Document radio button.

After you've selected the options in the dialog box, choose OK. Both the Insert Sound and Sound Clips dialog boxes will disappear, and a small sound icon will appear in your document.

Insider Tip

Here's a slick trick. Want to be able to control all your document's sounds without having to go to the Sound Clips dialog box? Just right-click on any sound icon in your document and choose Transcribe. A control panel—a special Sound property bar—will appear at the top of the screen, like this:

Of course, you can also get this bar to display by choosing Insert | Sound | Transcribe. From this bar you can Rewind, Fast-forward, Replay, Play, or Stop play of the selected sound. This feature makes transcribing recorded document comments easier—but you can use it for a quick check of sounds in any document.

Be sure to explore the other features in the Sound Clips dialog box, too. To access these features, choose Insert | Sound. You'll see the Sound Clips dialog box (Figure 12-3). From here, you can even Record a new sound (if your sound hardware supports it), Edit the descriptive name you gave a sound, Transcribe the sound (which makes the Sound property bar appear), Delete the sound, or Save an embedded sound file as a separate file.

Adding Endnotes

Don't forget that Corel WordPerfect has an amazing array of document-creation abilities. You can corral those abilities into your web documents. For example, you might find a way to use Corel WordPerfect's automated endnote feature in your web documents.

When you create endnotes in your web documents, they're automatically turned into hyperlinks so readers can jump immediately to your parenthetical comment, additional information, or reference. Look at Figure 12-4 to see both the Footnote/Endnote dialog box and the document that already includes a hyperlinked endnote.

Inserting an endnote is easy—just choose Insert | Endnote. You'll see the dialog box shown in Figure 12-4. From here, if you want to create an Endnote, choose Create. Of course, you can also Edit existing endnotes or even change the number's value or numbering style (using Options).

You'll probably find endnotes useful when placing less-relevant information in your web pages. Remember, it won't cost anything extra to add a little more information, since you're not printing it on paper.

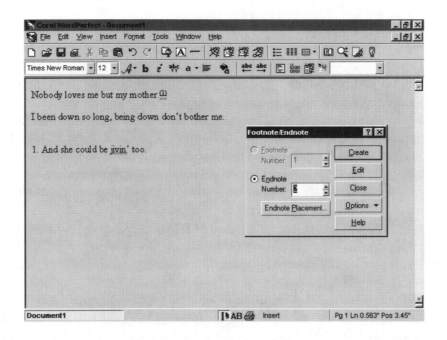

FIGURE 12-4   The Footnote/Endnote dialog box and a document that already includes a web-ready, hyperlinked endnote

Insider Tip

Even as web-savvy as your web site visitors will undoubtedly be, they may not know how to return from an endnote reference to their previous location in the document. When they click on a hyperlink endnote reference, they'll be taken to the endnote at the end of the document. Especially in a long document, these endnotes may be screenfuls of information away. Here's the trick—they just need to click the "back" button on their web browser. In fact, if you want to be extra helpful, you could add a brief note at the end of each endnote that says something like "Click Back in your browser to return to your place in the document."

Fancy Web Typography

Earlier in this book, you learned that Corel WordPerfect follows HTML customs in allowing only minimal font specifications. And in Chapter 18, if you read ahead, you might have discovered that Java-based HTML pages provide only a little more font control. If you're brave, you can move beyond those limitations.

Corel WordPerfect supports HTML 3.2's font specifications—the font face and font size tags. These special tags allow you to specify the exact typeface and relative size you want to use in your web documents. Sounds attractive, both from how it will make your pages appear and how much control it will give you. But it's not without its perils. Don't try this at home until you've read this entire section.

NOTE: *Since these tags are part of HTML 3.2, if a web browser doesn't support this newer version of HTML, it will ignore them entirely. The latest versions of Netscape Navigator (3.0 and higher) as well as Microsoft Internet Explorer (3.0 and higher) support these tags.*

Before you learn how to specify these attributes in Corel WordPerfect, take a look at some of the HTML behind the automation. First, look at the font *size* attribute. The short explanation: you're not really specifying the font's size in points as you would on a printed page. Instead, it's a general size relative to the default size of the rest of the text. Now, the details. In HTML, this tag appears as <FONT SIZE="#">, where # is the font size from 1 to 7 (no decimals). The default font size is usually 3, so, for example, if you specified a point size of 18 points, Corel WordPerfect would translate that point size into an HTML font size of 5. Here's where things get a bit dicey. The HTML tag placed in your document for this example won't read <FONT SIZE="5">— that would be far too simple. Instead, Corel WordPerfect creates a tag that tells the browser to show the font relative to the default size (3, in this case). So, the HTML tag will read <FONT SIZE="+2">.

TIP: *If you're feeling bold, you can fiddle with web page layouts that use Netscape Navigator's <BASEFONT="#"> tag. The default value for this tag is 3—but if you want the default text to be larger or smaller, try changing this value.*

The font *face* tag is simpler in concept than the font size tag. Here's the basic idea: if you want to specify a font for a particular block of text, you can do it (you'll learn how in a moment). If the web page visitor's computer doesn't have the font you specify, the browser will make its best guess at the equivalent—probably either Times or Courier. In HTML 3.2, you can specify three suggested typefaces—in descending order. But with Corel WordPerfect, you can specify only one. And when you're converting a document from HTML to Corel WordPerfect format, if there is more than one font listed in the font face tag, Corel WordPerfect will look only for the first typeface before it uses the default one.

Insider Tip

If you know that most of your web site visitors use Windows 95, you can safely specify a font such as Arial—since it's installed with Windows 95. Other common fonts include Helvetica, Times, Garamond, and even Comic Sans (for Windows 95). Choose a font that you know your web page viewers most likely have—or your design time will be in vain. And be sure to preview your pages without the font installed just to see if you need to tweak your page design to make it attractive either way.

Now to the fun part—specifying a typeface and size. To do so:

1. Choose Format | Font. You'll see the Font dialog box (Figure 12-5).

Normally, you'd restrict your formatting choices to the Styles (HTML Elements) list. However, since you're trying some advanced techniques, don't restrict yourself.

2. Select the typeface you want to use in the Font Face list.

3. If you want to specify a type size, select it from the Font Size list or type it into the text box.

4. When you've finished, select OK, then type your text.

 REMEMBER: *For information about the other features in the Font dialog box, including Appearance and Text Color, see Chapter 6.*

You'll want to experiment with this feature—choose View | View In Web Browser often—but with it you can create unique, dynamic, attractive pages.

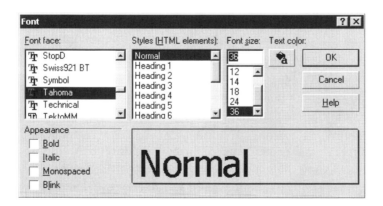

FIGURE 12-5 The Font dialog box—any typeface you choose will appear on the web page if the page is viewed on a system that includes that font

Inserting Custom HTML Tags

If you're an experienced HTML jockey, you may be using Corel WordPerfect as a tool to convert Corel WordPerfect–format documents to HTML. Or you may want to use some existing HTML without figuring out how to replicate it in Corel WordPerfect. Either way, you're not limited to the HTML formatting Corel WordPerfect supports—even though Corel WordPerfect supports most HTML abilities.

If you want to use HTML tags for which Corel WordPerfect doesn't include support, you can insert Custom HTML tags. Custom HTML is text that will appear without conversion when the document is saved as HTML. Make no mistake: you don't "insert" custom HTML as you have inserted dates, sounds, and other miscellany in this chapter. Instead, Custom HTML is a special formatting code, like bold or underline. Custom HTML code appears on screen in Corel WordPerfect as red, double-underlined text.

To insert Custom HTML, just choose Format | Custom HTML. You won't see any immediate change in your document…until you begin typing. The codes you type will appear, as mentioned earlier, in red, double-underlined text in the most recently used font style and size. When you're finished typing any Custom HTML, press the RIGHT ARROW key to move the insertion point into normal text again.

You may want to insert Custom HTML to specify a three-level font face, for example, or perhaps to use HTML frames—a capability Corel WordPerfect does not yet support.

Insider Tip

When Corel WordPerfect imports or exports a document that contains HTML tags it doesn't support or it doesn't recognize, it does so as Custom HTML. They'll appear in your document as Custom HTML when you open a document that contains these unrecognized codes—then they'll be exported along with any Corel WordPerfect–based changes you made when you publish the document to HTML.

Using SGML Features for HTML Editing

No matter how robust a program's HTML import and export abilities are, the program will add or modify some of the original document's HTML as it's edited and saved. But unlike other programs, Corel WordPerfect provides a powerful module that can help power HTML users get around this issue.

This module—available when you perform a custom suite installation—is Corel WordPerfect's SGML (standard generalized markup language) module. *SGML* is an international standard for format-rich documents that can be read by different programs on different computer platforms. It's also the progenitor of HTML—HTML began as a subset of SGML, but has grown to be much more than that.

SGML markup tags are similar to those in HTML, and Corel WordPerfect's SGML abilities allow you to import HTML documents with all the original formatting intact—even when you save them as HTML again. If you're performing high-level HTML acrobatics, you will want to install the SGML module so that you can edit HTML—from forms to frames, from heading elements to complex tables—without affecting a single one of the original codes.

Inserting Java Applets

Here's the end of the "...and that's not all" list. It's a snazzy bonus feature and if you're familiar with Java applets, this can be very handy. If you're not, then just skip this section: there is far more to Java applets than this book's focus allows.

NOTE: *Interested in learning more about Java or JavaScript? You may want to look at these other books by Osborne/McGraw-Hill:*

The comprehensive reference tome, Java: The Complete Reference, *by Patrick Naughton and Herbert Schildt, ISBN 0-07-882231-9 (1997).*

The more manageable guide, The Java Handbook, *by Patrick Naughton, ISBN 0-07-882199-1 (1996).*

Or the guide to JavaScript, JavaScript Essentials: Creating Interactive Web Applications, *by Jason Manger, ISBN 0-07-882234-3 (1996).*

In short, Java is a programming language designed to be platform and operating-system independent. Sun Microsystems developed the language—now becoming a full-fledged programming language—to increase the flexibility and power of the Internet and the Web. You've no doubt seen Java programs—called *applets* (mini-applications)—as you've browsed the Web. They commonly provide animated graphics, rotating advertising banners, or animated link buttons.

If you want to use Java applets on your web pages, you'll need to do two things first: install the Java support into Corel WordPerfect, and have the Java applet on your web server. If you're unfamiliar with creating, placing, compiling, and storing Java applets, you can consult one of the references noted earlier, or consult your webmaster or system administrator. Installing Java support into Corel WordPerfect is easy, though: just run the Corel WordPerfect Suite setup program. When prompted, choose Custom Installation. Choose the components under Corel WordPerfect and be sure to check the Java Applet Support check box. Once you've done so and installed this component, you'll be ready to place applets in your web documents.

To place a Java applet in your web document, choose Insert | Java | Create Applet. (If you want to modify the applet's properties later, select it and choose Insert | Java | Modify Applet.) You'll then see the Create Java Applet dialog box, shown in Figure 12-6.

It's important to understand that Corel WordPerfect is not a tool for *creating* Java applets. However, if you have an already-made applet, Corel WordPerfect can place it in your documents. It will place the information you type within a special HTML tag: the <APPLET> tag. Here's what you'll need to type in each of the fields shown in Figure 12-6.

The first group of fields, Class Information, includes two fields. The Class field, refers to the Java *class,* or applet itself. Here you'll need to type (or use the browse tool to locate) the file that contains the Java applet. (This information is placed within the APPLET tag as the value of the CODE attribute, if you're curious.) The second sounds more confusing than it is. "Code Base" refers to the *absolute path* of the applet and any related files—the folder where the applet will be stored. The location of any other folders referred to in this dialog box, including the Class (or applet filename), will be found in relation to the folder specified in the Code Base field. It'll help here if you know where your applet will be stored on your web server—and if you have access to that location while you're building the page.

Create Java Applet

Class information

Class:

Code Base:

OK

Cancel

Parameters...

Size/position information

Width: 100   Horizontal Space: 0   Help

Height: 30   Vertical Space: 0

Alignment: Default

Other information

Name:

Alternate Text:

Click Here To See Applet

FIGURE 12-6   Corel WordPerfect's Create Java Applet dialog box, which allows you to add already-made applets to your web pages

Once you've filled in that information, you can specify the Size/Position Information fields. A Java applet takes up space on a web page, much as a graphic does. By specifying this information, you can reserve this space before the applet downloads (again, much like you can with a graphic image). Specify both the Width and Height—in pixels. You can get this information from the person who programmed the applet or supplied it to you. If you want a certain amount of space around the applet, specify that amount of space, again in pixels, using the Horizontal Space and Vertical Space fields. The final position setting allows you to set the Alignment of the applet just as you can with other page elements (choose the alignment you want from the drop-down menu).

If you're planning to use JavaScript (or LiveConnect) to send information or messages to the Java applet, you can give the applet a name in the Name text box. As mentioned earlier, since you can mark off a certain amount of space on the web page for the applet, just as you can with graphic images, you can also specify some alternate text—text that will appear if the applet hasn't loaded. You can do so in the Alternate Text text box.

If you are aware of any parameters that need to be set for the applet, you can specify their names and values using the dialog box that appears after you choose Parameters. When you're finished specifying all of the applet details, choose OK.

If you want to see the applet working in your document, you'll need to actually publish it to HTML—not just view it in the web browser. The temporary copy of the page created when you view the page in the web browser won't include the correct applet path.

In this chapter, you've learned some advanced tricks for creating high-octane, high-performance web pages. In the next chapter, you'll learn about adding interactivity to those pages with web forms.

Making Your Pages
Interactive:
Creating Web Forms

13

The HTML pages you've learned about so far in this book have been much like the pages in more familiar media. They resemble a page of a book or magazine—with many layout options (but none of the printing costs). In some ways, these pages resemble television as you add animations, video clips, or sounds. In any case, so far you've learned only how to show pages to web visitors—not how to listen to the visitors.

NOTE: *In web publishing jargon, only showing pages to visitors is sometimes called pushing information. This broadcast or publishing approach to web publishing is referred to as the push model. Listening to what web visitors want or allowing them to choose the type of information they want is called a pull model, perhaps because the viewers are "pulling down" the information they want.*

But when you combine HTML's cross-platform, cross-operating system layout abilities with some widely available, "back-end" programming, you can move beyond what a book, magazine, or even television can do: you can get instant feedback from your visitors. The easiest way for you to get this feedback is with HTML-based web forms.

An HTML-based web form consists of HTML tags that look just like any other HTML page's source code. (And you'll create it in Corel WordPerfect much the same way as you would any other HTML page.) The secret to the form's interactivity is what it does *after* your site's visitor fills it out. When a visitor clicks the submit button on a web form, it sends a message consisting of all the form's data to an address you've specified. Special programming scripts, usually CGI (common gateway interface)-based, can process the form data and post it to a database; create new, customized web pages; or just about anything you choose. In this chapter you'll learn the basic components of a form and the options Corel WordPerfect has available for you. You will also learn how to create a form that you can use in your web site.

Gathering Feedback with Forms

The whole reason to create an online form is to gather information from your web site's visitors. Forms are especially helpful if your web site is patterned around a particular product or service. You might ask for feedback about your web site or your products. This instant feedback is essential to any business that wants to be responsive to its customers. And even if your web page isn't designed as a business, in a sense, it is—it's providing a service to people who will come to see it. Remember, if you don't listen to your customers, somebody else will—and your customers will follow them. Also, if your customers have a chance to send in instant opinions regarding your products or services, they will feel as though their "voices" are being heard. Overall, web forms allow you to get information instantly from your readers without spending a lot of money on mailers, comment cards, and so on.

 NOTE: *For more information about gathering feedback from your web site visitors, see Chapter 2.*

The following provides a general overview of what happens when your web site visitor encounters a form:

1. The form is filled out   The web site visitor uses the form tools (text boxes, radio buttons, and so on) to complete each field in the form.

2. The form is submitted   When the visitor completes the form, the submit button is selected. The submit button triggers an HTML function that combines the name of each of the form's fields with the information the visitor typed.

3. The form data is processed   This set of field names and data is combined into a message submitted to the address included in one of the hidden fields included in the form. A special program on the web server processes the form data and does something with it—submits it to an order processing center, creates a user profile, or just about anything.

Getting Started with Web Forms

Now that you have a general idea of how a web form works, it's time to learn the basics of creating a form. You could, in theory, insert web form fields or objects into any web page, but it's a good idea to keep the web form on its own page.

NOTE: *Here's a little web form jargon you'll want to know. A web form object simply means one of the controls, boxes, or other mechanisms you place on a page. A web form* field *generally refers to the part of a form object where the person completing the form fills in some information. For example, you might create a text box object called "E-mail address," where the field would consist of the person's e-mail address.*

To set up your web page for a form, from Corel WordPerfect's Web Editor:

1. Choose File | Internet Publisher.

2. Choose New Web Document, or open an existing web document by choosing File | Open, and selecting the file.

3. Choose Insert | Create Form.

When you choose Create Form, Corel WordPerfect will insert two yellow form tags—one for the beginning of the form and one for the end—in your document, as shown here:

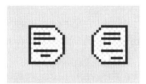

These form tags should remain respectively at the beginning and end of your form. All the form fields are placed between these two tags.

When you have the yellow form tags on your screen, the Forms property bar appears onscreen as well (see Figure 13-1). This property bar provides instant access to every major type of form object—from radio buttons to list boxes. But before you create a form, it's important for you to understand each control's abilities and function.

TIP: *The Forms property bar will appear only when the cursor is between the yellow form beginning and ending markers. If the property bar disappears, it's a safe bet you've wandered outside the form area.*

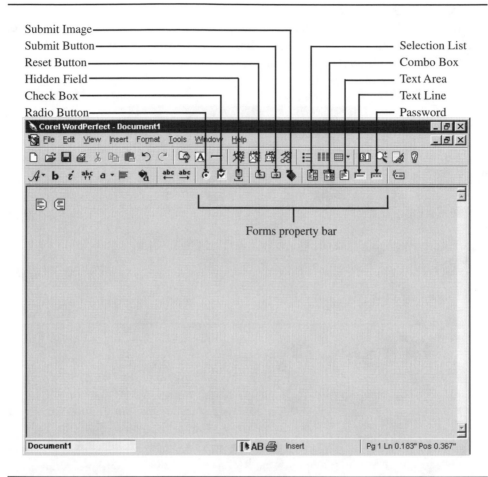

Submit Image
Submit Button
Reset Button
Hidden Field
Check Box
Radio Button

Selection List
Combo Box
Text Area
Text Line
Password

Forms property bar

FIGURE 13-1 The Forms property bar appears when you're working with a form. From here you can insert many of the components that make up a form.

Using Radio Buttons in Forms

On screen, a radio button looks like a small, empty circle to the left of a text phrase. When the radio button is selected, a black circle appears within the previously empty one. Radio buttons allow web page visitors to select *only one* choice from a number of options. To insert a radio button into your web form, click the Radio Button button on the Forms property bar.

With the radio button and with every form object you insert, you'll want to customize its "properties," which include its name, initial setting, and more. Once a radio button is inserted into your form, you can change its properties just by double-clicking the radio button. The Radio Button Properties dialog box will appear:

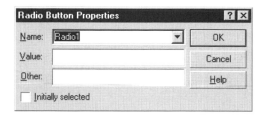

From here you can adjust the Name, Value, and Other settings (see Table 13-1).

Radio Button Property	Description
Name	The "internal" name of the radio button. This name will be passed along to the form processing script as the name of the form "field" or option. Each radio button in a group should have the same name.
Value	The "value" the selection will pass along to the form processor. For example, if the text next to the button reads "United States of America," the value might be simply "USA." While the name of each radio button in a group should be the same, the values should differ.
Other	Unused.
Initially Selected	If you want the group of radio buttons to have a default choice, check this. When the form appears, this radio button will already be selected.

Radio Button
Properties

TABLE 13-1

Insider Tip

Important—if you're creating a group of radio buttons, name each radio button with the same name. Corel WordPerfect makes it easy: once you've inserted one radio button and given it a name, you can then choose that name from the <u>N</u>ame drop-down menu in the Radio Button Properties dialog box. When you give each radio button in the group the same name, the HTML page knows to allow only one to be selected at a time *and* will pass along to the form processor *only* one value that corresponds to that name.

Once you've adjusted the radio buttons' properties to your liking, choose OK to dismiss the dialog box. Then type the text you want to appear next to the button. Remember, this text needs to be descriptive enough to provide adequate detail but not so long that it gets ignored.

Using Check Boxes in Forms

Check boxes are similar to radio buttons, but check boxes aren't necessarily part of a group of options. You can check one, some, or all—whichever you want. It's common to position the check box to the left of the text corresponding to the check box. If a check box has been checked when the form is sent back from the reader, the information for that check box is also sent.

To insert a check box into your web form, click the Check Box button on the Forms property bar. You'll now want to customize the check box properties. Double-click the check box. The Check Box Properties dialog box will appear—except for the heading, it's virtually identical to the Radio Button Properties dialog box. From here you can adjust the <u>N</u>ame, <u>V</u>alue, and <u>O</u>ther settings (see Table 13-2).

NOTE: *You can also view a form object's properties dialog box by right-clicking the object and choosing Pr<u>o</u>perties from the pop-up menu.*

Once you've entered the check box properties you want, choose OK to dismiss the dialog box. Then type the text you want to appear next to the check box.

Check Box Property	Description
<u>N</u>ame	The "internal" name of the check box that will be passed along to the form processing script as the name of the form "field" or option. Unlike radio buttons, each check box *must* have a unique name.
<u>V</u>alue	The "value" the selection will pass along to the form processor. Values for check boxes will probably correspond to the text next to the box.
<u>O</u>ther	Unused.
<u>I</u>nitially Selected	Check this box if you want the check box to be checked when the form initially appears.

Check Box
Properties

TABLE 13-2

Using Hidden Fields in Forms

The Hidden Field button will insert a hidden field into your form. Obviously, hidden fields aren't much use to someone filling out a form. Instead, *hidden fields* commonly are used to pass information about the form to the server. Generally, you'll find two uses for a hidden field. First, you use them to tell the server your form's name. Second, a hidden field might contain the information controlling the form's output location.

NOTE: *You will want to check with your Internet service provider (ISP), your webmaster, or whomever is in charge of the server at your web site. They can tell you the information they require to properly process a form, including the hidden fields they require. Don't be intimidated: they should be able to provide you with samples and complete information.*

To insert a hidden field into your web form, click the Hidden Field button on the Forms property bar. You'll then want to customize the properties of this hidden field. A small red icon will appear in the document, and the Hidden Field Properties dialog box will automatically appear, as shown here. From here you can adjust the <u>N</u>ame and <u>V</u>alue settings (see Table 13-3).

Unlike most other form objects, a hidden field requires no explanatory text because the users will never see it.

Insider Tip

A hidden field can appear anywhere within the form as long as it falls within the yellow form begin and end markers (of course, Corel WordPerfect doesn't let you place one anywhere else). However, most ISPs or webmasters will suggest that you include the hidden fields at the very top of the form.

Hidden Field Property	Description
Name	The "internal" name of the hidden field. This name will be passed along to the form processing script as the name of the form "field" or option. Each hidden field should have a unique name. This name is generally dictated by the server or form processing software.
Value	The "value" that the hidden field will pass along to the form processor. This is often the name of the form or the destination for the form data.

Hidden Field Properties

TABLE 13-3

Using Reset and Submit Buttons in Forms

The next two buttons you encounter on the Forms property bar are opposites; they erase or save a form's data. A reset button clears all of the data the user has entered into the form. It will also set all the fields to their default state, which is usually blank. You don't need to have a reset button on your web form if you don't want one, but they're often provided just to be polite. To insert a reset button on your web form, choose the Reset Button button from the Forms property bar.

You absolutely *must* include a submit button on every web form you create. The submit button is usually the last form object to appear on your form. When clicked, this button tells the browser to send the information to the appropriate output destination. If you have a form and want to put it to use, you must have a submit button.

TIP: *There's always an exception—you don't always have to have a submit button on your web form if there's only one field in your form. If you only have one field on your form, pressing the* ENTER *key will automatically submit the data. However, it's a good idea to include a submit button all the time.*

To insert a submit button on your web form, choose the Submit Button button from the Forms property bar. Once you've created either a reset or a submit button, you can edit its properties. To do so, double-click the button. You'll then see the Button Properties dialog box. From here you can adjust the Name, Label, and Button Type settings (see Table 13-4). When you're finished adjusting the button properties, choose OK.

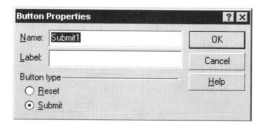

Button Property	Description
<u>N</u>ame	The "internal" name of the button. Each button must have a unique name.
<u>L</u>abel	The text that appears on the button as it is displayed on screen. For example, you might change the default "Submit" label to "Send it in!"
<u>S</u>ubmit/<u>R</u>eset	If you want to change a button to the opposite type, just select the appropriate radio button here.

Submit and
Reset Button
Properties

TABLE 13-4

Using an Image as a Submit Button

You've probably seen a web page or two that uses special, custom graphics on its buttons. With the Submit Image button, you can do just that. Use of an image is a bit trickier than use of a standard button, however. To create a submit button that uses an image instead of text, click the Submit Image button on the Forms property bar.

When you select this button, you are automatically taken to the Insert Image - Graphics dialog box (see Figure 13-2). From here, search for and choose the desired image and press <u>I</u>nsert. The image will then be placed into your form.

Once you've inserted the image, it will appear in your document. You can use the black handles to scale the image as you like. (See Chapter 7 for more information on using and modifying graphics in your web documents—you can use all of those image tools on this image as well). Once you've fine-tuned the image, you will need to play with its properties to turn it into a real button.

Insider Tip

You don't want to create a button that consists of just a nifty picture. The best image buttons help reinforce the site's identity *and* communicate to the site's visitors what the button will do. For example, a submit button may include the word "submit" along with a nice arrow—all within a graphic that looks like a button. The clip art included with Corel WordPerfect isn't really designed to create web page buttons, but you will find some useful graphics in the suite's clipart collections. You can use Corel Presentations to create these graphics and save them as GIF or JPEG images.

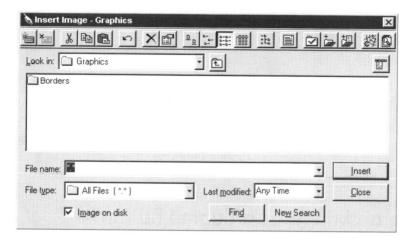

FIGURE 13-2   The Insert Image - Graphics dialog box allows you to insert images inside your web forms

To turn your image into a submit button, *don't* double-click it as you have other form objects. Instead, *right-click* the image and choose <u>H</u>TML Properties from the pop-up menu. You'll then see the HTML Properties dialog box. Click on the Submit Form tab to create a button (the other tabs are discussed in Chapter 8). You'll see this dialog box:

Now, in the Field Name text box, type a field name for the image button to turn it into a "real" button. Note that Corel WordPerfect will not allow you to use spaces in the name because HTML doesn't allow them. When you're finished, choose OK.

Insider Tip

If you want the submit button to return certain information to your server—and your Internet service provider or webmaster has given you the proper information—you can take advantage of an additional capability of the Submit Image feature. It will return the x and y coordinates as well. You might be able to use this to include several buttons in one image—each of which submits the form but returns a different value. Warning: this is an advanced feature and is best used in close collaboration with the technical or server side of things.

You'll now turn from objects that have more to do with the form's processing to create options that allow users to provide you with input.

Using Selection Lists

The next two buttons on the Forms property bar create selection lists and combo boxes for the web visitor to choose from. These two controls are virtually identical, except that the *selection list* by default displays five selections from a scrollable list. The *combo box* displays one selection from a pull-down menu. Either form object can allow multiple selections (in other words, more than one choice). However, if you're planning to allow multiple selections, the selection list is easier for visitors to use.

TIP: *If you plan to allow multiple selections from a selection list, you might want to mention that in the descriptive text you place next to the selection list. You may even want to remind users of how to select more than one option (in Windows, hold down the CTRL key).*

To insert a selection list into your web form, click the Selection List button on the Forms property bar:

To insert a combo box into your web form, click the Combo Box button on the Forms property bar:

Once you insert one of these objects, double-click it to display the Listbox/Combobox Properties dialog box (see Figure 13-3). From here, you can name your list box and set up its options, including the values listed in the box.

To set up your list box:

1. In the Name box, type the name you want to use as the "internal" name of the list box that will be passed along to the form processing script.

 **NOTE:**   *Each list box must have a unique name. Your form results will be unpredictable if not downright unintelligible if two form objects share the same name.*

You will next want to add all the options you want to appear in the selection or combo box. Repeat steps 2–6 for as many options as you need to add.

2. Choose Add to add an option to the list box. You'll see the Add Option dialog box:

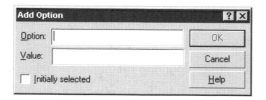

3. In the Add Option dialog box, type the name of the choice you want to appear on screen in the Option text box.

4. In the Add Option dialog box, type the value you want the form to pass along as form data in the Value text box.

5. If you want the option to be selected by default (highlighted when the form is loaded), check the Initially Selected check box.

6. Choose OK to close the Add Option dialog box.

If you need to change any of the options, choose Modify from the Listbox/ Combobox Properties dialog box. If you want to delete an option, choose Delete.

Once you've listed multiple options, you can make further modifications:

■   If you want to change the order in which the options appear, highlight the option you want to move, then choose either Move Up or Move Down to move the option in the list.

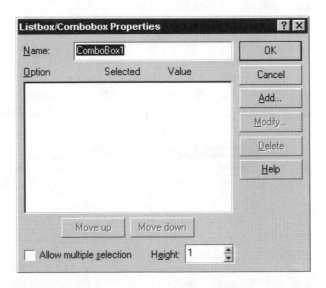

FIGURE 13-3   Do all your list box and combo box formatting from the Listbox/Combobox Properties dialog box

- If you want to allow people to choose more than one of the options listed, check the Allow Multiple Selection check box.

- While you can't change the horizontal size of either a selection box or a combo box, you can change the number of lines displayed at any one time. Type the number of lines you want displayed in the Height box.

NOTE: *By default, a selection box is five lines high and a combo box is just one line high. You can change the height of either type; however, changing a combo box to more than one line high is silly since it is a pull down menu.*

When you are finished with your choices in the Listbox/Combobox Properties dialog box, choose OK to close the dialog box and to list all your options in the list box.

Using Text Area Form Objects

When you need room on a form for your web page visitors to enter text, you can choose either a *text area* (for a lot of text) or a *text line* (for smaller amounts of text, discussed in the next section). Text areas are good for paragraphs or sentences of information—like feedback on products, opinions about a company's customer service, or suggestions for a better web site. Text lines are useful for fill-in-the-blanks information like names, cities, and e-mail addresses.

To insert a text area, choose the Text Area button from the Forms property bar. After inserting a text area, format it accordingly by double-clicking it and using the options provided in the Text Area Properties dialog box, shown here. From here you can change the name, size, text-wrapping options, and more (see Table 13-5).

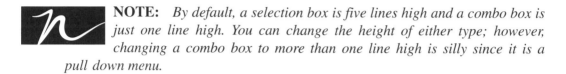

Text Area Property	Description
Name	The "internal" name of the text area that will be passed along to the form processing software. Each text area *must* have a unique name.
Initial	What will initially appear in the text box. You don't *have* to put anything here, but sometimes it's appropriate.
Other	Unused.
Columns and Rows	Adjust the size of the text area by changing the values in these two fields.
Max Char	The largest number of characters you want to allow in the text area. You may want to limit the size of the field based on the screen size, the database you're posting it to, or just to keep the data file size small.
Text Wrapping	None does not allow the text to wrap at all. You may want to avoid this unsightly setting.
Wrap At Window	Allows the text to wrap, but submits the text in "unwrapped" form to the server. You will probably choose this option most often.
Wrap And Send	Sends the text to the server complete with newline characters where the text wrapped.

Text Area
Properties
TABLE 13-5

Once you've entered the text area properties you want, choose OK to dismiss the dialog box. If you've set a limit on the text area size, you may want to mention that in some text next to the box.

Using Text Lines and Password Fields

In most cases, you won't need a full-blown text area for the information you want. A text line allows you to add one line of text to your form. Text lines are useful for fill-in-the-blanks information like names, cities, and e-mail addresses. A password looks like and is set up similarly to a text line, yet it is used for passwords or other information that should be shielded from view. When the password is typed, instead of displaying on screen the letters typed, the form shows them as asterisks.

To insert a text line, choose the Text Line button from the Forms property bar:

To insert a password field, choose the Password button from the Forms property bar:

Format your password or text line by double-clicking it and utilizing the Text/Password Properties dialog box, shown here. From here you can change the name, size, length options, and more (see Table 13-6).

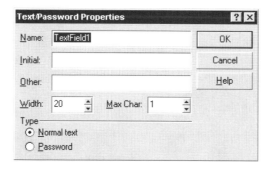

Once you've entered the text line or password properties you want, choose OK to dismiss the dialog box. Then type the text you want to appear next to the text line. If you've included a maximum number of characters, you will probably want to say so.

Creating a Simple Web Form

Now that you know the functions of each button, let's create a simple web form for practice. To create a simple web form:

1. Choose File | Internet Publisher | New Web Document.

2. Highlight Create A Blank Web Document, choose Select.

3. Choose Insert | Create Form.

Your page will now include two yellow form tags. Your cursor will rest between them (remember, they mark the beginning and end of your form).

4. Type **Please give us your favorite Web site address** and press ENTER.

5. Select the Text Line button from the Forms property bar and press ENTER.

TIP: *To change the size of the text line, double-click the text line and in the Width text box of the Text/Password Properties dialog box, type the size you want.*

6. Then select the Submit Button button from the property bar.

Text Line/Password Property	Description
Name	The "internal" name of the text line or password that will be passed along to the form processing software. Each field *must* have a unique name.
Initial	What initially appears in the text line or password. You don't *have* to put anything here, but sometimes it's appropriate.
Other	Unused.
Width	Specify the length of the text line or password field (in characters). This value will often be the same as the Max Char value.
Max Char	The maximum number of characters you want the field to accept. For example, a U.S. ZIP code field could accept ten characters (five digits, a hyphen, then four more).
Normal Text/Password	Because text lines and password fields are so similar, you can switch a field from one to the other simply by choosing the appropriate radio button.

Text
Line/Password
Properties
TABLE 13-6

You should now have a form similar to the one shown in Figure 13-4. This form can be used for a web page designed to keep track of people's favorite web sites. You see, forms don't have to be lengthy to be considered forms—they just have to have the right components.

Creating a More Complex Web Form

Now that you have created a simple web form, you can see how easy the process is. Creating a complex form is the same as creating a simple form, but with more fields and features, thus it takes some planning. It's best to plan your form's content and layout *before* you create it in Corel WordPerfect. Planning will save you time in the long run.

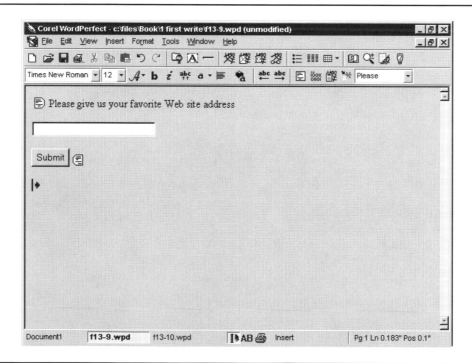

FIGURE 13-4 An example of a simple web form

Let's create the sample form shown in Figure 13-5. This form would be used for a company to obtain the demographics on the people visiting their web site or to receive comments. It would also be used to gather comments about their company, product, or web site. Notice how this form has used every web form feature available in Corel WordPerfect, except for the password field.

Insider Tip

The web form shown in Figure 13-5 not only uses most of the form features available, but it's also set up inside of a table. This allows for the form fields to be lined up perfectly. Using tables takes the hassle out of lining up the fields yourself. It's a great way to produce attractive, well-designed forms without a lot of effort or planning.

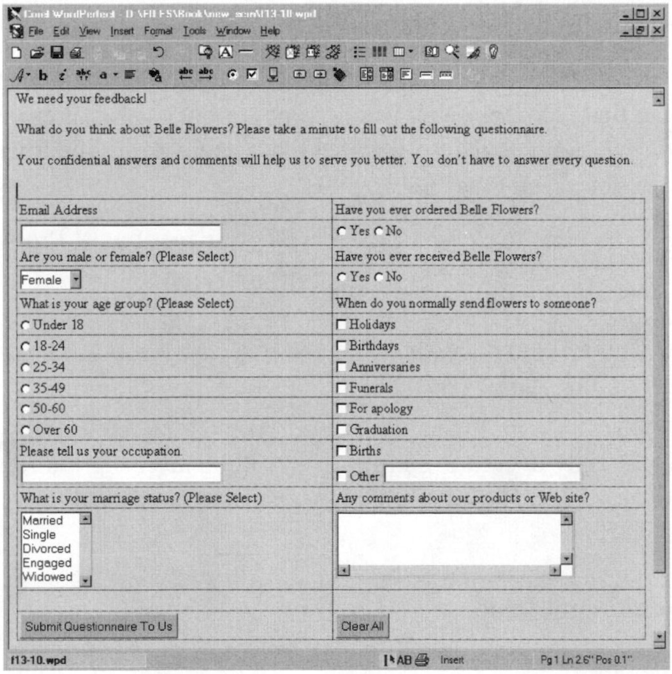

FIGURE 13-5 A more complex web form—it can be used to gather comments about a company, product, or web site

To create this web form:

1. Choose File | Internet Publisher | New Web Document.

2. Highlight Create A Blank Web Document, choose Select.

3. Choose Insert | Create Form.

Your page will now include two yellow form tags. Your cursor will rest between them (remember, they mark the beginning and end of your form). From here:

4. Type the name of the company, such as **Belle Flowers**.

 NOTE: *To change the font for the company name, highlight it, select Format | Font, choose Heading 1 from the Font/Size text box, and than choose OK.*

5. Choose Format | Justification | Right; then select the Submit Image button.

6. Highlight ROSE.WPG from the list of graphics and choose Insert. (You can choose any graphic you want, really, since this is just practice.) The graphic that is inserted will be too large for the page. To resize it, click on one of the corner brackets and drag the corner toward the image until it's the size you want. Press ENTER.

7. Type some other text, such as **We need your feedback!** Press ENTER twice.

 NOTE: *Format this font the same way you formatted the company name. Use Heading 2 this time.*

Now we are ready to create the form. We will be inserting the form inside of a table. This way, all of the fields will look even and symmetrical.

To insert a table:

1. Choose Insert | Table.

2. Under Table Size, type **2** in the Columns text box, and type **17** in the Rows text box.

3. Choose OK.

A table will appear on the screen and the cursor will be in cell A1. The first thing to do to this table is remove all of the cell borders. To do this:

1. Right-click the table and choose F<u>o</u>rmat from the QuickMenu.

2. Type **0** in the Table Borders text box and choose OK.

With the cursor in the first cell, you are ready to begin adding the form fields:

1. Type **Email Address** in the first cell, and press the DOWN ARROW once to move to the cell below.

2. In this cell, insert a text line for the reader to type in his or her e-mail address. Simply click the Text Line button on the property bar.

3. Change the width of the text line by double-clicking it and changing the width by typing **25** in the <u>W</u>idth and Max Char text boxes. Type **Email** in the <u>N</u>ame field, then choose OK. Press the DOWN ARROW once.

The first question is finished. The rest is just as easy—it just takes a bit of time. For the next section of the form:

1. Type **Are you male or female? (Please Select)** and press the DOWN ARROW once.

2. Here you will insert a combo box by selecting the Combo Box button from the property bar.

3. Double-click the combo box and from the Listbox/Combobox Properties dialog box, set up the list.

4. In the <u>N</u>ame text box, type **Gender**.

5. To set up the list, choose <u>A</u>dd. The Add Option dialog box will appear.

6. In the <u>O</u>ption text box, type **Male**. In the <u>V</u>alue text box, type **male** again, and choose OK. Repeat the same instructions to add **Female**, and choose OK to close the dialog box.

For the age group section, type the question as it appears in Figure 13-5. Then add radio buttons by selecting them from the property bar. Type the age groups after each radio button and press DOWN ARROW to move to the cell below. Then create the occupation field and text line the same way you created the e-mail address field.

For the next field:

1. Type **What is your marriage status? (Please Select)**, and move the cursor to the next cell.

2. Press the Selection List button from the property bar, and then double-click the select list.

3. From the Listbox/Combobox Properties dialog box, type **Status** in the Name text box and choose Add.

4. Type **Married** in the Option text box and **married** in the Value text box and choose OK.

5. Add **Single**, **Divorced**, **Engaged,** and **Widowed** using the same method. You can also change the order of the list by using the Move Up and Move Down buttons inside the dialog box.

6. Choose OK when finished entering all the options.

The last field in this column is the submit field. This field is essential to the entire form. If this field isn't included, then the form has no value. To insert a submit field:

1. Place the cursor in the appropriate cell, and select the Submit Button button from the property bar.

2. Double-click the field to activate the Button Properties dialog box.

3. In the Label text box, type **Submit Questionnaire To Us** and choose OK. This will change the display name of the button.

Next, move the cursor over to the first cell of the next column. Using the instructions for the previous fields, create the first five cells of this column, as shown in Figure 13-5. Next, add a list with check boxes. The reason you'll use check boxes here is that there may be more than one answer. The reader can choose none, one, some, or all from the list of choices. To insert a check box:

1. Choose the Check Box button from the toolbar.

2. Type the text right after the check box.

3. Highlight the text you just typed, and press CTRL-C to copy it to the Clipboard.

4. Double-click the check box to modify its properties.

5. Place the cursor in the Value field, and press CTRL-P to paste the check box text.

6. If you want the check box already checked, choose the Initially Selected check box.

7. Choose OK.

Repeat these instructions for each of the items on the list. When you come to the last item:

8. Insert a check box. No need to mess with the value on this one, since the value will appear automatically in the text line.

9. Type **Other** and press SPACEBAR once.

10. Insert a text line. The text line's value will be any "other" occasion.

The next field asks for comments or suggestions from the reader. This is an important section to include in any online form. To add a text area like that shown in Figure 13-5:

1. Place the cursor in the appropriate table cell.

2. Select the Text Area button from the toolbar.

3. Double-click the text area to activate the Text Area Properties dialog box.

4. Type **Comments** in the Name text box.

5. Change the size by typing **30** in the Columns text box.

6. Change the maximum characters by typing **200** in the <u>M</u>ax Char text box. Choose OK.

Two cells below the text area field is the Clear All button. This button is inserted as follows:

1. Place the cursor in the cell, and select the Reset Button button from the property bar.

2. Change the display name by double-clicking it and typing **Clear All** in the <u>L</u>abel text box and choosing OK.

Underneath the entire table is a hidden field. This field contains the information about where the form will be sent once it's submitted from the reader. This field is just as important as the submit field—without it, the submit field is useless. To add this field:

1. Place the cursor below the table and select the Hidden Field button from the property bar. The Hidden Field Properties dialog box will appear.

2. In the <u>N</u>ame and <u>V</u>alue text boxes, you will need to type in certain information provided by your web administrator.

Hidden fields contain the information on where the form will be sent once it's submitted. Simply typing in an e-mail address isn't going to get your forms sent back to you. You will need to contact your web administrator to find out the number of hidden fields your form may require, and the correct names and values to use. You will insert the names and values in the Hidden Field Properties dialog box, which appears when a hidden field is inserted.

 NOTE: *Many Internet service providers use common gateway interface (CGI) to process data sent between web forms and the server.*

Web forms look intimidating to the non–HTML guru, but as you can see, they are rather simple. The best forms are easy to read, not too lengthy, and are well designed. No web surfer wants to spend too much time filling out a hard to read, messy online form. Keep your web visitors happy by giving them the opportunity to place direct orders or give comments, complaints, or suggestions instantly.

Converting Corel WordPerfect Documents to HTML

Sometimes you don't want to create a web page from scratch, with or without the help of the Web Page Expert. In fact, most companies have a lot of existing files they want to make available in an intranet or on the Internet. Luckily, Corel WordPerfect makes it easy to convert WordPerfect documents to HTML format (and vice versa). In fact, nearly all of the basic document formatting your documents contain will probably translate to HTML. If that sounds like a qualified endorsement, it is. Because HTML doesn't support the rich formatting features that Corel WordPerfect does, you may have to experiment a bit with your documents to see if you need to make any little formatting adjustments before you make the conversion.

What Formatting Corel WordPerfect Converts

Earlier in this book, you learned about some of the things Corel WordPerfect does when it converts documents to HTML format. In Chapter 6, you learned how each text attribute (bold, italic, and so on) is converted to HTML (see Table 14-1).

Later, you learned that Corel WordPerfect automatically converts graphic images when you publish them to HTML. Regardless of their original format, Corel WordPerfect will change them to one of the two web-supported formats (GIF or JPEG). Any graphics already in the CompuServe Graphics Interchange Format (GIF) will remain in that format. Others will be converted to JPEG. Wallpaper or background images that use 256 or fewer colors are converted to GIF format. If the images use more than 256 colors, they're converted to JPEG.

How Corel WordPerfect Converts Key Font Attributes When a Document Is Published to HTML

	Converted Exactly	Converted, But Not Necessarily Supported By All Browsers	Changed	Deleted
	Bold	Redline	Shadow (inaccessible under Web Editor menus) is converted to Blink. Internal hypertext links' color is changed to blue (or the custom color you specified for links) from green.	Hidden
	Italic	Strikeout		Double underline
	Underline			
	Subscript			
	Superscript			
	Font color			
	Font size			

TABLE 14-1

Some Corel WordPerfect features don't convert to HTML. When you convert a Corel WordPerfect document to HTML, these formatting codes are deleted:

- Double underline

- Drop caps

- Footnotes

- Headers and footers

- Page numbering

- Vertical lines

- Watermarks

NOTE: *While watermarks are not supported when you convert documents to HTML, you can achieve a watermark effect by creating a background image for your HTML documents. See Chapter 7 for details.*

Indents and tabs are converted to spaces. You can view any document summary information your Corel WordPerfect document contains while in Corel WordPerfect, but the document summary will not be viewable on the Web. Also, if your document contains a hypertext link to a macro, it will not operate.

Converting Documents Using Internet Publisher

Corel WordPerfect makes it easy to convert documents with its automated Internet Publisher. In fact, it's the only way to convert HTML documents unless you plan to get your hands dirty with writing HTML.

To format a Corel WordPerfect document as an HTML document:

1. Open the Corel WordPerfect document by choosing File | Open.

2. Choose File | Internet Publisher.

3. From the Internet Publisher dialog box (see Figure 14-1), choose Format As Web Document.

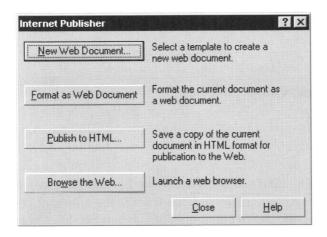

FIGURE 14-1   To convert a Corel WordPerfect document to HTML, use Internet Publisher's Format As Web Document option

After warning you about the consequences of converting a document to HTML (just choose OK), Corel WordPerfect will format the current document as a web document and open the Web Editor to put all the web tools in easy reach. It's a good idea to save the file under a different name by choosing File | Save As before you make any more changes.

When you've finished making any editing changes you want to make, choose File | Internet Publisher | Publish To HTML. From the Publish To HTML dialog box, choose the filename you want to publish the document to and choose OK.

Of course, you can change any document from HTML format to Corel WordPerfect format as well. To do so:

1. Open a web-formatted document.

2. Choose File | Internet Publisher.

3. Choose Format As WP Document. (This option changes depending on the format of the document you have open.)

4. Choose File | Save As to save the file in Corel WordPerfect format.

Tips and Tricks for Converting to HTML

As mentioned at the beginning of this chapter, there are no hard-and-fast rules about how *your* specific document will translate to HTML. As a general rule, however, the less formatting your documents contain, the more accurately they will translate to HTML. Additionally, the more you use Corel WordPerfect's styles, the better off you'll be.

For example, documents or letters already formatted by use of Times Roman or a similar typeface that contain few if any graphics, lines, or other special formatting will translate easily. Many government agencies and legal offices have successfully translated archival materials for ready, online reference.

Insider Tip

Corel WordPerfect Suite doesn't currently support batch conversions, however. In other words, you must load each document into Corel WordPerfect, format it as a web document, and publish it as HTML rather than processing a group of files at once. You could create a macro to do that, or you might want to look at products such as Corel's WEB.Transit, which can process a number of Corel WordPerfect files into HTML files. You can customize some of the details for the translation and then load the converted files into Corel WordPerfect for final editing.

On the other hand, if you've spent a lot of time formatting a Corel WordPerfect document, plan on spending some time tweaking that formatting for HTML. The more complex the design and layout of a document, the more work you'll need to do to make it look good in HTML. For example, say you've created a document that contains a graphic with text wrap set to "no wrap" so the text overprints the graphic. When that document is converted to HTML, the text *will* wrap around the graphic because of HTML's limitations. The same goes for a contoured text wrap (where the text wraps around the image, not the box borders).

 CAUTION: *While Windows 95 allows long filenames that include spaces, some web servers don't. Be careful naming your files so they'll be usable on the Web when you publish them to HTML.*

If you're consistently making the same types of changes to your documents, you may want to use a macro. While this book doesn't have space to provide complete details on creating macros, it's easy to create macros that simply record what you've done—much like a video camera capturing your motions to replay them later.

Insider Tip

Corel provides some macro information in a special Macro Help file you can access when you're installing Corel WordPerfect. To install this special Macro Help file, run Corel WordPerfect Suite's installation program, choose a custom installation and check the Macro Help file option in the Corel WordPerfect option screen. For the only complete, detailed, how-to macro reference, contact Gordon McComb, noted Corel WordPerfect macro guru and author. His self-published book is essential for people who plan to write their own Corel WordPerfect macros. For more information, visit **www.gmccomb.com/wp/**, e-mail **gordon@gmccomb.com**, or send a letter to Gordon McComb's Automation Masters, 2642 Hope Street, Oceanside, CA 92056.

Here's an example of a simple Corel WordPerfect macro that can help you translate your Corel WordPerfect documents to HTML beyond what Corel WordPerfect already provides. Many businesses, especially those whose livelihood focuses around documents, take advantage of Corel WordPerfect's document summary feature. This feature lets you add information *about* a document to the document itself, including a descriptive name that can appear in the File Open dialog box. However, this summary doesn't make it to the HTML document when you publish the document to HTML. You can make a simple macro, however, that takes the descriptive name and makes it the document's title. To create a simple macro:

1. Make sure the current document is in web format. If it isn't, choose File | Internet Publisher | Format As Web Document.

2. Choose Tools | Macro | Record. You'll then see the Record Macro dialog box (it looks almost exactly like the File Open dialog box).

3. In the <u>N</u>ame text box, type a clever name such as **docsumm** (Corel WordPerfect will automatically add the WCM extension). Press ENTER.

You're now recording the macro. (Notice the special macro toolbar that appears.) All of your actions will be recorded into the macro file. The following steps will walk you through copying the information from the document summary into special HTML.

TIP: *Corel WordPerfect will only record the result of the keys you press or the menu items you choose—not the exact motions of your mouse or the spelling errors you make. Still, try to minimize the errors you make or the backtracking you do. This way, your macro will run faster.*

1. Choose <u>F</u>ile | P<u>r</u>operties. You'll see the Properties dialog box (Figure 14-2).

2. Highlight the text in the Descriptive Name text box, and press CTRL-C to copy it to the Clipboard.

FIGURE 14-2   The Properties dialog box

3. Choose OK to close the Properties dialog box.

4. Choose Format | HTML Document Properties to open the HTML
Document Properties dialog box, shown here:

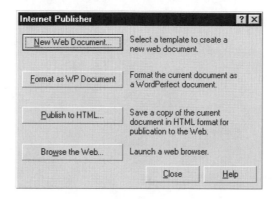

5. Press ALT-C to move the cursor to the Custom Title text box.

6. Press CTRL-V to paste the descriptive name into the text box.

7. Choose OK to close the dialog box.

8. To stop recording the macro, click the Stop button on the macro toolbar or
choose Tools | Macro | Record. (The Record option acts as a toggle.)

That's it! To play the macro on a new document, just choose Tools | Macro | Play.
Choose *docsumm.wcm* from the file list and choose OK.

The most important thing to remember when converting Corel WordPerfect
documents to web pages is to have patience. You'll need to spend some time working
with heavily formatted documents to get them the way you like them. But the time
will be well spent once your attractive pages appear on the Web.

Part
III

Creating Web Pages with Corel Quattro Pro, Corel Presentations, and More

Web Publishing with Corel Quattro Pro

15

Corel Quattro Pro is a great tool to work with numbers and numerical data. It provides complete, easy-to-use spreadsheet tools built on years of experience. It was the first spreadsheet to read, write, and link to web documents. The latest versions of Corel Quattro Pro continue this legacy of spreadsheet power plus trend-setting Internet connectivity.

When you work with spreadsheets and notebooks in Corel Quattro Pro, you don't need to work in isolation. In fact, even early Quattro Pro for Windows versions (including the one in the Borland Office Suite) provided unparalleled network connectivity. Exclusive technology made it easy to share spreadsheets and data across networks, with each affected spreadsheet being automatically updated with a form of "publish and subscribe."

NOTE: *"Publish and subscribe" is a bit of computer jargon. If you want to share a spreadsheet or bit of information with others, you make it available by publishing it on the network. Others can subscribe to that spreadsheet or piece of data and incorporate it into other spreadsheets. Subscribers are automatically given the latest information as it's published. This terminology is largely obsolete, however, since most information is now shared by the use of HTML, an intranet, or the Internet.*

This history of network friendliness continues with Corel Quattro Pro 8. Corel Quattro Pro makes it easy to incorporate data from the Web into your spreadsheets, and, in turn, publish those spreadsheets to the Web by use of HTML, Corel Barista, or Envoy.

In this chapter, you'll first learn the basics of creating Corel Quattro Pro documents to be distributed on the Web—as well as how to load HTML documents into Corel Quattro Pro. You'll also pick up a few pointers for creating spreadsheets designed to be distributed via the Web. You'll then learn how to insert links to data on the Web in your spreadsheets. And you'll learn how to create hyperlinks to web pages in Corel Quattro Pro spreadsheets.

Creating Corel Quattro Pro Documents for the Web

Corel Quattro Pro can both read and write HTML 3 documents. In other words, you can save your spreadsheets in HTML format *and* you can read HTML documents into Corel Quattro Pro spreadsheets.

Insider Tip

If you're interested in converting existing Corel Quattro Pro spreadsheets into HTML or HTML tables to Corel Quattro Pro spreadsheets, Corel Quattro Pro is your best tool. But for advanced HTML page layout and abilities, you may want to consider using Corel WordPerfect or Corel Presentations instead. Corel Quattro Pro is the perfect tool for working with numbers and tabular data, but for fine-tuned web layout, it may not be the most appropriate choice.

It's simple to save a spreadsheet page in HTML format. In fact, you don't have to do anything special at all. But be warned: the spreadsheet page as you see it will not look exactly as it does onscreen (or on paper) when you publish it to HTML. In fact, when you publish a Corel Quattro Pro spreadsheet to HTML, you should plan on publishing only the tabular data—the rows and columns of information—on just the current page with minimal formatting intact. Charts, graphs, embedded graphics, and hyperlinks will not translate to HTML.

Unlike Corel WordPerfect, Corel Quattro Pro is not designed as a document creation tool. Instead, it's designed to help you make sense of numbers and present those numbers clearly. Its web abilities are part of presenting numbers—and as such, make great tools for creating HTML tables. When you save a Corel Quattro Pro spreadsheet to HTML, you'll get a basic HTML table that contains the values and labels from the spreadsheet page you've saved. Take a look at Figures 15-1, 15-2, and 15-3 to compare a Corel Quattro Pro spreadsheet page as seen onscreen to the way it appears in Netscape Navigator when published to HTML and Corel Barista.

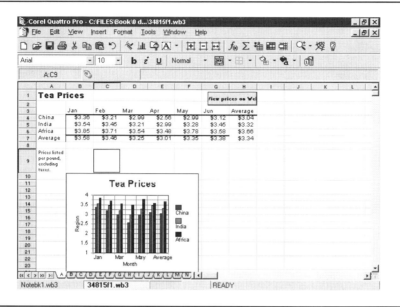

FIGURE 15-1 A sample spreadsheet page onscreen in Corel Quattro Pro

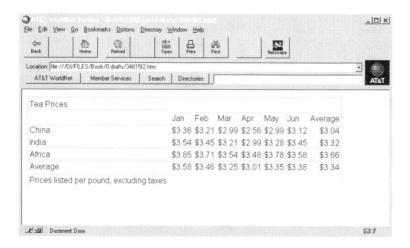

FIGURE 15-2 The Figure 15-1 spreadsheet published to HTML format

CAUTION: *You can publish only the current Corel Quattro Pro page to HTML. Multipage notebooks aren't supported in HTML, so you must publish only one page at a time.*

 TIP: *Be careful of long, text-only cells. Even if they appear to span cells in your spreadsheet, HTML will automatically size columns based on the widest cell in the column. It's easy to get a column that's much wider than you want it to be!*

Saving a Corel Quattro Pro Spreadsheet as an HTML Table

It's simple to save a Corel Quattro Pro spreadsheet as an HTML table. Remember that any charts, graphics, or hypertext links will not translate to HTML. You will be saving the spreadsheet portion of the current page only. To save a Corel Quattro Pro spreadsheet as HTML:

1. Make sure the Corel Quattro Pro file you want to convert is open and you're viewing the spreadsheet page you want to save as HTML.

2. Choose File | Save As.

3. In the For Type pull-down menu, choose HTML.

4. Type the filename you want to use in the Name text box.

5. Choose Save.

If you want to preview your Corel Quattro Pro document in its HTML format, you'll need to open your web browser, then open the file from there. In Netscape Navigator, you can open a file by choosing File | Open Page.

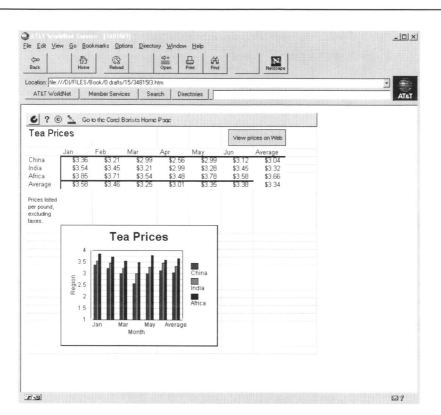

FIGURE 15-3   The Figure 15-1 spreadsheet published to Corel Barista

Saving a Quattro Pro Spreadsheet Using Corel Barista or Envoy

If you want more control over the look of your spreadsheet when it's published to the Web, you will want to take advantage of Corel WordPerfect Suite's other web publishing options. Both Corel Barista and Envoy can help you preserve more of your spreadsheet's formatting when it's published to the Web. And both can protect its information from being copied or edited. To learn more about the advantages and disadvantages of each method, see Chapter 18 (Corel Barista) or Chapter 19 (Envoy).

Corel Barista

Corel Barista takes advantage of the power of Java. By doing so, it can reproduce elements and formatting on your web pages that HTML can only imagine. Corel Barista's Java-based technology breaks the limitations HTML imposes and more accurately reproduces your page layout, including fonts, graphics, and so on. In short, a Corel Barista page is an HTML-based document that contains special information beyond basic HTML codes. When the page is loaded into a Java-compatible browser like Netscape Navigator, the browser loads the Java classes—special Java programs—that interpret this special data and display the page.

To save your spreadsheet to an HTML page using the Java technology in Corel Barista:

1. Choose File | Send To | Corel Barista. The Publish The Current Document In Java Format dialog box, shown here, will appear:

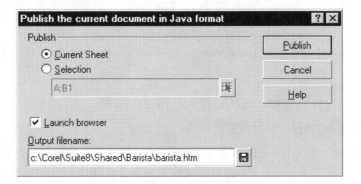

 NOTE: *For details about the Publish To Corel Barista dialog box, see Chapter 18.*

2. Choose whether you want to publish the page (Current Sheet), or a range of cells (Selection); then enter a filename in the Output Filename text box and choose Publish.

3. If you checked the Launch Browser check box, Corel Quattro Pro will automatically launch your web browser to show you the page.

NOTE: *Remember to copy the Corel Barista class files to the same directory as your files. For more details, see Chapter 18.*

Envoy

Publishing your Corel Quattro Pro spreadsheet to Envoy works much the same way as does publishing to Corel Barista if you have Corel WordPerfect Suite 8 Professional (the Professional version includes the full version of Envoy, not just Envoy Viewer). Envoy is not an HTML- or web-based document format. Instead, it's a way of creating application-independent, format-rich documents. With special browser plug-ins, you can view Envoy documents in your web browser. However, since the Envoy viewer is freely distributed, virtually anyone can view an Envoy file using that viewer.

When you publish a document to Envoy, you can use either the Envoy 7 printer driver or the Send To command. Because the Envoy 7 printer driver is installed when you install Corel WordPerfect Suite 8 Professional, you can "print" to Envoy from any application (including Corel Quattro Pro) just like printing to a printer. To print to Envoy, choose File | Print. Choose the Envoy 7 driver from the drop-down list of printers, complete any dialog boxes, and you're set! (See Chapter 19 for more details.)

Opening Web Documents in Corel Quattro Pro

Corel Quattro Pro's support for the Web extends beyond just *saving* documents in Web-compatible formats. It can also *read* HTML documents. Don't get carried away, however, and assume that Corel Quattro Pro is designed to lay out complex web pages. Remember, its strength is that it's a tool focused on helping you better understand your data. If the HTML document you open in Corel Quattro Pro is a table containing lots of numerical data, you're in for a treat. Corel Quattro Pro loads this tabular data easily and quickly—and provides you with its full complement of tools to manipulate and format that data.

To open an HTML document in Corel Quattro Pro, open it as you would open any other document:

1. Choose File | Open. Since Corel Quattro Pro displays only Quattro Pro documents by default (*.wb*), you may want to list all files or HTML files.

2. In the <u>N</u>ame text box, type ***.*** and press ENTER.
   Or, from the For <u>T</u>ype drop-down menu, choose HTML.

3. Select the file you want to open from the list and choose <u>O</u>pen.

Corel Quattro Pro will load your HTML file and do its best to reproduce the formatting within the spreadsheet's cells. As mentioned before, tables translate most faithfully to spreadsheet format.

But opening HTML files isn't the only use for Corel Quattro Pro and the Internet. The Internet has become the world's network—and as such, you can access any resource or any file published on it, no matter where it resides. Corel Quattro Pro makes it easy to open documents located anywhere on the Internet. And because it provides comprehensive file import and export abilities, you can open any file in any supported format—from HTML to Lotus 1-2-3, from Excel to (obviously) Corel Quattro Pro.

To open a file from a web site, ftp site, or gopher on the Internet:

1. Choose <u>F</u>ile | <u>O</u>pen.

2. In the Name text box, type the URL for the document you want to open.
   For example, you might type **ftp://ftp.fictitious.com/public/stats.wb3**.

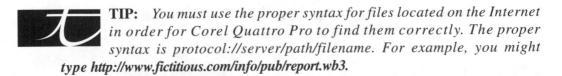

TIP: *You must use the proper syntax for files located on the Internet in order for Corel Quattro Pro to find them correctly. The proper syntax is protocol://server/path/filename. For example, you might type http://www.fictitious.com/info/pub/report.wb3.*

Insider Tip

Corel knows you might not always be connected to the Internet, so you don't have to be continuously connected to access files across the Internet. When you specify a file located on the Internet, Corel Quattro Pro looks on the Net for the file and makes a copy on your hard drive. You can then disconnect from the Internet while you work with the file. You cannot save the file onto the Internet; however, you can save any changes on your hard drive and then upload the file as you normally would.

Instant Internet Links with QuickButtons

If you're creating a complex spreadsheet or slide show, you may want to provide an easy, attractive way to connect to a specific web site or Internet resource. Corel Quattro Pro's QuickButtons do just that—they're customizable, graphic buttons that appear anywhere you want them. You might use a QuickButton to allow someone viewing your spreadsheet to connect to detailed corporate earnings information as published in an annual report on a web site. Or you might connect to an ftp site to allow a spreadsheet user to download a related spreadsheet.

It's easy to create a QuickButton. To do so:

1. Choose Insert | QuickButton.

2. The cursor will then change to the special QuickButton cursor:

3. Click and drag the QuickButton cursor to create a button where and in the size you want.

Or, click the QuickButton cursor where you want the button to appear. This creates a QuickButton in the default size.

> **TIP:**   *Once the QuickButton is in place, you can change its size or location anytime you like. Click on the QuickButton to select it. Drag any of the black, square handles to resize the QuickButton. Or move the cursor over the selected QuickButton, then click and drag the QuickButton to move it.*

4. To customize the QuickButton's text, right-click the button and choose Button Properties. Choose the Label Text tab in the Button Properties dialog box. Type the new text label you want in the Enter Text text box and choose OK.

Not only can you customize the QuickButton's text, you can also customize the appearance of a QuickButton. You can add a drop shadow, change the button type, and even change its border. To change these options, right-click the QuickButton and choose Button Properties. But that's not the only thing you can change: you can also paste a bitmapped graphic onto the button. To do so:

1. Copy the graphic you want onto the Windows Clipboard. Remember, the graphic must be in Windows bitmap format.

2. Return to Corel Quattro Pro, select the QuickButton, and choose Edit | Paste.

TIP: *To select the QuickButton without activating it, right-click the QuickButton, then press ESC.*

You're now ready to link the QuickButton to an Internet resource.

1. Right-click the QuickButton; choose Button Properties from the pop-up menu.

2. Choose the Macro tab, then choose Link To URL.

3. In the URL text box, type the Internet resource to which you want the button linked. For example, you might type **http://www.corel.com** or **ftp://ftp.corel.com**.

4. Choose OK, then OK again to save your changes.

Creating Hyperlinks in Corel Quattro Pro

Similar to Corel WordPerfect, with Corel Quattro Pro you can create a hyperlink in any cell. You might create a link that takes you to a web page with more information, say, on an annual report. It works like the links you create in button form. For more information on the types of hyperlinks you can create, see Chapter 9.

To create a hyperlink in a cell:

1. Select the cell in which you want to create the hyperlink.

2. Choose Insert | Hyperlink. You'll then see the Edit Hyperlink dialog box, shown here:

3. Type the web address you want to use in the <u>L</u>ink To File Or URL text
box. You can, of course, create a hyperlink to a file you have stored on
your computer, on your local area network, or on a wide area network as
well as to an Internet resource.

Insider Tip

If you want to find the page to which you want to link, choose the
file-folder icon to the right of the text box in the Edit Hyperlink dialog
box. Then, in the File Open dialog box, you can choose one of your
Internet bookmarks from the Favo<u>r</u>ites menu. Once you choose the
URL you want, you'll be taken to the Corel Internet Namespace dialog
box, where, if you're connected to the Net, you can preview the web
page or link to another before you accept the final link.

Once you've created a hyperlink, to edit or remove it, just highlight the cell, then
choose <u>I</u>nsert | H<u>y</u>perlink again. Make any editing changes to the URL you like and
choose OK. Or, to remove the link and convert the existing URL to plain text, choose
<u>R</u>emove Link. But Corel Quattro Pro can do more than just link to web documents.
It can actually use the power of the Internet to provide data to your spreadsheets.

The Web as Data Server: Inserting a URL into a Cell

Corel Quattro Pro can do more than just *link* to the Internet, however. You can incorporate information from data on the Internet into your spreadsheet cells. The most common example of this is to update stock prices. But that's not the only way you could use it—it might make it simple for your company to assemble information from various sites. For example, a manufacturing site in Ireland might place information about the day's manufacturing totals in a Corel Quattro Pro spreadsheet stored on a protected ftp site. Regardless of your location, you could incorporate those totals into a worldwide summary spreadsheet automatically. Here's how:

1. Move to the cell in which you want to make the reference.

2. Here's the tricky part—type the link in Corel Quattro Pro's notebook/page/cell reference format:

    +[*Drive*:*Path**Filename.Extension*]*Page*:*Cell reference*

3. Press ENTER to save the formula in the cell.

NOTE: *You'll only need the plus sign at the beginning if this is the only thing you're typing in the cell. (The plus sign tells Corel Quattro Pro that the text following it isn't just a text label.) If you're including your reference to the Internet resource as part of a formula, you can omit the plus sign.*

For example, if you wanted to link to a Corel Quattro Pro spreadsheet (or *notebook*) stored on your hard drive, you might type **+[c:\myfiles\stats.wb3]A:C4**. This would tell Corel Quattro Pro you want to look at the value in cell C4 on page A of your stats.wb3 file. This same approach works with Internet resources. Remember, though, that instead of the *drive*:*path**filename.extension* syntax, you'll want to use *protocol*://*server*/*path*/*filename.extension* syntax instead. So to access a similar file stored on an ftp site, you might type this formula:

+[ftp://ftp.fictitious.com/mfg/stats.wb3]A:C4

You could use a similar formula to access a file stored on a web site: you'd just use an Internet address beginning with "**http://www**" instead.

Insider Tip

Corel Quattro Pro's formulas aren't case sensitive, so you can enter them in all uppercase, all lowercase, or a mix of the two. But Internet files *can* be case sensitive, so be careful to use the appropriate case when you're referring to a file located on the Internet. For example, most UNIX-based web servers see a difference between "FISH.HTM" and "fish.htm."

REMEMBER: *You can only read files located on the Internet. But since you're pulling information from Internet resources when you create an in-cell link, this doesn't limit Corel Quattro Pro's abilities in any way.*

Once you've saved the formula in the cell, Corel Quattro Pro will connect to the Internet to load the information you've described. It will automatically update the links as you open the file each time. If it cannot find the information or cannot connect to the Internet, it will give you an error message and ask you to change the information in the cell.

Spreadsheet Design Considerations for the Web

If you're going to make HTML the final format of your spreadsheet, plan for it! It's like creating a document in Corel WordPerfect you know will be printed in booklet form: if you know the final output format, you can better plan the way the information will be presented.

On the other hand, if you are planning to simply make your spreadsheets (notebooks) available via the Internet in Corel Quattro Pro format, you don't need to do anything special. If others will be linking to your spreadsheets, though, be sure to keep the cells consistent so that the references in their spreadsheets remain correct. When others link to information in your spreadsheets or workbooks, they will appreciate your keeping the same information in the same files, on the same notebook pages, and in the same cells. In fact, they'll be eternally grateful when you don't cause them additional work in using their automated, linked spreadsheets.

Formatting Column Titles for the Web

When you publish a spreadsheet to HTML, Corel Quattro Pro will convert each spreadsheet column to a column in a table. If you're like most people, you will often have a description, a label, or a footnote that creeps across several columns. If you leave this long line of text in the spreadsheet, it will stretch the column it's in to fit the text inside. This will make spreadsheets look downright ugly. Keep your columns narrow.

Insider Tip

If you must include a large line or block of text, here's a trick that will help Corel Quattro Pro format your HTML table correctly. Select the cells your text is in. When you save the spreadsheet as HTML, the text inside the box will wrap within the cell just as it does onscreen. If you don't like the way the text looks when it wraps, you can also use the new Cell Join feature. It's a bit trickier, though. Here's how:

1. Select the block of cells across which your text spreads.

2. Then choose Format | Selection.

3. Under the Alignment tab, check Join Cells (make sure Wrap Text is unchecked) in the Cell Options group box.

4. Choose OK.

Onscreen, the text will stretch across the cells just as you like—but when it's saved as HTML, the text will wrap just as it did by use of the Wrap Text feature.

Formatting Tricks: Using Empty Rows

It's not just columns you'll want to watch out for; most Corel Quattro Pro (and, for that matter, spreadsheet) users use empty rows to assist in grouping information on a page. When you publish a spreadsheet page to HTML, these empty rows appear only as slightly thicker lines between cells. If you want to ensure that these empty rows appear on your HTML page, there's a work-around. It's not pretty, but it works. Just place a period (.) in any cell on the row you want to appear empty. You might even want to place it in the far right cell. You can change the color of the text in that cell to white so it doesn't appear on your screen (it will appear in the final HTML table). In short, using empty rows to format your spreadsheet page won't work well when you're publishing to HTML, but it works just fine publishing to Corel Barista or Envoy.

Other Formatting Tips and Tricks

You might have picked up on another formatting tip in the last paragraph: font colors won't translate when a spreadsheet is saved as HTML—neither will lines, cell shading, or colors. Remember, Corel Quattro Pro's HTML publishing abilities are designed to create quick, attractive HTML tables with little fanfare. To preserve the layout of carefully designed spreadsheets, publish your spreadsheet to Corel Barista or Envoy, both of which preserve cell shading, lines, cell colors, and font colors.

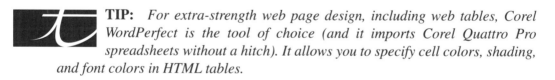

TIP: *For extra-strength web page design, including web tables, Corel WordPerfect is the tool of choice (and it imports Corel Quattro Pro spreadsheets without a hitch). It allows you to specify cell colors, shading, and font colors in HTML tables.*

As with colors and lines, saving a spreadsheet to HTML doesn't bring along "floating" items (text boxes, buttons) and charts. Again, however, publishing your spreadsheet to Corel Barista or Envoy will include all of these items.

When you're planning your spreadsheet for publication to the Web in a format other than Corel Quattro Pro, keep in mind these considerations—and a couple others as well. Unfortunately, when you're publishing a web document from Corel Quattro Pro, neither Corel Barista nor Envoy recognizes buttons that link to web sites (as they do with Corel WordPerfect). But while publishing a spreadsheet to HTML limits you to only the current page, both Corel Barista and Envoy support multipage spreadsheets.

No matter how your spreadsheets relate to the Web, you will find that Corel Quattro Pro is a flexible, powerful tool. You've learned in this chapter how Corel Quattro Pro makes it easy to link your spreadsheets to Web- or Internet-based information. You've learned how to connect to the Internet instantly from within your Corel Quattro Pro spreadsheets from the toolbar or from special, custom-designed buttons. Now you know how to publish Corel Quattro Pro spreadsheet information to the Web in HTML, Barista, or Envoy formats—and when and why you'd want to use each format. But Corel Quattro Pro isn't the only application (besides Corel WordPerfect) in the suite that provides web connectivity. Take a look at the next chapter to learn about Corel Presentations' powerful web features for both graphics and interactive Internet presentations.

Web Publishing with Corel Presentations

16

orel Presentations gives you the freedom to create and present high-quality business communications. This advanced presentation program is actually two impressive programs in one: a versatile business presentations package *and* a sophisticated business graphics tool.

With enhanced HTML, Corel Barista, Envoy, and even ActiveX support, you can publish slides, slide shows, and graphics on the Web—and create your own web graphics. Corel Presentations helps you reach an entirely new audience in two ways: by creating web graphics (or pages) and by creating presentations that can be turned into live, dynamic web-based presentations.

In this chapter, you'll learn how to get started creating, editing, or modifying an image for use on the Web. You'll also learn the basics of creating a presentation. You won't spend much time with these, however. Instead, you'll learn about publishing your presentations to the Web or to other electronic, portable media by use of Corel Presentations' Internet Publisher and the new Show On The Go.

Creating Web Graphics with Corel Presentations

Corel Presentations uses two types of graphics formats—*bitmap* (point) and *vector* (draw). A bitmap image is a medley of tiny dots called *pixels.* You can create and edit bitmap images in Corel Presentations' Bitmap Editor, where each pixel can be altered individually. A vector image is a single object made up of connected elements called *vectors.* Any objects you create in the Corel Presentations drawing window, such as charts, text lines, and shapes, are vector objects (see Figure 16-1).

Since bitmap images are created pixel by pixel, they may lose resolution when enlarged or printed, becoming fuzzy or jagged. If your printer has various dpi (dots per inch) settings, you'll get the best printed resolution by using the highest setting. Vector images, on the other hand, are formulated through mathematic calculations, so they retain their original high-resolution quality when enlarged or printed.

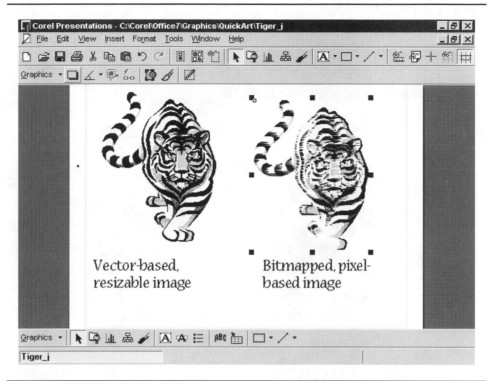

FIGURE 16-1 Vector images are whole objects made up of vectors; bitmap images are collections of pixels

Creating Bitmap Images

Corel Presentations comes with a variety of clipart images, but you're not limited to using them. Advanced drawing tools and features in the Bitmap Editor make it possible to draw almost anything. Of course, you need to have a little creativity and imagination—the program isn't capable of deciding *what* you want to draw, at least not yet.

Before you can create an image, you have to open Corel Presentations. To launch Corel Presentations:

1. Click Start on the Windows 95 menu, then choose Corel WordPerfect Suite 8 and select Corel Presentations 8. Or, double-click the Corel Presentations shortcut on your desktop.

2. In the Create New tab of the New dialog box, shown here, select Presentations Drawing, then click OK.

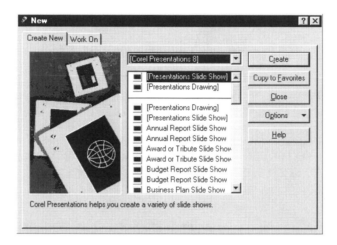

The Corel Presentations window (see Figure 16-2) is similar to the other suite applications, with program-specific menus and toolbars. Also, notice the Slide Show/Drawing Tool palette displayed at the bottom of your screen. As you begin using the different features in Corel Presentations, you'll find this palette provides instant access to dozens of tool options and features.

To create an image in the Bitmap Editor:

1. Choose Insert | Bitmap. Or, click the Bitmap button on the toolbar.

2. A hand holding a square, as shown here, appears in the window. Click once to open the Bitmap Editor.

The Bitmap Editor (see Figure 16-3) has all the tools you need to create and edit images. As with the main Corel Presentations window, a palette is also at the bottom

Drawing window

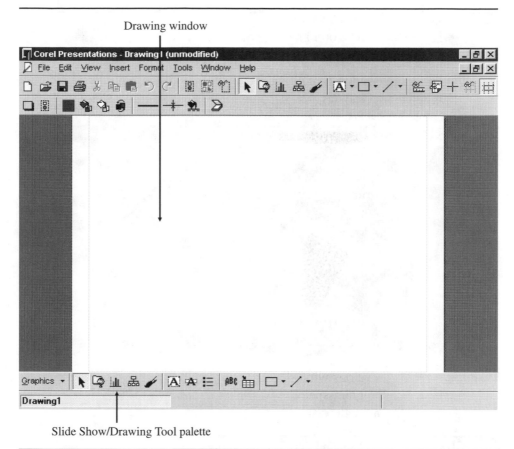

Slide Show/Drawing Tool palette

FIGURE 16-2 The Corel Presentations window with the Slide Show/Drawing Tool palette

of the Bitmap Editor. This is the Bitmap Tool palette and it contains all the drawing tools you need to create a bitmap graphic. Specific drawing features for each tool will appear on the property bar when the tool is selected.

TIP: *You can move the palette to any spot on your screen by clicking and dragging it.*

Now you're ready to create your image. From here on, the best way to learn how to create the bitmap is to experiment with the different features. Table 16-1 contains a list of the different features you'll find on the Bitmap Tool palette, along with a description of what they do.

Property bar

Toolbar

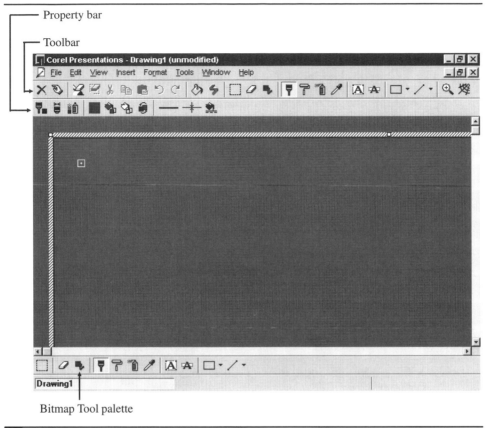

Bitmap Tool palette

FIGURE 16-3   The Bitmap Editor with the Bitmap Tool palette

When you're finished creating the image, you need to save it. If you plan to use the image on the Web, make sure to save it as either a GIF or JPEG—the only two graphics file formats the Web supports. Use GIF for images with few colors, such as a two-color logo, and JPEG for images with many colors.

To save your new drawing in JPEG or GIF format:

1. Choose File | Save As.

2. From the Type drop-down box, choose either Joint Photographic Experts Group (JPEG) or CompuServe Bitmap (GIF).

3. Type the filename you want to use in the Name text box.

4. Choose OK.

Tool	Name	Use To
	Select Area	Select a portion of the bitmap to cut, copy, erase, move, or apply special effects to
	Eraser	Erase portions of a bitmap image
	Selective Replace	Replace foreground colored pixels with background colored pixels
	Paint Brush	Paint a freehand bitmap image using colored lines and patterns
	Flood Fill	Replace the color or pattern of a group of connecting pixels with another color or pattern
	Air Brush	Spray colors into a bitmap
	Pickup Color	Copy a color used within the bitmap or object
	Text Box	Create a text box
	Text Line	Create a text line
	Closed Object	Create squares, circles, rectangles, ellipses, polygons, arrows, and more
	Line Object	Draw straight, curved, angled, Bézier-curved, circle/ellipse sections, and more

Bitmap Editor
Tool Palette

TABLE 16-1

Now close the Bitmap Editor by choosing the Close Bitmap Editor button on the toolbar to return to the main drawing window.

Insider Tip

You don't need to save your drawings in JPEG or GIF formats if you're going to create your pages using Corel WordPerfect or another Corel WordPerfect Suite tool. These programs automatically convert graphic images in other formats to JPEG or GIF when they are published to HTML.

Your image will appear selected in the Corel Presentations drawing window (see Figure 16-4). As with creating the image in the Bitmap Editor, you can use the tools on the toolbar and property bar to edit and modify the image (don't be afraid to experiment—you can always choose Undo!). For example, click Graphics on the Slide Show/Drawing Tool palette to see a pop-up menu of different positioning options, shown here:

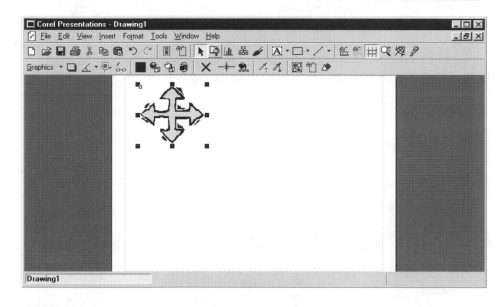

FIGURE 16-4   Both the toolbar and property bar contain powerful tools for modifying and editing images

Converting Vector Images to Bitmap Images

Use Corel Presentations' Convert To Bitmap feature to change selected vector objects, such as text lines, charts, figures, graphics, and drawings, to a bitmap format. Vector objects with a Quick 3-D or a QuickWarp effect applied to them can also be changed to a bitmap format. Once a vector image is converted, you can use the tools in the Bitmap Editor to modify the image.

Convert To Bitmap is also useful for existing bitmap images. For example, if you have a large bitmap image that you want to use as an icon on a web page, you can size the image, then reconvert it to a bitmap. This method will also help to reduce the file size of the bitmap.

Depending on the speed of a viewer's connection, viewing pages with large graphics can become extremely frustrating if the connection is slow. Because bitmap images tend to redraw faster than vector images, they are more useful in slide shows and in web pages that you want to publish on the Internet.

To convert a vector object to a bitmap image:

1. Select the object(s) you want to convert to a bitmap.

2. Click Tools | Convert To Bitmap.

The first time you use this feature, you'll receive a message box defining what the feature does, as shown here:

Select the Disable This Message Permanently check box, then choose Convert (it won't appear again).

 TIP: *If you change your mind immediately following the conversion, you can return the image to its original vector-based format by clicking Edit | Undo.*

To save objects as bitmaps:

1. Click File | Save As.

2. Select a bitmap format from the For Type drop-down list, such as BMP, CPT, GIF, JPG, MAC, TGA, or TIFF.

3. Specify a folder and filename in the Name text box, then click Save.

4. Select a predefined size, or specify the units of measure and values for the width and height of the image.

5. Select a resolution from the Resolution list, then click a color option.

 **NOTE:** *Corel Presentations will automatically add the appropriate bitmap file extension, based on the format you selected. By default, it will also save images as WPG files.*

Creating Presentations for the Web

Corel Presentations 8 offers a new, easy way to publish your documents to the Web. It's an Internet Publisher function much like the one in Corel WordPerfect, but specially tailored for creating presentations that you want distributed or even viewable on the Web. It bears repeating here that Corel Presentations isn't designed as a web page creation tool. It's an excellent tool for creating web graphics, as you learned in the previous section. And, as an industrial-strength, business-presentation software package, it also creates attention-grabbing presentations. With version 8, these presentations can be distributed via the Internet and published to the Web.

To see the options Corel Presentations offers for creating web-based presentations, load the Corel Presentations Internet Publisher by choosing File | Internet Publisher. You'll then see the Internet Publisher window, shown in Figure 16-5.

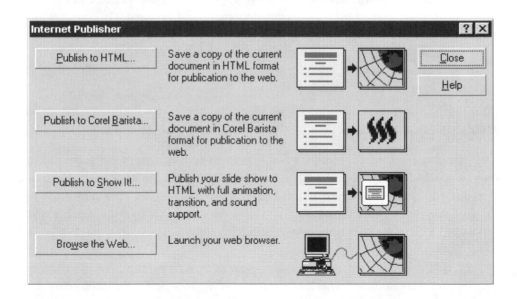

FIGURE 16-5 Corel Presentations' main Internet Publisher window—choose any of the first three options to publish your slide show to the Web

Next you'll learn about the first option—publishing your Presentations slide show to an HTML-based slide show.

Publishing Your Slide Show to HTML

In the Internet Publisher window (see Figure 16-5), the first option listed is to publish your slide show to HTML. Since a slide show is graphically rich and full of color (at least, in most cases), publishing a slide show to plain-vanilla HTML would be underwhelming at best. Instead, Corel Presentations' HTML publishing abilities are turbocharged to allow you to publish your slides to HTML with full color and layout intact. You'll be able to customize many options as you go.

To publish your slide show to HTML:

1. Make sure you have your slide show loaded.

2. Choose File | Internet Publisher.

3. Choose the Publish To HTML option.

If you haven't previously saved your document or if it has unsaved changes, Corel Presentations will ask you if it's okay to save the document before you proceed. If you agree, it will save your document and proceed. (If you say "no," Internet Publisher will stop and you'll be returned to your slide show.)

You'll then see the first in a series of dialog boxes that will walk you through each of the customization options for publishing your slide show to an HTML-based document or set of documents.

Choosing a Layout

The first dialog box you'll see, shown in Figure 16-6, asks if you want to create your own, custom slide layout or if you prefer to use one of the four predefined layouts. (Even if you decide to use one of these predefined layouts, it's a good idea for you to read the rest of this chapter so you'll understand exactly what each setting represents.) Here's a brief decription of each layout:

TIP: *A "layout" in this instance refers to a predefined way of arranging the slide and its navigation elements on the web page. You can create your own layout and save it so you can reuse it again.*

- The *Frame-Enhanced Page* option is useful when you know that those who will be viewing your slides have frame-compatible browsers like Netscape Navigator 3.0 or greater. The Frame-Enhanced Page option publishes your slide show to a single HTML page that includes navigation tools in frames (other panes) in the browser window.

- The *Multiple Pages* option publishes your slide show to one file that includes multiple pages for each slide.

- The *Single Page* option publishes your slides individually, each to a separate HTML file.

- Finally, the *Thumbnail Page* option publishes your slide show to one file that contains thumbnails of each slide in the presentation.

These layouts and their values are shown in Table 16-2.

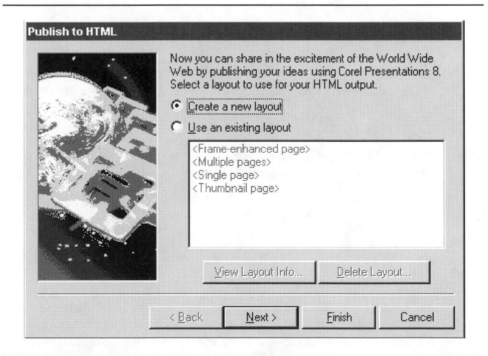

FIGURE 16-6 Choose to create your own web page layout or use one of the predefined layouts for your slide show

Page Information	Frame-Enhanced Page	Multiple Pages	Single Page	Thumbnail Page
Display slide titles	Yes	Yes	Yes	No
Display slide notes	Yes	Yes	Yes	No
Display speaker notes	Yes	Yes	Yes	No
Display goto bar	Yes	Yes	Yes	No
Auto-running show	No	No	No	No
Display TOC as	Thumbnails	Thumbnails	None	Thumbnails
Footer Information				
My home page	None	None	None	None
My e-mail address	None	None	None	None
Other information	None	None	None	None
Include show file	No	No	No	No
Display date	No	No	No	No
Display copyright	No	No	No	No
Graphic Information				
Show size	640x480	480x360	480x360	480x360
Graphic type	GIF	GIF	GIF	GIF
Color settings	Use browser's colors	Use browser's colors	Use browser's colors	Use browser's colors
Background wallpaper	None	None	None	None

Settings
for the
Predefined
HTML
Presentation
Formats

TABLE 16-2

To select one of the predefined layouts, choose <u>U</u>se An Existing Layout and then choose the one you want from the list. To be able to specify each option and create your own web page layout, choose <u>C</u>reate A New Layout. No matter which option you chose, you'll move to the next step.

Choosing a Title and a Destination

In this dialog box, shown in Figure 16-7, you'll have the opportunity to revise your slide show's title and specify the location to which you want the slides published. In the Title Of Slide Show text box, Corel Presentations has already placed the title you've specified for your show on its title page. If you don't want that title, type a new one in that text box. Then, in the Publish Files To text box, you can specify a directory to which you want your web show published. You'll generally specify a "holding" or temporary directory on your hard drive before you upload the files to the Web.

ADVANCED OPTIONS   You can also specify some more detailed settings. To do so, choose Advanced. You'll then see a dialog box with some more specific settings, shown here:

Advanced Settings   ☒

File options ─────────────────────────────

Filename of initial HTML file: index.html

Extension for other HTML files: html

☑ Do not publish skipped slides

☑ Save images and sound clips in an 'Images' sub-folder

☐ Update HTML files only (Does not create slide images)

[OK   ]   [Cancel]

First, if you want Corel Presentations to publish your slide show using a filename other than index.html for the main document, type that filename in the Filename Of Initial HTML File text box. This file will be the central file for your slide show, to which all other pages are linked. If you want the other pages to have an extension other than HTML (perhaps just HTM), type that extension in the Extension For Other HTML Files text box.

You can choose three more settings in this Advanced Settings dialog box. In Corel Presentations, you can keep a large presentation and designate certain slides to be skipped during the presentation. If you want your web-based presentation to skip those same slides, do nothing—that's the default option. However, if you want all the slides in your presentation to be published whether or not they're designated as "skipped," uncheck the Do Not Publish Skipped Slides check box.

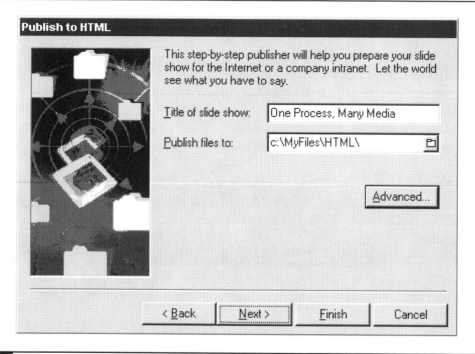

FIGURE 16-7   Type the slide show's title—if you don't want to use the title of your first title slide—and the destination for the HTML and image files

NOTE: Designating certain slides as "skipped," along with other information including presentation basics, is outside this book's scope. To learn more about the basics of creating a Corel Presentations slide show, see Corel WordPerfect Suite 8: The Official Guide, by Alan Neibauer (Osborne/McGraw-Hill, 1997).

Next, like Corel WordPerfect, Corel Presentations places any associated images and sounds in a folder inside the folder you've just published the HTML files to. If you don't want them placed in a separate folder (it's not mandatory, it's just tidier), uncheck the Save Images And Sound Clips In An "Images" Sub-folder check box. Finally, if you've previously published this slide show and you don't want Corel Presentations to take the time to create new images of each slide but *do* want to change some of the options that appear on the HTML pages, check the Update

HTML Files Only option. This is a good option to use when you've decided to change a slide show's layout, but don't need to reconvert each slide image.

When you've finished changing any advanced settings, choose OK. To move on to the next main dialog box, choose Next.

Specifying a Layout Type

If you told Corel Presentations you want to create your own layout, you'll see the next slide, which allows you to specify one of the four main layout types—frame-enhanced page, multiple-pages, single-page, or thumbnail (see Figure 16-8). To specify the slide layout type you want, choose the thumbnail sketch of the layout by clicking on the sketch itself. In the Border Around Slide section, for the first three types of layouts, you can also specify exactly how much of a border—or margin—you want around each slide's graphic image on each page. The default is 4 pixels; however, you can choose either no border (None) or the exact number of

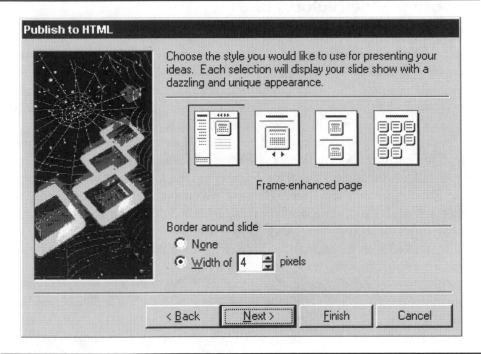

FIGURE 16-8   Specify the slide layout type you prefer

pixels you want in the Width Of Pixels text box. When you've chosen a layout and a border size, choose Next to move on to the next question.

Insider Tip

While working on any of this series of dialog boxes, you can back up and change any settings you've previously set. Just choose Back to move back one dialog box. If you've given up on the whole thing, choose Cancel. Or, if you want to just leap ahead and take all the default settings for those settings you haven't yet set, choose Finish. You can use all these functions to have exact control over just which settings you modify...without spending time reviewing settings you don't want to change.

Choosing Slide Features and Navigation Buttons

The next dialog box (see Figure 16-9) presents options for frame-enhanced, multipage, and single-page slide shows. (If you chose the thumbnail layout, you'll see a different dialog box next, and it's explained shortly.) This dialog box presents a list of features you can include in your slide shows, plus your choice of navigation button styles. Note that not all of the options will appear with each of the layout types.

In the series of check boxes on the left side of the dialog box, you can specify which information about the slides you want to include on each web page. Choose any or all of the Slide Title, Slide Numbers, Slide Goto Bar, Speaker Notes, or Auto-Running Show check boxes. The first two options are self-explanatory. A slide goto bar provides you with quick access to any slide in the presentation, giving slide show viewers the ability to jump among slides. Speaker notes include any speaker notes you've created with the slide show in the web-based pages. An auto-running show automatically cycles through the web pages and slides without user intervention.

You can also specify a table of contents style. The default layout styles create a table of contents that consists of thumbnail sketches of each slide. This can produce a page that contains a lot of graphics. If your slides contain small text, the thumbnails may not provide a lot of detail to the web reader. However, a thumbnail TOC is neat looking and impressive. Specify the type of TOC you want in the Table Of Contents section by choosing either the Text or Slide Thumbnails radio button. If you choose

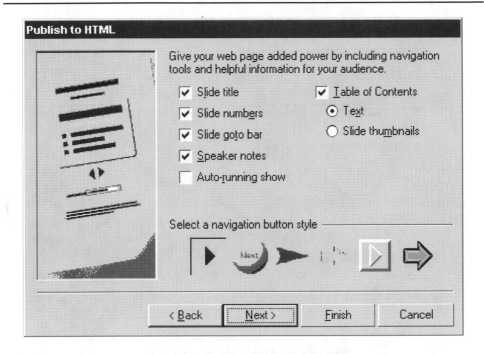

FIGURE 16-9 Select the features and the navigation button style you want in your web slide show

to create slide thumbnails, more options will appear. Choose the thumbnail size you want from the Size drop-down list: Small, Medium, Large, or Custom. The pixel size of the thumbnail you selected will appear next to the Result field. If you chose a custom size, you can specify that size in pixels by choosing Custom Size. (More details about this in the next section, "Specifying Thumbnail Settings.")

The last section on this dialog box allows you to choose a navigation button style. These navigation buttons will allow web viewers to navigate among slides in your presentation and will appear on every page. Choose the style by clicking on it. Then choose Next to move on to the next dialog box.

Specifying Thumbnail Settings

Don't forget, however, that if you chose to create only a thumbnail presentation, you will have seen a different dialog box next (see Figure 16-10).

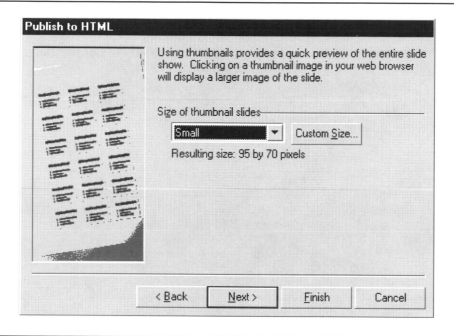

FIGURE 16-10   Specify the thumbnail size you prefer, small, medium, large, or custom size

If you're using one of the other three layout types, you can skip ahead, but if you're creating a thumbnail presentation, read on. If you did select that layout type, you'll see a dialog box that provides the same options that appear in the other layouts' dialog box (Figure 16-9). In this dialog box, you can specify the thumbnail size (Small, Medium, Large, or Custom) from the Size Of Thumbnail Slides drop-down list. If you want to create a custom size, you can do so by choosing the Custom Size button. Type the Width (in pixels) you want. The default is to keep the width and height proportional to the original dimensions of your slide show, so the Keep Height Proportional To Width check box is already checked. If you don't want to do that, you can uncheck the box and type the Height you want in the box that appears. Choose OK when you're finished. Then choose Next to move to the next dialog box.

Setting Slide Footer Information and Other Settings

In this next dialog box, shown in Figure 16-11, you can specify information that will appear in the footer of each page (plus a little extra). You'll see this dialog box

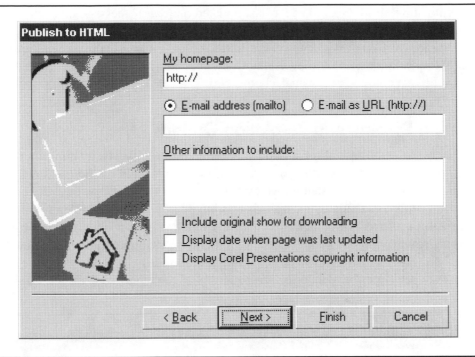

FIGURE 16-11 Specify a little more information here about yourself and what you want published

regardless of the layout you've selected. This dialog box allows you to customize each page to include vital information plus a downloadable slide show.

In the first three text boxes, you can include information about yourself and your web site plus any other information you'd like. For example, you might want to include information about where the presentation was originally given, or include your company's copyright notice. If you want to include it, you can type your own or your company's home page URL in the My Homepage text box. And if you want to make it easy for people to contact you, you can type your e-mail address in the E-mail Address text box. Both of these will automatically be created as hyperlinks. If there's any additional data you wish to include on the bottom of every page, you can add that in the Other Information To Include text box.

Now you can specify three more slide show settings. First, if you want to include a downloadable copy of the original Corel Presentations slide show for your web viewers who have Corel Presentations, check the Include Original Show For

Downloading check box. To add a "last updated on (date)" message on each page, check the Display Date When Page Was Last Updated check box. To tell web visitors your pages were created with Corel Presentations and include a copyright notice for Corel Presentations, check the Display Corel Presentations Copyright Information check box. When you're finished, choose Next.

Setting Display and Resolution Options

The next dialog box (see Figure 16-12) allows you to specify exactly how you want your presentation to appear on your web visitors' displays. In the first section, you can specify the display resolution you want your slide show to look best at. Unless you're guaranteed that all your web visitors have high-resolution systems, you are safest in accepting the default value—the lowest resolution—which is 640x480 pixels. However, if you want a different size, choose the appropriate radio button.

Next, you'll determine how large you want each slide to be on the web page size you just specified. The default is three-quarters of the page. You can set the slide

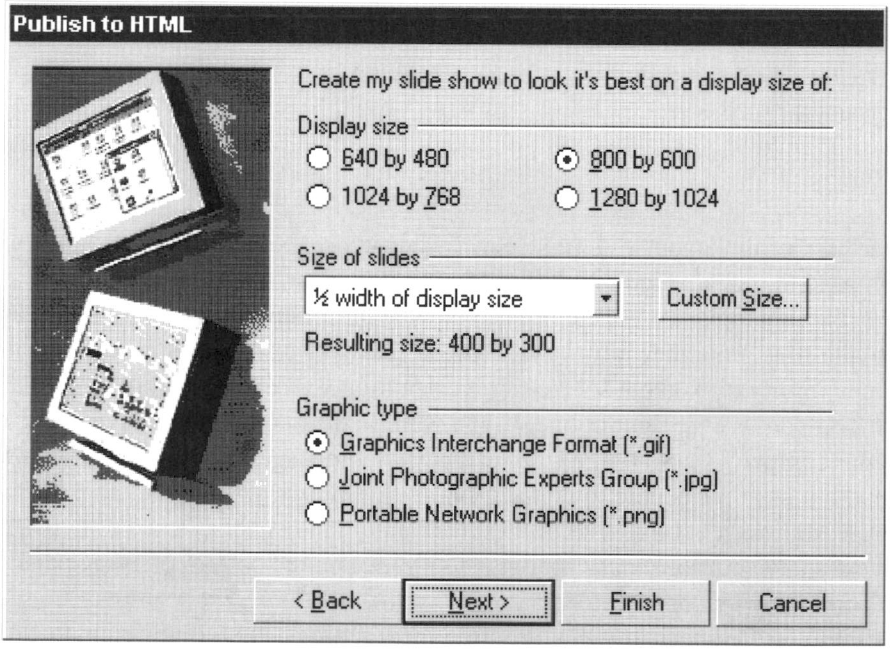

FIGURE 16-12 Specify the settings for your presentation to look its best on your web visitors' displays

size to one-quarter, one-half, three-quarters, full-width, or a custom percentage of the page size. Choose the slide size you want from the Size Of Slides drop-down list. If you want a custom size, choose Custom Size, enter the settings you want, and choose OK. (Custom size settings were explained earlier under "Specifying Thumbnail Settings.")

Finally, although all the default layouts include GIF as the default graphics type, you can choose any of three types from the Graphic Type list: Graphics Interchange Format, Joint Photographic Experts Group, or Portable Network Graphics. Once you've determined the graphic type you want, you will see the last settings dialog box.

Adjusting Colors and Other Elements

In the dialog box shown in Figure 16-13, you can change the colors of the links and other elements in your slide show. (For a detailed explanation of each type of link, you can see Chapter 9.) In most cases, you can stick with the default selection—Use Web Browser's Colors. The colors used as default hues in most people's web browsers are what they've come to expect, so using those colors will help communicate the status of your page's hyperlinks more directly. However, if you want to change the color settings, choose Use My Color Settings. The color options—grayed out until you choose Use My Color Settings—will appear as do those in Figure 16-13. Use the pull-down menus to select the colors you want for each element listed in the dialog box.

Insider Tip

If you're a power web user, you can also enter the hexadecimal values for the colors you want to use. Check the Use RGB Hex Values check box. The drop-down lists will change to text entry boxes, wherein you can type the values you want. Unless you're doing it for good reason, you can pretty much leave this option alone. It's good for when you're trying to ensure consistency with other pages, especially those programmed by someone who uses these values (you can get them from an HTML document's source code as well). Otherwise, choosing this option serves largely as a reminder of why it's so much easier to use automated tools like Corel Presentations for web page creation—so you don't have to refer to hexadecimal hue tables to figure out what "purple" means to HTML.

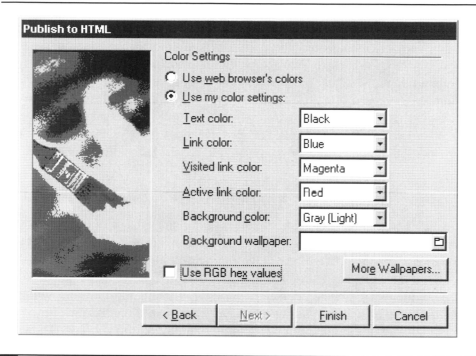

Publish to HTML

FIGURE 16-13   Specify the color settings you want to use for your Corel
Presentations web pages

At this point, you can also specify a background wallpaper. If you know the name
of the file you want to use, type it in the Background Wallpaper text box. Or use the
File Open dialog box by clicking the small file folder icon to the right of the box.
Choose More Wallpapers to view a list of premade wallpaper images. When you're
finished with this dialog box, choose Finish.

Saving a Custom Slide Layout

If you've created a custom layout, you'll see the Save Layout dialog box. It'll ask
you for a new name for your layout. If you want to save your settings for later use,
type a name for your layout and choose Save. If you don't care to keep the settings,
choose Do Not Save. At this point, a neat, animated dialog box will show you the
progress as Corel Presentations creates your web pages—and then they'll be ready
to view on the Web!

Depending on the settings you created, your presentation will include navigational buttons on every page. It'll include a separate, hyperlinked table of contents page. If you asked it to, it will also include a Go To Slide bar for each page so visitors can move to any slide. It could also include any speaker notes you have prepared for a slide. No matter what you've included, your pages will be attractive, easy to use, and persuasive.

Insider Tip

Your newly created Corel Presentations web slide show is fully integrated with Corel WordPerfect 8's Internet Publisher. If you want to modify your pages, you can simply open your new HTML-based presentation in Corel WordPerfect and use all of its web editing abilities.

Publishing Your Presentation to Corel Barista

If you want your presentation to take advantage of Corel Barista's advanced, Java-based formatting abilities, choose the Publish to Corel Barista option in the Internet Publisher dialog box. You'll then be taken directly to the standard Corel Barista publishing options. See Chapter 19 for more details.

Publishing Your Presentation Including Animation and Sound

The third option—Publish To Show It!—in Corel Presentations' Internet Publisher allows you to take your presentations one level beyond the attractive, graphically rich HTML-based presentation you created using the first option. In addition to all that the Publish To HTML option includes, this option preserves your slides' animation, sound, and other multimedia features, including transitions.

NOTE: *These features will require a faster web connection and multimedia capabilities on both the web viewer's browser and computer. Those considerations aside, you can create a snazzier web-based presentation with this option.*

To publish your presentation to the Web preserving these multimedia capabilities, choose Publish To Show It! from the Internet Publisher dialog box. You'll see four dialog boxes that are just the same as those you saw for the Publish to HTML option discussed earlier. The first asks you for a slide show title and file location. The second asks you to specify the footer information, just as you did for the basic HTML presentation. Then you can specify the presentation's display size and proportions. Finally, you can specify any custom link colors or backgrounds you want to use. When you choose Finish, Corel Presentations will create a slide show you can play on the Web that includes complete animation and multimedia.

Insider Tip

It's sometimes easy to be confused about the difference between the Show It! HTML/web abilities and the new Show On The Go feature. Reading this chapter has probably given you a pretty good idea of what these HTML abilities do—they create an HTML-based presentation that any web browser can display. In contrast, Show On The Go creates a presentation that's self-contained, but in a special format. This special format creates a file that can be run all by itself to display the Corel Presentations slide show without needing Corel Presentations. It creates what's called an executable file (EXE). You can e-mail this file or make it available on your web site, but it's not an HTML-based file.

Browsing the Web from Corel Presentations

Corel Presentations' Internet Publisher also includes a quick way to launch your web browser and wander around the Net. From the Internet Publisher dialog box, choose Browse The Web. Corel Presentations will bring up your default web browser and allow you to surf the Web using whatever your default Internet connection may be.

Now that you've learned about Corel Presentations' Internet Publisher, you're ready to use this powerful tool to persuade, present, and convince using the World Wide Web. Next, you'll learn about some other Corel WordPerfect Suite web abilities.

Web Publishing with Other Corel Applications

You've now spent a lot of time learning how to create web pages with Corel WordPerfect, a powerful tool for virtually any kind of web page—from a home page to an interactive form. You've also learned how Corel Quattro Pro can publish your numbers to the Web. Then you learned how Corel Presentations can create both graphics for the Web and publish interactive presentations you can show on the Web.

But what about the rest of Corel WordPerfect Suite? The three main applications you've already learned about constitute the bulk of the web page creation tools in the suite. With their powerful HTML publishing abilities, combined with the Java-enhanced abilities of Corel Barista, you can publish virtually any page you can imagine. However, in the standard edition of Corel WordPerfect Suite, you will find other tools to help you achieve your web publishing goals.

First, you'll learn how the other products in Corel WordPerfect Suite can help you with your web publishing tasks. You'll then take a special, advance look at what you can expect in the Corel WordPerfect Suite 8 Professional edition.

Web Publishing with Other Suite Applications

While none of the suite's other components pack the web publishing power of Corel WordPerfect, Corel Quattro Pro, or Corel Presentations, they're still useful. These tools help you manage your system, files, and web projects.

Image Editing with Corel Photo House 2.0

The perfect complement to Corel Presentations is Corel Photo House. It's designed to be a quick and easy way to create, edit, and add special effects to bitmapped images and photos. You can touch up photos or even apply effects to them much like those you see from high-end photo editing software. For example, the photo in

Figure 17-1 shows an image that has had the default impressionist effect added—an effect that makes the image appear as if it were made of dots.

While these effects and tools are certainly professional strength, they're easy and (really) fun to use. When you launch Corel Photo House, an easy-to-understand notebook on the left of the window helps you choose the task you want to perform. Clicking on other tabs in the notebook allows you to choose colors, brushes, special effects, and photos included with the program. This notebook makes the program so easy to use that you could avoid the menu bar entirely.

This quick access to powerful bitmap-editing features adds up to higher productivity for web page creators. When you need to add some zip to a bitmap, put some sparkle in a stock photo, or inject some interest into a mug shot, Corel Photo House is a fine choice. Of course, it can save images in all the major graphics formats, from Windows bitmap (BMP) to JPEG, so its tools are web-ready.

FIGURE 17-1   An image being edited in Corel Photo House—note the "notebook" on the left side of the window that helps you work on projects, choose colors, select brushes, apply effects, and more

Organizing your Typefaces with Bitstream Font Navigator

If you're creating image maps, menu bars, or logos that you'll be using in your web pages, you're probably doing so in order to use some interesting fonts. Regular HTML supports only a couple of typefaces—each of which anyone can change in his or her browser to goof up your page's layout—and Corel Barista supports the basic fonts supported by Java 1.0 (Courier, Arial/Helvetica, and Times Roman). But if you're taking advantage of what images can do to add visual interest to your pages—and even using Corel WordPerfect's Text Box feature to preserve text formatting in your Corel WordPerfect documents—then you need some way to keep track of your fonts.

Of course, you've noticed that the Corel WordPerfect Suite ships with a boatload of fonts. And you certainly won't use them all at once. So, to help you preview, install, group, and manage your fonts, Corel has included Bitstream's Font Navigator in the suite.

TIP: *Take advantage of the built-in wizard that launches the first time you run the program. It will search your hard drives for installed or uninstalled fonts. And if you have your suite CD in the drive, you can also ask it to check the suite CD for its fonts as well. The few extra minutes up front will pay off in how easy it will be to work with your fonts.*

Bitstream Font Navigator provides a straightforward, drag-and-drop way of managing large numbers of typefaces (see Figure 17-2). If you're designing multiple web sites, each with its own special typeface sets, you can create *font groups* for each set of typefaces. In Font Navigator, you can drag these groups to and from the Installed Fonts list to install or remove them from your Windows system. And perhaps niftiest of all is the customizable preview window pane that allows you to see what any font looks like before you install it.

Internet Browsing, Mail, and News with Netscape Navigator 3.0

Netscape Navigator is the world's most-used web browser. Version 3.0 is by far the most popular 32-bit version. Version 3.0 includes all the features that exemplify accessing Internet information at its best. Netscape Navigator supports all advanced

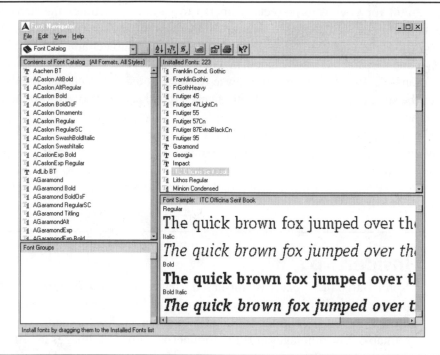

HTML tags as well as advanced features such as Java-enhanced applications. If you've worked on the Web, chances are you're familiar with Navigator.

But Navigator's abilities don't stop with web browsing. You can also use the integrated mail and news abilities to communicate with others. If you're using a standard, dial-up connection, you'll be able to handle all your e-mail needs. And if you're interested in the Internet community, you can use the news reader to keep up on Usenet newsgroup happenings.

Once you've installed the program, you can access a wealth of information about Navigator using cool, web-based help, tutorials, and information.

Using the Bonus Clip Art, Fonts, and Photos

Like many Corel products, Corel WordPerfect Suite contains thousands of useful images, fonts, and photos. But the hard part is choosing which of these will be the most useful for your web projects. Clipart images are sometimes the hardest to choose simply because there are so many of them! But Corel has made it easier for you to choose among the images by grouping them by subject and style. You can consult the clipart catalog included in your package (unless you purchased the educational package). Or, you can browse for images using the viewer window in any of the suite applications' File Open (displayed when you choose Insert | Image) dialog boxes.

When you're choosing an image to be used on the Web, you'll want to remember a few key things. First, choose relatively simple images. Remember, if your page includes too many large, intricate graphics, it will take longer to download. If your page takes a long time to download, web visitors may abandon it before it even fully loads.

Insider Tip

Corel Barista re-creates vector-based images as *vector images*. The unique Corel Barista Java classes actually *draw* vector images in the browser window. Unlike publishing to plain HTML, which saves bitmap or vector images in JPEG format (or keeps GIF images in GIF format), Corel Barista retains the information required to redraw the graphics. While this creates high-quality images, complex images can require some time to redraw—just as large, bitmap images can take some time to load.

Besides avoiding images that are unnecessarily complex, you may also want to avoid images that use a wide variety of colors. Of course, the conversion filters built in to Corel WordPerfect Suite applications will convert the colors as the images are saved in JPEG format. But to retain the most control over how your images will appear on the Web, it's best to stick with fewer, more commonly used colors.

Choosing Fonts for Your Web Pages

Just as you don't want to overuse images, it's also possible to overuse fonts. However, since in most cases your web pages will contain only the default fonts your browser supports, this is rarely a worry. Don't forget that you *can* use any of the hundreds of fonts Corel WordPerfect Suite includes in text boxes (see discussion in Chapter 8) that will faithfully reproduce all your font information as JPEG graphics in your web pages.

To choose the perfect font for your pages, Corel has included helpful font groupings. When you install fonts using the Corel WordPerfect Suite setup program, you can choose from a number of font sets, including sets to help you with snappy business documents, attractive invitations, and eye-catching advertisements.

As a general rule, the simpler the typeface, the more likely it is to be readable on the Web. You will generally want to avoid ornate or script fonts, such as those used in announcements and invitations. You'll also want to avoid using fonts in extremely small sizes—when they're converted to 96 dpi (dots per inch) images for use onscreen, they'll often be hard to read and lose detail. Choose fonts with clean lines, like Futura. And, as discussed earlier, choose fonts you're planning to use consistently throughout your site that reinforce your company's image and style.

TIP: *For more tips on typography on the Web, visit type expert Daniel Will-Harris' web site at **www.will-harris.com**. Will-Harris, who assisted Corel in choosing, classifying, and organizing the fonts that came with your suite, offers helpful tips plus an interactive font selection system.*

Images and Your Software License

Keep in mind that just because you received these images, fonts, and sounds along with your Corel WordPerfect Suite, you don't "own" them. As with your license to use the software (guess what—you don't really "own" that, either), you have a license to use the images, sounds, and fonts. For the most part, you're on safe ground when you use the images, sounds, and fonts to create documents during the regular course of business. But if you're looking at creating something that will be resold, including packaging or an electronic product, there's a good chance that this won't be covered by your license. And there has been some debate in software circles about the advisability of including images on your web site that could possibly be extracted and used by someone else who doesn't have the license to use them.

CAUTION: *When in doubt, consult your lawyer or other competent, professional legal counsel. (This advice is not considered professional advice; instead, it's general information.) If you are in doubt, contact Corel Corporation for the exact terms of your image license and consult your lawyer.*

To be safe, you can try a few different techniques when you use images and photos from your Corel WordPerfect Suite CD-ROM. First, you might want to modify each image somewhat so that it's not exactly what appeared on the original disk. In fact, in the digital image arena, while you will never own the copyright to the original image, you *can* own the copyright to the modifications you've made. Second, whether or not you modified the image, you should place a copyright notice somewhere near the image stating that Corel and its suppliers own the image (that is, "© Corel Corporation and its suppliers"). You might even use Corel WordPerfect's graphics caption capability for this (discussed in Chapter 7).

Third, you might try incorporating the image into a larger graphic. For example, if you're using a digital photo of a baseball, you might run type around or across the image to make it more difficult to extract the original image from the graphic you've placed on the Web.

Don't let these guidelines dissuade you from using your Corel WordPerfect Suite clip art, photos, and sounds in your projects. Instead, be smart and prudent as you use them in your web-based documents.

Quick File Viewing with Quick View Plus

Power Corel WordPerfect Suite users have long taken advantage of a special feature: Quick View Plus. It's been part of the suite for the last version or so and provides an invaluable tool to the power web publisher.

In short, install it. If you're using Windows 95, you may already have a miniversion of Quick View on your system. But this full-blown, latest addition of Quick View Plus takes all of Inso Corporation's file translation know-how and puts it only a click or two away. Once you've installed it (it's available from the main CD-ROM installation menu—the one you see when you put the CD in the drive), you'll have a new icon in your Windows 95 taskbar that will automatically launch the program. But the second thing it'll do is even more exciting—right-click on any file in Windows Explorer or in your Corel WordPerfect Suite File Open dialog boxes, and you'll have two new options in your pop-up menu: Quick View Plus and Quick Print. Quick Print will print the file you've selected without having to launch the application with which it was created. And the Quick View Plus selection launches, not surprisingly, Quick View Plus. This extremely fast, low-overhead program can read virtually any file format you can think of, including the latest versions of business applications like those in the suite.

Insider Tip

For a list of all the file formats Quick View Plus supports, be sure to read the readme file included with the program—it will automatically be displayed as you install the program. To learn about new file format filters, you can visit Inso Corporation's web site at **www.inso.com**.

Once Quick View Plus has loaded an image, you can view it in different ways, zoom in on it, or do any number of other things. As a web publisher, you'll find the ability to instantly view a document invaluable as you organize your web pages and web site.

Quick View Plus can integrate itself into your web browsers and other applications so that if you download a file, the file can automatically download itself into Quick View Plus if you don't have the original application. This gets you out of the dreaded "unknown file type" error message. Quick View Plus is a powerful tool that's essential for power suite users—especially web publishers.

Web Publishing with Corel WordPerfect Suite 8 Professional

The innovations in Corel WordPerfect Suite 8 won't stop with the initial release. Of course, as this book is being written, Corel is still adding capabilities to Corel WordPerfect Suite 8, because they want to pack it with as much value as they can. Some of these capabilities, like CorelCENTRAL, they'll send free of charge to registered customers; others, like additional PerfectExpert projects, they'll post on their web site free for downloading. In any case, Corel will also release an even more powerful, industrial-strength version of the suite—called the Professional edition.While the contents of the Professional edition are subject to change, Corel has divulged enough details to provide you with an inside look at the web publishing tools you can expect.

Web Publishing with CorelCENTRAL/ Netscape Communicator

Perhaps the most cutting-edge of the products expected in Corel WordPerfect Suite 8 Professional is CorelCENTRAL—the product of Corel's collaboration with Netscape. CorelCENTRAL incorporates all the features of Netscape Communicator and exclusive features you won't find anywhere else.

From a strict, web publishing point of view, CorelCENTRAL itself isn't focused on web publishing. What it helps you do is simple: it's a way to organize your contacts, time, and projects, plus a way to communicate and share that information with others using the Internet. To do these things, Corel relied on its know-how in web collaboration and information management (remember InfoCentral from past suites?) and Netscape's proven web abilities. The result builds on Netscape's state-of-the-art web suite, Netscape Communicator.

You may want to familiarize yourself with Netscape Communicator before you look at what CorelCENTRAL adds. Netscape Communicator supersedes the excellent 32-bit browser included in the suite now (Netscape Navigator 3.0). Netscape Communicator is a suite of Internet tools within the Corel WordPerfect Suite. This integrated set of tools includes a new version of Netscape Navigator (for web browsing, ftp access, and so on), Netscape Messenger (e-mail), Netscape Collabra (for electronic discussions), Netscape Composer (for web page authoring), Netscape Conference (for real-time electronic conferencing), and more. It's an easy-to-use set of tools for finding, publishing, and sharing information on the Internet.

 TIP: *For up-to-the-minute information about Netscape Communicator plus the possibility of trying out a beta version, visit Netscape at* ***www.netscape.com***.

CorelCENTRAL extends these abilities to help you share address information, schedules, appointments, and tasks across the Internet. Besides being a powerful personal information manager, CorelCENTRAL extends that information management to project, time, and people management via the Internet.

Corel Time Line

Corel Time Line is a great way to keep track of projects, resources, and schedules for any undertaking. You may find it most useful to track major web publishing projects. Of course, you can publish its reports and timetables to HTML documents for easy sharing across an intranet, local area network, or Internet.

Since it's a project management tool, Time Line is not the type of product you would use to create web pages and web sites. Instead, it can help you keep track of those kinds of development projects. It can also provide information you might place on a web page if you want to share the status of a project with others.

Corel WEB.SiteBuilder 2.0

Corel WEB.SiteBuilder is an essential part of Corel WordPerfect Suite's web publishing tools. While Corel WordPerfect, Corel Quattro Pro, Corel Presentations, and others contain powerful page creation tools, Corel WEB.SiteBuilder goes beyond creating pages. Corel WEB.SiteBuilder helps you plan your web site, create its structure, upload it to your web server, and then maintain it. In fact, with Corel WEB.SiteBuilder you have a full complement of web site tools—you're set to be a webmaster!

This essential utility brings the other web elements of the suite together. You can create a web site using the Site Builder Expert. You'll enhance the site by incorporating the pages you created using other elements of Corel WordPerfect Suite. You'll then upload that site to your web server. Finally, you'll be able to use the troubleshooting and maintenance tools Corel WEB.SiteBuilder includes to keep your web site in top shape.

Corel WEB.SiteBuilder helps you in your web site creation phase no matter whether your site is already created or if you're starting one from scratch. You can open an existing site—even one you're still working on—and make any changes to it you like.

TIP: *If you want to analyze the structure of an existing web site, Corel WEB.SiteBuilder will allow you to load an external web site as well. Just watch out—some sites can take a long time to load. To stop a site from loading entirely (much like you can stop a web document while it's loading in Netscape Navigator), just click the Stop button on the toolbar.*

When you create a web site using Corel WEB.SiteBuilder, you can use the powerful yet simple Site Builder Expert. This Expert walks you through a few simple steps to create a site. Each page is built upon a predefined template that you can modify. Corel WEB.SiteBuilder includes a wide variety of templates. And these

templates and styles can easily be modified with the changes implemented across the site—using only a few clicks.

NOTE: *Remember, all of these capabilities are based on prerelease software, so they are subject to change before the final release of Corel WordPerfect Suite 8 Professional.*

Envoy 7 (Full Version)

To fully take advantage of Envoy, you'll need the full-blown version, not just the Envoy viewer that ships with Corel WordPerfect Suite 8 in its standard edition. You can learn more details about using Envoy in Chapter 19.

Insider Tip

If you're upgrading from your copy of Corel WordPerfect Suite 7 or Corel Office Professional 7, you probably already have a copy of Envoy 7. Since you don't terminate your license to use previous versions of the software, you can leave your installation of Envoy 7 on your system when you upgrade to Corel WordPerfect Suite 8—and then you'll have full access to Envoy's abilities.

Envoy provides you with the ability to retain almost all of the layout characteristics of your original documents—including fonts, graphics, tables, columns, hyperlinks, and more. The Envoy documents you create can be viewed with the freely distributable Envoy viewer or even with a cool Netscape Navigator plug-in that displays Envoy documents right in the web browser. It's a great choice for publishing documents with very intense layouts. And with Envoy, you can also restrict people reading the document from printing, copying, or otherwise modifying or distributing the information it contains.

Corel Paradox 8

The latest version of this database and database development software promises to be impressive. Besides an enhanced, easy-to-use interface and hand-holding wizards, its Internet abilities are amazing. For example, you can use Corel Paradox 8 to instantly create HTML files containing information from a database. It'll publish HTML tables or database reports to dynamically created web pages—and your web site visitors' web browsers will automatically update the pages.

If you're looking for web server software, Corel Paradox 8 comes with two different web server software programs. Both can be used to publish files on your local area network, intranet, or even on the Internet. If you're a beginning web publisher, you'll probably use the Personal Web Server, which, without any programming, runs as an easy-to-set-up-and-administer, stand-alone web server. If you're looking to add capabilities to an existing server, and if you're technically advanced enough to use it, Paradox also includes an OCX control called the Borland Web Server Control. This control is managed through its own set of OLE automation methods and properties.

Web Publishing with Other Corel Software

While Corel WordPerfect Suite provides a full range of web page creation tools, Corel Corporation offers other products that complement those you now own. Depending on your needs, you may want to look at any or all of these packages. (All the packages listed here are available for Windows 95 or Windows NT.)

Corel WebMaster Suite

Corel's WebMaster Suite provides tools to help you create, manage, and maintain a web site. The package contains a variety of programs, each tailored to help you automate a different aspect of your web work. Perhaps the most useful piece of software is Corel WEB.SiteManager. This package removes all the drudgery of web site creation, maintenance, and repair. It sports a variety of views to help you visualize and organize your site's contents. It also enables you to perform a variety of maintenance tasks, including sitewide search-and-replace and virus scanning. You can also use it to locate broken links to pages both inside and outside your web site—and repair them.

Corel WEB.DESIGNER is the HTML authoring portion of the suite. Like Corel WordPerfect, it offers full HTML support within a WYSIWYG (what you see is what you get) environment. It also includes templates for full pages or just portions of a page. Even if you've already created pages with Corel WordPerfect, you may find Corel WEB.DESIGNER useful to create quick pages using the templates or to tweak pages you've already created. Corel WEB.DESIGNER integrates with the other tools in the Corel WebMaster suite.

These other tools include Corel WEB.DRAW, a drawing program tailored to web graphics creation; Corel WEB.MOVE, for creating animated images for your pages; and Corel WEB.WORLD, for creating virtual worlds your web visitors can explore. If you're interested in publishing existing databases to the Web, the suite also includes Corel WEB.DATA. In addition, the suite has 8,000 GIF-format clipart images ready for use in your site (you can browse them quickly with the included Corel WEB.GALLERY image organization software).

Corel VENTURA 7

For industrial-strength document processing and layout that's ready for full-color commercial duplication, Corel VENTURA 7 is the perfect complement to Corel WordPerfect Suite. While the package includes additional software, Corel VENTURA is the cornerstone. Its strongest ability—besides DTP (desktop publishing) abilities that stand up to any other professional publishing software package—is its multiple master pages. What this means is that you can create one layout using any variety of colors, and Corel VENTURA will allow you to publish this layout in multiple formats—a standard, 8 $\frac{1}{2}$ x 11-inch page, for example, as well as a CD-ROM or web-sized, horizontal screen image. These layouts all come from the same layout file.

Like Corel WordPerfect, Corel VENTURA includes Corel Barista as well as plain HTML abilities. And when you publish Corel VENTURA documents to the Web, they retain hyperlinks and create special ones for tables of contents, footnotes, and so on. You can automate your document creation with VENTURA libraries, drag-and-drop images, a script editor, and more. In the Corel VENTURA package, you'll also find:

- Corel WordPerfect 7

- CorelDEPTH, for adding 3-D elements to your images

- Corcl CAPTURE, for capturing images from your computer screen

- CorelMEMO, for adding annotations to your documents

- Corel VERSIONS, for keeping track of document revisions

- Corel PHOTO-PAINT 6, for complete photo and bitmap editing abilities

- Corel CD CREATOR 2, for easy CD-ROM creation

- Full SGML support

In short, if you're looking for a complete DTP solution or creating long, design-intensive, full-color publications, Corel VENTURA's for you.

CorelDRAW 7

CorelDRAW has won hundreds of awards and has a long reputation as the most powerful, PC-based drawing software available. In its newest incarnation, version 7, CorelDRAW has been honed into a finely tuned, professional-strength illustration package (see Figure 17-3).

You'll appreciate its full range of features and how easy it is to use. Even if you've never used CorelDRAW before, you'll be able to create complex images with ease. New features like CorelTUTOR and ever-ready hints make sure you

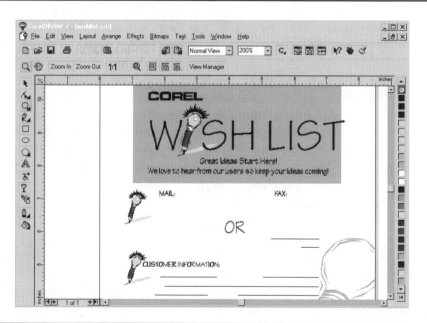

FIGURE 17-3   Create complex images and professional drawings with CorelDRAW 7

always keep your bearings. You'll also be able to edit large images with CorelPHOTO-PAINT 7, powerful image-editing software that's fully compatible with Adobe Photoshop filters and plug-ins. You can even create three-dimensional renderings and images using CorelDREAM 3D.

The package also includes Corel TEXTURE, an easy-to-use tool for creating natural textures like paper, marble, clouds, metal, or wood. After you've scanned an image with CorelSCAN, use Corel OCR-TRACE to convert scanned or bitmap images to vector-based, editable CorelDRAW images. As with Corel VENTURA, you can also add instant, 3-D effects to text and images with CorelDEPTH or capture screen images with CorelCAPTURE. You'll also find other bonus utilities, 32,000 clipart images, 1,000 fonts, 1,000 photos, 450 CorelDRAW templates, 750 floating objects, and 250 3-D models.

In short, if you're interested in creating professional illustrations or in taking your web graphics to the next level, you need to get CorelDRAW, a professional-strength suite of image creation and editing tools.

CorelXARA!

CorelXARA! is an underrated, 32-bit graphics program. Corel began selling CorelXARA (developed by Xara, Ltd., a British company) only a couple of years ago. Why is CorelXARA underrated? Because it's not as comprehensive a package as CorelDRAW, nor does it fit conveniently into a software industry cubbyhole. Instead, CorelXARA is designed to create images quickly and intuitively. It doesn't include all the features of CorelDRAW, nor does it include the bonus applications. It's a relatively small, targeted tool that's perfect for quick web graphics.

The latest version, 1.5, includes powerful Internet features as well. It edits both bitmap and vector images, and creates image maps, transparent GIFs, and even animated GIFs. It supports the default color palettes for both Netscape Navigator and Microsoft's Internet Explorer. It can create compact, high-quality GIF files using its special dithering abilities plus optimized palette abilities (meaning it can create special palettes to capture the colors in your image).

If you're looking for a quick, well-tailored tool for web image creation, CorelXARA's worth picking up. As do most Corel products, CorelXARA includes thousands of clipart images plus hundreds of photos, fonts, and textures.

While the core applications in Corel WordPerfect Suite provide excellent web publishing power, you now know how the other parts of the suite you own can help you realize your web vision. With the new Corel WordPerfect Suite 8 Professional, you'll be able to accomplish your web publishing projects even more easily. Of course, Corel produces a wealth of other tools to help you turbocharge your web business. No matter which tool you choose, you've already learned the basics of producing a high-quality, effective web site.

PART

IV

Publishing Web Pages: HTML, Envoy, and Corel Barista

Web Publishing with HTML
and Corel Barista

18

Once you've created, converted, or modified a document you want to place on the Web, the final step is to publish it to HTML. Because Corel WordPerfect's Web Editor provides an HTML-oriented editing environment, you'll have few, if any, surprises when your document is converted to HTML format. In fact, Corel WordPerfect provides the closest to WYSIWYG web editing you can get.

In this chapter, you'll learn the two ways Corel WordPerfect Suite helps you publish documents to HTML. The first is straightforward: Corel WordPerfect Suite can save any document in HTML format. It's a simple process from any core suite application like Corel WordPerfect, Corel Quattro Pro, Corel Presentations, and so on. And it creates rich, attractive HTML-based pages.

But you can easily go beyond plain HTML to produce Java-enhanced pages. Corel WordPerfect Suite is the only suite to offer Corel Barista—a special capability that allows you to publish web pages in standard HTML format *with* special Java features. These Java applets and extensions make your web pages rich with design and layout aspects that plain HTML just can't provide.

You'll first learn how to publish documents to HTML. Then you'll learn the basics of Corel Barista and why it's better than HTML. Finally, you'll learn how to use Corel Barista and glean a few web site design tips.

Web Publishing to HTML

When you publish a document to HTML, Corel WordPerfect Suite saves a copy of that document in HTML format. By default, the file will be saved with the same filename—only with an .HTM file extension. Any images, graphics, charts, sounds, or other related "content" files on the page are stored in a folder in that file's folder (the default name is the document name with an .IITG extension) directory.

Once you've published a file to HTML, you can copy the HTM file and any related HTG folder to a local web (intranet) or to the Internet. For details about copying these files and folders to the proper place, consult either your company's system administrator or your Internet service provider.

Insider Tip

To see your documents as they'll appear in your web browser—usually Netscape Navigator—after you publish them to HTML, click the Preview In Browser icon or choose View | View In Web Browser. After the final step in the following procedure, your Corel WordPerfect Suite application will load your default browser with your file loaded.

To publish a document to HTML:

1. Choose File | Internet Publisher.

2. Choose Publish To HTML. You'll see the Publish To HTML dialog box:

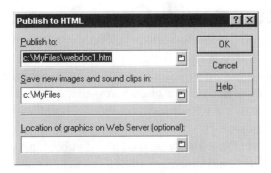

3. In the Publish To text box, type the name of the HTML file you want to use.

Note that the name of the associated HTG folder (containing any associated graphics) changes to match the filename automatically. You can also click the file folder icon at the end of the text box to browse for a filename you want to use.

TIP: *You might want to create a special folder just for your files that are ready to be uploaded to the Web. Then you can copy all the files and folders in that web folder when you upload them to your intranet or to the Internet.*

4. When you've settled on a filename, choose OK.

NOTE: *Any graphics you've used in the document that are already in GIF format will remain in GIF format. Others will be converted to JPEG format. Wallpaper or background images that use 256 or fewer colors are converted to GIF format—those with more than 256 colors are converted to JPEG.*

Your document will be converted to an HTML document as described earlier. For more details on file conversion to HTML, see Chapter 14. Now that you've learned how simple it is to publish your documents to HTML, read on to learn how easy it is to leap beyond plain HTML to Java-charged pages using Corel Barista.

Web Publishing with Corel Barista

If you're talking to a friend—perhaps a dyed-in-the-wool user of another office software suite—and you're looking for some way to prove Corel WordPerfect Suite's superiority, you've turned to the right chapter. There is no other technology—in an office suite or elsewhere—that creates HTML pages using Java technology as easily and effortlessly as does Corel WordPerfect Suite. In fact, Corel's Barista technology is theirs and only theirs.

So far in this section, you've learned about publishing your web pages to plain HTML files and in the next chapter, you'll learn to publish them to Envoy. If you've read this book all the way through—or even just published a few Corel WordPerfect documents to HTML—you're painfully aware of HTML's limitations. And while Envoy's ability to faithfully reproduce page layouts is admirable, it can sometimes incur an overhead you're not willing to accept. With Envoy, for example, you not only must keep track of all the files and monitor their file size, but also must ask your readers to download the Envoy Viewer or the Envoy Plug-in to view the files.

Corel Barista includes none of the limitations of HTML or Envoy. Corel Barista produces HTML files that include nothing but HTML code—so their file size remains small. And since they're HTML-based, they load and display rapidly.

Why Corel Barista Outdoes HTML

Corel Barista can do everything HTML can do…and more. It doesn't support just the usual features and formatting that HTML does. Instead, it uses Java technology to reproduce formatting and layout elements HTML can't. Since Corel Barista uses Java, it's compatible with almost any operating system and browser, just like HTML.

When you create HTML files using Corel Barista, you're really creating files full of special information that will help a web browser using the Corel Barista Java class files. This special information tells the browser how to re-create the layout of your pages as faithfully as possible. This layout includes all of HTML's abilities and more. Here's a sampling:

- Complete hypertext linking is preserved, including Corel Quattro Pro's QuickButtons.

- Documents are turned into pages (based on the page size you specified in your application). You can move among pages using a cool navigation button that appears with the page number on each page.

- Formatting features such as columns, text that wraps around an image, and so on, are preserved as well.

- Unlike Envoy, Corel Barista's use of Java eliminates the need for another application or for a browser plug-in.

- Again unlike Envoy and similar technologies, all the document's text can be indexed by web search engines (Yahoo, Excite, Infoseek, and so on).

- Your web page visitors don't have to wait for the entire page to be downloaded, because Corel Barista uses streaming technology to display some page elements while it's rendering others—so there's a shorter wait for the page to display.

- Corel Barista supports multiple color models for onscreen display. These color models include device-independent color specifications.

- Corel Barista contains strong support for bitmapped images, unlike some electronic document formats that are based entirely on vector technology.

- Corel Barista allows you to use all the fonts supported by Java 1.0 that go beyond those in plain HTML: Courier, Helvetica, and Times Roman. A future version of Corel Barista is planned to allow more fonts as part of its support for Java 1.1.

 **NOTE:** *Corel Barista is also integrated into other Corel products that help you create web elements. Corel WEB.DESIGNER helps you create animations, and Corel Web.DRAW helps you create graphics and image maps—all of which can be saved as elements on a Corel Barista, Java-enhanced HTML page.*

How Corel Barista Works

As you learned earlier in this chapter, Corel Barista extends HTML's abilities but creates actual HTML documents. This sounds confusing, and unless you've boned up on arcane Java programming, it is. But you don't need to know the exact programming principles or code that make it work. Instead, you *do* need to have a general idea of how it works so you can best use it.

When you publish a document using Corel Barista, here's what happens:

1. An HTML file—embedded with special tags and codes—is created. Of course, you can specify the folder and filename. (A sample Corel Barista document is shown in Figure 18-1; the HTML source file is in Figure 18-2.) The HTML file, saved with an HTM extension, contains very little understandable HTML code. Instead, it has custom HTML tags, which contain information the Corel Barista classes use to re-create the page's initial layout.

2. A folder with the page's contents—graphics, and so on—is also created. For example, the folder that accompanies the document shown in Figure 18-1 contains windmill.wpg (converted to GIF format), the graphic shown on the page. It appears in the same directory as the HTM file and has the same name as the HTM file but has an HTG extension. Don't forget to upload this folder to the web server along with the HTML file.

3. When you upload the HTML file and the "contents" folder to your web server, upload the Corel Barista Java class files along with the file (or at least, along with the first file you upload). You'll learn how shortly.

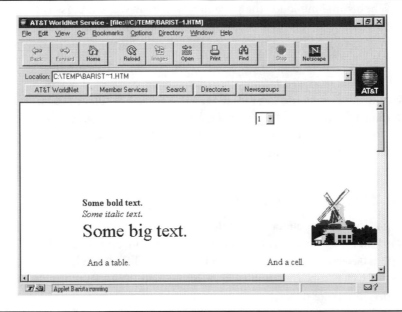

FIGURE 18-1 A sample document published to Corel Barista–enhanced HTML

```
<HTML>
<HEAD>
<TITLE></TITLE>
</HEAD>
<BODY>
<APPLET CODE = "Barista.class" width = 816 height = 1106>
<param name =Version value = "1000">
<param name =FontnameList value = "Times New Roman,TimesRoman">
<param name =J3FontnameList value = "TimesRoman,TimesRoman">
<param name =BackgroundColor value = "00FFFFFF">
<param name =XYDPI value = "96">
<param name =NumOfPages value = "2">
<param name =G1 value = "2 96 240 2 1 00000000 ">
<param name =G1S value = " 5 0 0 0 0 1 0 1 0 0 0 ">
<param name =G2 value = "2 96 238 2 1 00000000 ">
<param name =G2S value = " 5 0 0 0 0 1 0 1 0 0 0 ">
<param name =G3 value = "2 96 236 2 1 00000000 ">
<param name =G3S value = " 5 0 0 0 0 1 0 1 0 0 0 ">
<param name =G4 value = "2 96 234 2 1 00000000 ">
<param name =G4S value = " 5 0 0 0 0 1 0 1 0 0 0 ">
<param name =G5 value = "2 96 232 2 1 00000000 ">
<param name =G5S value = " 5 0 0 0 0 1 0 1 0 0 0 ">
<param name =G6 value = "2 96 230 2 1 00000000 ">
<param name =G6S value = " 5 0 0 0 0 1 0 1 0 0 0 ">
<param name =G7 value = "2 96 228 2 1 00000000 ">
<param name =G7S value = " 5 0 0 0 0 1 0 1 0 0 0 ">
```

FIGURE 18-2 The HTML tags and codes in an HTML document created with Corel Barista

4. When someone loads the page in a web browser, the class files are downloaded along with the page. The Corel Barista Java class files are loaded first; then the page contents are processed by use of the Java files.

That's Corel Barista in a nutshell. Of course, it does a lot of work when it processes a document for the initial HTML file and when it processes the Corel Barista data in the file in the browser. Read the upcoming section "Using Corel Barista" to learn how to perform each step in the overall process. First, however, you might want to know a little more about what a Corel Barista class file is.

About Barista Class Files

Java, a platform-independent programming language, can create *applets*. Applets are simply small applications that can be invoked from an HTML file. Java program files, called *classes*, contain these applets. The Corel Barista class files, each with a CLASS file extension, are actually little applications that can re-create every aspect of your original page onscreen.

These Java classes—exclusively created by Corel—must be uploaded to your web site in order for your Corel Barista pages to display correctly. Of course, your Corel WordPerfect Suite license includes permission to copy those files to your web server, but you may want to check the fine print for details if you plan to copy them to multiple servers.

 TIP: *Be sure to include not just the files in the Corel Barista folder, but also any other folders and their contents (such as .htg folders containing the page's graphics).*

These special class files are downloaded by each web page visitor upon the first visit to a Corel Barista page during each web session. (The class files remain on the local system until the web browser is closed.) These class files allow individual visitors to view Corel Barista pages properly.

Insider Tip

If you are sharing files with individuals who are creating files with Corel Barista under Windows 3.1, they will be unable to view the Corel Barista files they create on their machines, but they should be able to upload them to a web server. This is because the class files Java uses have a five-character file extension (CLASS) rather than the standard, DOS/Win 3.1 three-character extension. See "Uploading Corel Barista Files to Your Web Server" later in this chapter for more tips for Windows 3.1 users.

Using Corel Barista

You've learned on a general level how a Corel Barista page is created—and what happens when it's copied to the web server and downloaded. Now you'll learn how to create Corel Barista files from Corel WordPerfect Suite applications—and virtually any Windows 95 application. You'll then learn exactly what you'll need to do when you copy the Corel Barista files to your web server, and even some tips for helping your web page visitors view those pages.

Using Corel Barista from a Corel WordPerfect Suite Application

The core applications in the Corel WordPerfect Suite have Corel Barista integrated into all that they do. Other applications—described shortly—can publish to Corel Barista using the Print command.

To publish the current document to Corel Barista:

1. Choose File | Send To.

2. Choose Corel Barista. You'll then see the Send To Corel Barista dialog box, shown in the following illustration:

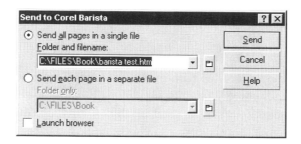

3. First, you'll be able to choose whether you want to publish your document to a single Corel Barista document (with all the pages in one file) or to publish each page to an individual Corel Barista document.

■ To publish your document to a single Corel Barista file that contains multiple pages, choose Send All Pages In A Single File. Type the name of the folder and filename you want to publish your document to (for example, you might choose **c:\myweb\index.htm**).

TIP: *By default, Corel Barista will fill in the box with the current folder and filename of the document you're editing—only with an HTM extension. If you want to keep that name, just move on to the next step.*

■ If instead you want to publish your document to individual Corel Barista files, each page as its own file, choose Send Each Page In A Separate File. Type the name of the folder to which you want your pages published.

NOTE: *If you want to minimize the size of your Corel Barista–enhanced HTML files, you may want to choose the Send Each Page In A Separate File option.*

4. If you want Corel Barista to automatically launch your default web browser to preview your pages before you send them to your web site, make sure you've chosen the Launch Browser check box.

5. Choose OK to publish your pages to Corel Barista.

NOTE: *If it can't find the folder, Corel Barista will ask you if you want to create a new folder or if you want to go back and specify a different one. If you meant to create a new folder, just press ENTER.*

Once the pages have been converted and published to Corel Barista, you'll see a dialog box letting you know that. And if you've selected the <u>L</u>aunch Browser option, your browser will automatically launch with the Corel Barista file loaded.

Using the Corel Barista Printer Driver in Windows 95

With Corel Barista 2.0, included in Corel WordPerfect Suite 8, you can publish to Corel Barista from any Windows 95 application (just as you can with Envoy).

How Corel Barista works is just about the same, but how you get there is slightly different. To publish a document to Corel Barista from any Windows 95 application:

1. Choose <u>F</u>ile | <u>P</u>rint. You'll see a dialog box that's probably the standard Windows 95 Print dialog box. Most likely there will be a drop-down menu that lists printer names. In some dialog boxes it may be a Printer <u>N</u>ame menu, a <u>C</u>urrent Printer menu, or something similar.

2. Choose Corel Barista from the printer selection drop-down menu.

The Send To Corel Barista dialog box will appear, as shown in the previous section, "Using Corel Barista from a Corel WordPerfect Suite Application." You can then complete the dialog box options as described there.

Insider Tip
The dialog box works almost the same as it does when you publish to Corel Barista. However, if you want to add special effects, or fancy transitions that appear between Corel Barista pages, you can add them using the Special Effects Properties dialog box. Corel Presentations can take advantage of some of these features automatically.

Uploading Corel Barista Files to Your Web Server

Once you've created some Corel Barista–enhanced HTML files, you'll then need to upload them to your web server. However you normally upload files, you'll need to follow some special directions to use Corel Barista files on your web site.

When you created HTML files, you probably placed them in a certain folder on your hard drive. When you upload your files to your web server, you include both the HTML files (*.HTM) and their accompanying HTG folders that contain graphics and other material that appear on the HTML pages.

Insider Tip

If you didn't already plan to do so, you might want to create a replica of your web site on your hard drive for easy testing and manipulation. Transfer your Corel Barista files to the appropriate folder within the site replica.

When you upload Corel Barista files to your web server, you will upload the Corel Barista–enhanced HTML files (*.HTM), the accompanying HTG folders, *and* the Corel Barista class files. The class files are necessary for the web server to provide the proper information to web browsers when the HTML code requests the Barista Java applet. These class files are freely distributable.

You will only need to copy the files to your web server once if you place all your Corel Barista files in the same folder on the server. But the Corel Barista class files must be in the same directory as every Corel Barista page you create if you don't store them all in the same place. If you do find it necessary to store the class files more than once, at least you can be reassured that they only need about 200K.

The Barista class files, by default, are installed to your hard drive in a /corel/office8/shared/barista folder. Copy all the files in this directory—there'll be some CLASS files and some GIF files—*and* all the subdirectories and any files they contain.

 CAUTION: *Be sure to include all the files and all the subfolders in the Barista folder. If you miss some files or folders, your Corel Barista pages may not appear correctly.*

Obviously, it makes a lot of sense to keep all your Corel Barista files in the same folder on your web server or hard drive. If you keep them in one place, you won't have to copy the files more than once. And if Corel updates their Corel Barista classes, you can easily update them with one replacement

Insider Tip

Windows 3.1 users, as mentioned earlier in the chapter, can't upload the required Java class files because of the files' five-character extension. However, Corel includes a compressed file (barista.zip) with the Windows 3.1 versions of Corel WordPerfect Suite. Windows 3.1 users can upload this file to the web server along with their Barista pages. Then the webmaster or a Windows 95 user can unzip the files (using a utility that supports long filenames like PKZip for Windows) into the appropriate directory on the server. Remember, the appropriate directory is usually the same one as the original HTML (HTM) file.

NOTE: *If your web site is hosted on a UNIX-based web server, be sure that when you copy your Corel Barista classes to the server, you maintain the same upper- and lowercase letters in the filenames.*

Some Special Web Site Design Tips

Corel Barista provides you with amazing page layout abilities, all contained in standard HTML documents. In fact, there's really only one potentially significant drawback to Corel Barista. If those viewing your web pages aren't using a Java-enabled web browser (one that can't support Java applets), they will be unable to view your pages. But don't overestimate the extent of this.

Odds are, anyone viewing your page will be using a Java-enabled browser. Just about everyone on the Web is using a Java-enabled web browser today. The last few versions of both Netscape Navigator (included in Netscape Communicator) and even Microsoft's Internet Explorer support Java applets. And both AOL and CompuServe's latest versions provide browsers that support it as well.

But if you want to cover all your bases—and it's a good idea to do so—you may want to offer non–Java-enabled pages as well. Some sites do this already. They generally offer both a set of Java-enabled pages that are graphically rich and a set of pages that contain fewer graphics and no Java. You can do the same—just publish your pages to both plain HTML and to Java-enhanced HTML. Then you can adopt one of two approaches to integrating these on your site. You can load the simpler, plain HTML pages first, and offer a link to the Java-enhanced pages, or load the Java-enhanced pages first, offering a link on those to the less-fancy pages. Perhaps the safest route—and the one that doesn't involve actual, hands-on HTML coding—is the first one.

TIP: *If you decide to create two versions of your site, you may want to create two identical sets of folders (or directory structures) on your web server—one under a "Java" directory and one under an "HTML" directory. You can then create two sets of files, one that's plain HTML and another that's Corel Barista enabled.*

If you're a Java developer and want to know more about how Corel Barista works—and how you can take advantage of it—you can get more information at **www.corel.com/partners_developers/ds/barista/docs/index.htm**.

You've now learned the basics of the last step of your web publishing process—actually publishing your files to HTML or to Corel Barista/Java–enhanced HTML. In the next chapter, you'll learn an alternate method for publishing your pages if you've purchased the Professional version of Corel WordPerfect Suite—publishing to Envoy.

Web Publishing with Envoy 7

19

Envoy is designed to overcome incompatibilities between software programs. This innovative software allows you to share your documents with other people—even if they don't have the Windows application you created the file in. Because it's quicker and more cost-effective to print your documents electronically, Envoy is the perfect publishing tool. You can view, exchange, and distribute documents across different operating systems—or across the Internet. The people receiving your documents can print pages, add annotations, and read the document as if they had the same application you do.

In this chapter, you'll get an overview of Envoy, and learn its primary functions, how to print a document to Envoy, and how to view your documents on the Web.

Envoy Basics

Envoy is a medium or vehicle—a way of delivering layout-rich documents. It's a tool that helps you electronically distribute manuals or newsletters via e-mail or the Web. When a document is printed to Envoy and distributed, the document keeps its original format—fonts, page sizes—regardless of the computer the recipient is using.

 NOTE: *Corel WordPerfect Suite 8 includes only the Envoy Viewer. But Corel WordPerfect Suite 8 Professional contains the entire version of Envoy.*

There are four major components of Envoy: Envoy Viewer, Envoy Driver, Envoy Runtime Viewer, and Envoy Distributable Viewer. *Envoy Viewer* is the core of the program. It allows you to display Envoy documents, annotate (add comments to) them, use links, and print pages. *Envoy Driver* is a Windows 95 printer driver that creates the Envoy documents (EVY files) that can be automatically launched in the Envoy Viewer. *Envoy Distributable Viewer* allows you to create a folder that includes compressed versions of the Envoy Viewer and its help files so that you can compress them (using PKZip or a similar application) and distribute them. The *Envoy Runtime Viewer* allows you to create an executable file that includes both your Envoy document and an Envoy Viewer. Users just have to launch this file—it's a self- contained program—to view your Envoy document.

> **NOTE:**   *Since you're using Windows 95 or Windows NT, the distributable and runtime viewers you create will only be usable on those operating systems. The distributable and runtime viewers are platform specific. Contact Corel for more information about viewers for other platforms, including Windows 3.1x and Macintosh OS.*

Preparing Your Document

Before you publish to Envoy, there are two main rules you should follow for making better documents:

RULE #1   Keep everything organized. The best way to keep an Envoy document organized is to add a table of contents. From the table of contents you can insert hyperlinks to other areas of the document. This way, readers can jump to other areas of the document with a click of the mouse.

RULE #2   Pay close attention to your document's design. Make sure you design your documents with small margins—this will allow more text per page. It will also eliminate too much scrolling on the readers' part. Also, use a lot of color in your documents—the last thing you want to do is put people to sleep with boring pages.

Printing a Windows Document to Envoy

Once your document is created, whether it's in Corel WordPerfect, Corel Presentations, or any other Windows application, you are ready to publish it electronically through Envoy. Printing to Envoy is just like printing a document to your laser printer—but instead of printing on paper, it prints in Envoy.

Suppose you want to send your company newsletter to all of your advertisers. You created it in Corel WordPerfect 8 and want to send it electronically to save paper and mailing costs. With the newsletter onscreen, formatted the way you want it, choose File | Send To | Envoy.

If the program you're using doesn't include a Send To option, you can print to Envoy. Here's how:

1. Choose File | Print.

2. If the program uses the standard Windows 95 Print dialog box, you can then choose Envoy 7 Driver from the drop-down list of printers.

3. Make any adjustments you want to make—like number of pages—and choose Print.

When you send your files to Envoy, the computer basically takes a snapshot of your document. While printing to Envoy, it goes through a routine similar to that of printing to paper. Instead of coming out on paper, the document opens in Envoy and is displayed on your screen.

Once you print your document to Envoy, you can't edit the Envoy version. If an error, such as a misspelling, needs to be fixed, go back to the authoring application, make the change, and print the document to Envoy again.

NOTE: *An* authoring application *is the application that created the document and printed it to Envoy. Any Windows application can be the authoring application.*

Customizing Your Envoy Document

Once the file becomes an Envoy document, you can use Envoy's toolbar, shown here, to navigate through the file or customize it. Table 19-1 shows each toolbar button and its function.

Now that your document is an Envoy file, you can set it up with other functions and features to help your readers navigate through it more easily. You can't change

Tool	Name	Function
	New	Opens a new Envoy document
	Open	Opens an existing document into a new window
	Save	Saves the current document
	Print	Prints the current document to paper
	Find	Searches for text or annotations within the open document
	Select	Selects text or graphics (This tool selected by default)
	Scroll	Drags the current document view in any direction
	Zoom In	Zooms in on the main view by set amounts
	Zoom Out	Zooms out on the main view by set amounts
	QuickNote	Creates a new QuickNote in the open document
	Highlight	Highlights texts or graphics

The Envoy
Toolbar
Buttons

TABLE 19-1

Tool	Name	Function
	Hypertext	Creates a hypertext link to another location within the document
	Bookmark	Inserts a bookmark
	Web Links	Creates a link to the Internet
	First Page	Views the first page of the document
	Previous Page	Goes to the previous page
	Next Page	Displays the next page
	Last Page	Views the last page in the document
	Previous View	Returns to the previous view
	Next View	Returns to the next view
	Thumbnails	Shows or hides the thumbnail views
	Fit Width	Adjusts the view so the document fills the screen width

The Envoy Toolbar Buttons (*continued*)

TABLE 19-1

Tool	Name	Function
	Fit Height	Displays the document so you can see the full height of the page
	Help	Displays a list of Envoy Help topics

The Envoy
Toolbar
Buttons
(*continued*)

TABLE 19-1

the text or format in any way—but you can add annotations to it. There are five ways to annotate your document:

- Insert a QuickNote

- Highlight text

- Add hyperlinks

- Insert a bookmark

- Create links to web sites

QuickNotes

A QuickNote is very similar to the commonly used sticky notes found all over most offices. Even though you can't edit an Envoy document, you can add notes and messages to them. QuickNotes are placed directly on the document (see Figure 19-1).

To insert a QuickNote:

1. Select the QuickNote button from the toolbar.

2. Click on the document to insert a blank QuickNote.

3. Type the text you want in the note.

4. Click on the document outside the note when you're finished.

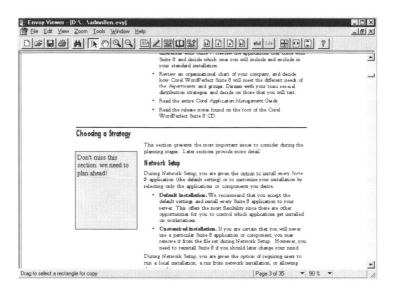

FIGURE 19-1 QuickNotes are placed directly on the document

TIP: *To delete a note, click on it once, then right-click and choose Clear from the QuickMenu. Or, click on the note and press DEL.*

You can change the properties of a QuickNote by right-clicking the note and choosing QuickNote Properties. From the Note Properties dialog box, you can change the text, toolbar icon, text color, and background color (see Figure 19-2).

TIP: *To change the size of the QuickNote, choose the QuickNote button from the toolbar, click in the document window, and drag the mouse to create the note size you want.*

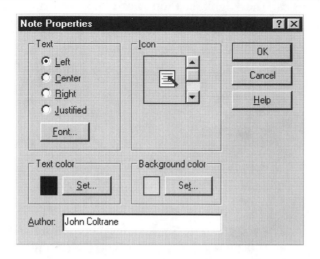

FIGURE 19-2   You can change the properties of a QuickNote from the Note Properties dialog box

Highlight Tool

The Highlight tool allows you to highlight parts of the document's text. This is helpful when you want to draw attention to a specific area. It's simple to use:

1. Click the Highlight tool on the toolbar.

2. Place the highlighter at the beginning of the text you wish to highlight.

3. While holding down the mouse button, drag the highlighter to the end of the desired text, and release the mouse.

4. Turn off the highlighter by clicking the Highlight button again or by pressing ESC.

TIP: *To delete the highlights, select the Highlight tool, right-click the highlighted text, and choose Clear from the QuickMenu.*

Just as with QuickNotes, you can change the properties of the Highlight tool. To do this, select the Highlight tool, right-click the highlighted text, and choose

Highlight <u>P</u>roperties. The Highlight Properties dialog box appears, shown here, letting you change the style from <u>N</u>ormal to <u>S</u>trikeout and change the highlight color.

To change the highlight color, choose Se<u>t</u>, and then choose from the list of colors in the Color dialog box. If the color you are searching for isn't there, you can create your own.

To make your own highlighting color:

1. Choose <u>D</u>efine Custom Colors from the Color dialog box (see Figure 19-3).

2. Click and move the mouse over the color grid to develop a color. Or, add your own settings in the text boxes available.

3. Choose <u>A</u>dd To Custom Colors after you've developed the color you want, then choose OK.

Creating Hyperinks

Hyperinks allow the reader to jump around the document. For example, links are used frequently in tables of contents. You can link each subject in a table of contents to its specific section within the document. This way, the user only needs to click on the subject to get to that section instantly.

To create a hyperlink:

1. Select the Hypertext button from the toolbar.

2. Highlight the text you wish to link.

3. Highlight the text you want the link to be connected to.

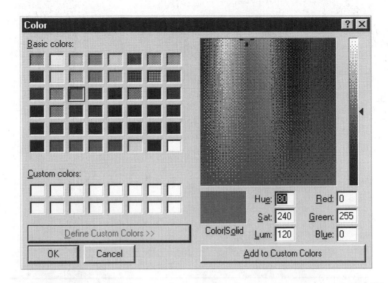

FIGURE 19-3 You can create your own unique colors in the Color dialog box

4. Select the Hypertext button from the toolbar to turn it off.

There you have it—a hyperlink. Now your readers can jump back, forth, and around the document with ease.

To change your hyperlink:

1. Select the Hypertext button from the toolbar.

2. Right-click the link.

3. Choose Properties from the QuickMenu.

4. From this Hypertext Properties dialog box, change the source text style and color, and change the link style if you like (see Figure 19-4). Then choose OK.

5. Select the Hypertext button to turn it off.

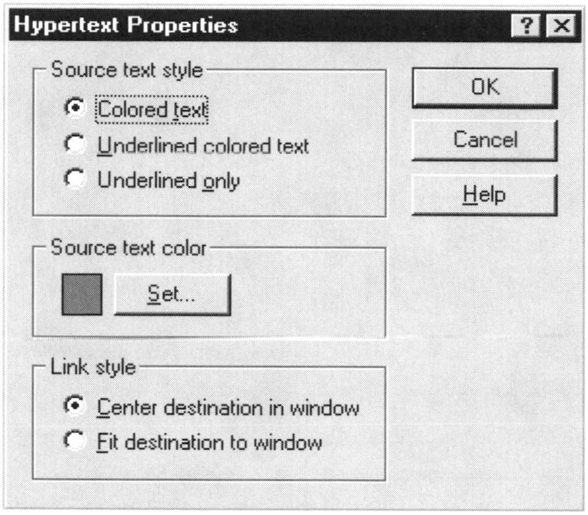

Hypertext Properties   ? X

─ Source text style ─
- ⦿ Colored text
- ◯ Underlined colored text
- ◯ Underlined only

OK

Cancel

Help

─ Source text color ─

Set...

─ Link style ─
- ⦿ Center destination in window
- ◯ Fit destination to window

FIGURE 19-4   Customize your hypertext links with the Hypertext Properties
dialog box

 NOTE: *To change the color of a hypertext link, follow the same instructions as for changing the highlighter color.*

Adding a Bookmark

A bookmark functions just like the bookmark in your favorite book—it holds your place. Use bookmarks in your Envoy documents to save places that you want to return to later.

To add a bookmark to your document:

1. Select the Bookmark button from the toolbar.

2. Move the bookmark pointer to the text you want to return to later, drag the mouse over it, and then release the mouse button. The Bookmark Properties dialog box will automatically appear, as shown here:

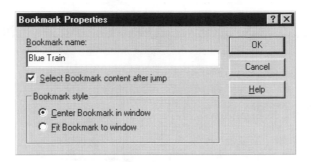

3. In the <u>B</u>ookmark Name text box, leave the inserted name or type a new one.

4. If you check <u>S</u>elect Bookmark Content After Jump, when you move to the bookmark, the text will be highlighted.

5. Choose a bookmark style. Either choose <u>C</u>enter Bookmark In Window, or choose <u>F</u>it Bookmark To Window.

6. Choose OK.

Repeat this same process for all of your bookmarks. When you want to go to one of your bookmarks, select the Bookmarks pull-down menu from the lower-right corner of your document window. From the list of bookmarks that appears, just select the one you want to go to and voilà—you're taken there!

Linking from Envoy to the Internet

Similar to a hypertext link, which links to areas within a document, Web Links connects to an actual site on the Internet.

 NOTE: *Obviously, the person reading the Envoy document must have Internet access in order to use this feature.*

To link to the Internet:

1. Select the Web Links button from the toolbar.

2. Click and drag over the text you wish to link. The Create Web Link dialog box will appear, as shown here:

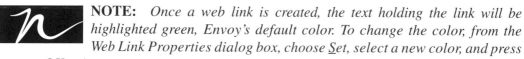

3. Type the web site address (URL) in the <u>D</u>estination text box. You can also enter a filename here if you want to link to another document. Or, if you want to move to a certain bookmark within the same document, type the name of the bookmark in the B<u>oo</u>kmark text box.

4. Choose OK.

NOTE: *Once a web link is created, the text holding the link will be highlighted green, Envoy's default color. To change the color, from the Web Link Properties dialog box, choose <u>S</u>et, select a new color, and press OK twice.*

As always, to change the web link properties, right-click and choose <u>P</u>roperties. The Web Link Properties dialog box allows you to change the source text style and color, and to modify the link locations (see Figure 19-5).

Saving Your Document

Once you've customized your Envoy document, you will need to save it. There are three formats in the Save As dialog box (see Figure 19-6) that you can save it under:

■ *Envoy Files* This format will require readers to have Envoy installed on their operating system. Or, they will need the Envoy Distributable Viewer program in order to open the document. This viewer allows the reader to see the document, but they can't use it to create an Envoy document.

■ *Text Files* This format only saves the document's text—without any of its formats.

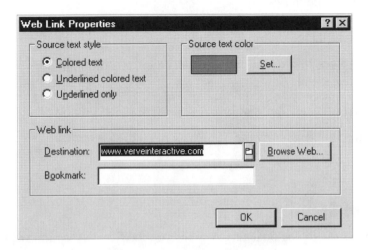

FIGURE 19-5   Change the links properties from the Web Link Properties dialog box

■ *Envoy Runtime Files* This saves the file as an executable program file.
It allows the user to read the file without having an Envoy Distributable
Viewer.

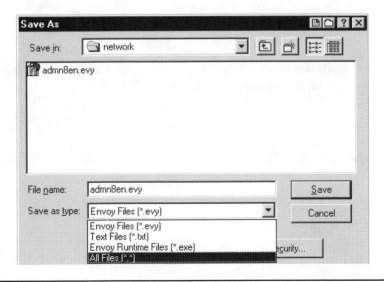

FIGURE 19-6   There are three formats for saving your Envoy document

To save your file in Envoy:

1. Choose File | Save As.

2. In the Save In text box, type or select the name of the folder you wish to save the file in.

3. Type a filename for your Envoy document in the File Name text box.

4. Choose a format from the Save As Type pull-down menu.

5. Choose Save.

Document Security

From the Save As dialog box, Envoy gives you the Security option, which allows you to assign a password and add different security levels to your document (see Figure 19-7). This security does not provide encryption—that is, it doesn't shield your documents from prying eyes. It does, however, limit what a user can do with your Envoy documents.

There are three levels of security to choose from:

- *Unrestricted* This option allows the user to read, print, and annotate the Envoy document.

- *View And Print Only* This option won't allow the reader to annotate the document.

- *View Only* This will let users only read the document—restricting them from annotating or printing.

To add security to your Envoy documents:

1. In the Save As dialog box, choose the Security button. The Security Settings dialog box will appear.

FIGURE 19-7   There are different levels of security to protect your Envoy documents

2. If you want to assign a password, select the <u>P</u>assword check box, and type the password in the text box.

NOTE: *The password you assign will only authenticate, or verify, the document. It does not add any document encryption or protection. You will want to use a dedicated file protection and encryption program to do that.*

3. To assign a level of security, choose from the three options available under Document Access (<u>U</u>nrestricted, <u>V</u>iew And Print Only, View <u>O</u>nly).

4. Choose OK and continue saving the document.

Viewing Envoy Documents

Suppose you're at work, and you just received a newsletter formatted in Envoy. Open it just like any other Windows 95 document.

To open an Envoy document:

1. Open Envoy.

2. Choose File | Open.

3. Select the file you wish to view.

Remember, now that the Envoy document is onscreen, you can't edit it, but you can add annotations.

Publishing on the Internet

Envoy documents can be published electronically on the Internet. Tumbleweed Software Corporation, the creators of Envoy, have provided a way to view Envoy documents on the Internet. From their web site, **www.tumbleweed.com**, you can download a free Envoy Viewer or Plug-in. These special extensions available from Tumbleweed allow you to view Envoy documents straight from a browser without launching Envoy separately. Anyone with Internet access can view Envoy documents whether or not they have Envoy.

NOTE: *Tumbleweed's web site gives you instructions for downloading the Envoy Viewer and Plug-in.*

Of course, you could simply upload your Envoy documents to your web server. If they're linked-to from your HTML documents, web site visitors will be prompted by their browser to either save the file or choose an application with which to open it. If they have Envoy, they can choose Envoy and their browsers will automatically launch Envoy with the document loaded. However, it's slicker to have the Envoy document appear within the browser itself.

Publishing this way is advantageous because Envoy documents don't have to be converted to HTML. Often when documents are converted to HTML, many of the formatting features are lost through the conversion process. With Envoy, none of the formatting is lost—it looks just the way you created it. It maintains the fonts you used, the layout, design, page size—just about everything. Envoy makes an electronic copy of your document without HTML's help.

Envoy is an effective tool for electronic publishing. Don't waste trees or time by distributing important documents by hand, on paper. Distribute them electronically—and give your readers a great tool for easy reading, navigation, and printing.

Part

Appendixes

Learning More: Additional Resources

This appendix provides some jumping-off points for you to learn more about the topics discussed in the book. You may find some more useful than others; in any case, you'll find a variety of sources, from lists of resources to pages of information. You may also want to consult one of the popular web search engines—Yahoo (**www.yahoo.com**), Excite (**www.excite.com**), Wired's HotBot (**www.hotbot.com**), or Alta Vista (**www.altavista.digital.com**).

Web History

In the beginning of this book, you learned a brief history of the Internet and the World Wide Web. You learned just enough to know your way around. If you'd like to learn more, here are a few web sites that can teach you about the history of the Internet and the Web:

Yahoo's index of Internet history sites.	**www.yahoo.com/Computers_and_Internet/ Internet/History/**
The Discovery Channel's excellent discussion of Internet history (Figure A-1).	**www.discovery.com/DCO/doc/1012/world/ technology/internetbest/opener.html**
The comprehensive NetHistory (Figure A-2).	**www.geocities.com/SiliconValley/2260/**
Highlights from PBS' recent series on the Internet (Figure A-3).	**www.pbs.org/internet**
Internet Valley's guide to Internet History.	**www.internetvalley.com/intval.html**
Yahoo's list of Internet information sites.	**www.yahoo.com/Computers_and_Internet/ Internet/Information_and_Documentation/**

The Electronic Frontier Foundation's "(Extended) Guide to the Internet."	**www.eff.org/papers/bdgtti/eegtti.html**
Stimulus' "Internet 101" basic training course (Figure A-4).	**www.stimulate.com/education/ internet101.html**
Yet another Internet 101 course (Figure A-5).	**www.sisna.com/users/scotting/**
Yahoo's list of Web and Internet beginners guides.	**www.yahoo.com/Computers_and_Internet /Internet/World_Wide_Web/Information_ and_Documentation/Beginner_s_Guides/**

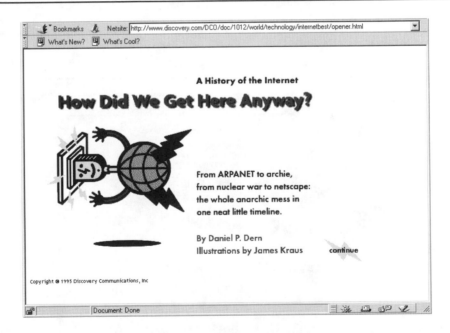

FIGURE A-1   The Discovery Channel's history of the Internet

FIGURE A-2   NetHistory

FIGURE A-3   Highlights from PBS' recent series on the Internet

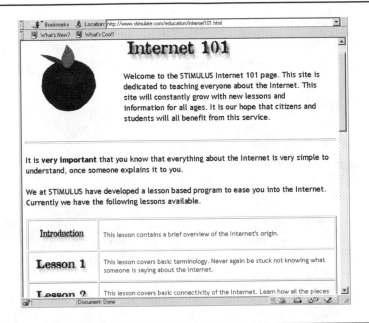

FIGURE A-4   Stimulus' "Internet 101" basic training course

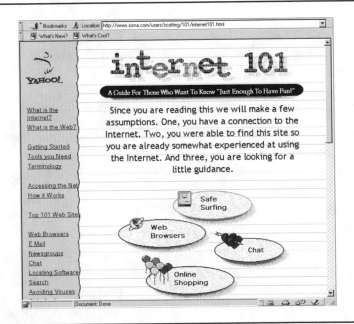

FIGURE A-5   Yet another Internet 101 course

Designing Web Sites and Web Pages

Unsurprisingly, the web is also full of great advice for planning, producing, and maintaining your web site and web pages. For tips about designing your web site, check these out:

Daniel Will-Harris' excellent font selection portion of his web site helps you choose the perfect face for your site and pages. Don't miss the rest of the site for additional advice (Figure A-6).	**www.will-harris.com**
An in-progress primer on all aspects of web page design and publishing.	**web.canlink.com/helpdesk/**
Want to make sure your HTML cuts the mustard? Here you can give it the browser taste test for a smorgasbord of HTML versions, clients, and more.	**www.webtechs.com/html-val-svc/index.html**
Self-styled web "zealots" share all they know with you to help expand your web expertise (Figure A-7).	**www.netamorphix.com/**
While it's difficult to take the company name seriously, you'll still find some useful design tips here (Figure A-8).	**www.stoopidsoftware.com/tips/**
Professor Pete also offers some useful web design tips on his site (Figure A-9).	**www.professorpete.com/**
Sun's semiauthoritative, useful guide to proper web style.	**www.sun.com/styleguide/**
Some web design tips and tools from the north.	**www.urban.no/tore/web/**
Yale's C/AIM department's web style manual (Figure A-10).	**info.med.yale.edu/caim/manual**
Want to know what *not* to do? Turn here (Figure A-11).	**www.webpagesthatsuck.com/**
How to design a "great" web site.	**www.unplug.com/great/**
How to create your own home page (called "HTCYOHP" here).	**www.intergalact.com/hp/hp.html**
Getting started with web design.	**www.msg.net/tutorial/**

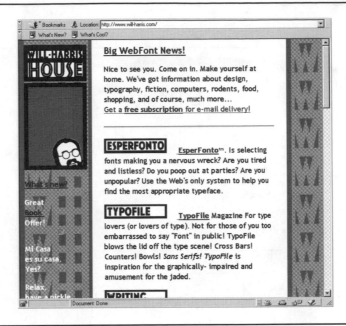

FIGURE A-6   The excellent font selection portion of Daniel Will-Harris' web site

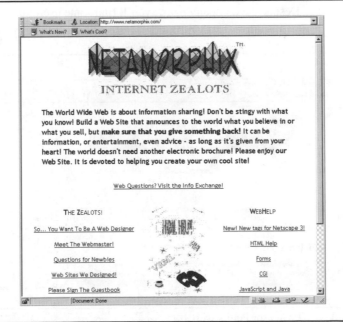

FIGURE A-7   Netamorphix

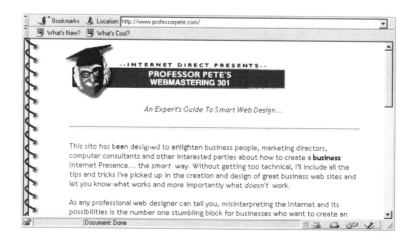

FIGURE A-8 Despite the company name, you'll find some useful design tips here

FIGURE A-9 Professor Pete's web site

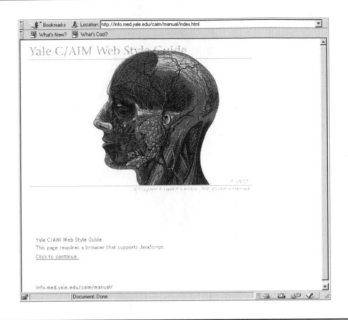

FIGURE A-10   Yale's C/AIM department's web style manual

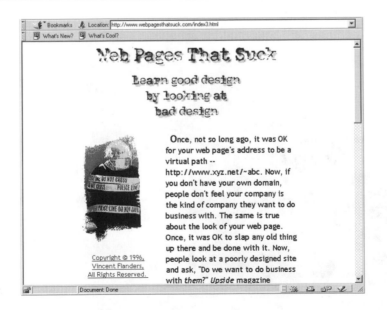

FIGURE A-11   The Web Pages That Suck site

Cool Background Graphics
Included with the Suite

B

One of the coolest things about Corel WordPerfect Suite 8 is that it's absolutely packed full of stuff. But it's easy to forget some of it because you're so overwhelmed with what's in there. This appendix is designed to help you take advantage of some of these extras. In Chapter 4, you discovered that certain graphics designed specifically for use as web page backgrounds ship with Corel WordPerfect Suite. But the suite CD-ROM includes a host of other graphics. One group, textures, is particularly well-suited for use as web page background graphics also.

To help you use these graphics, you'll find thumbnail images of each in this appendix. And these thumbnail images are helpfully sorted by the types of pages for which you might use them:

- Formal Business or Personal
- Casual Business
- Personal (Informal)
- Themed
- Use at Your Own Risk

NOTE: *You may notice that the graphics mentioned in Chapter 4—those specifically designed for use as web page backgrounds—are already in the web-standard GIF format. The images shown in this appendix are in Windows bitmap (BMP) format. Not to worry: remember that Corel WordPerfect automatically converts images to JPEG (or GIF if you prefer) when you publish your documents to the Web.*

Remember, the categories in which the images are placed here are based on the author's best judgment. You may find a particular image listed in, say, the formal category equally suitable for an informal, personal web page. Feel free to mix and match. This appendix provides a good starting point for your own designs, but is by no means dictating the proper use of these images.

Background Images for Formal Business or Personal Web Pages

The images shown here are best suited for use in a conservative, relatively formal web page. Since there's little difference between a formal web page used for a business and a formal one created by an individual, you'll find these images equally well-suited for both. Of course, you may find a particular image appropriate for a less-formal web page as well. Remember, it's easier to use a more formal background for a less-formal web page than to use an informal background for a web page that's purporting to be more formal or conservative.

Each of these images can be found in their respective folders within in the **\corel\suite8\graphics\textures** folder on your Corel WordPerfect Suite 8 CD-ROM. The image name will be listed here with the folder first, like this: **\design\bluetile.bmp**. To find that image, for example, you'd look in the **\corel\suite8\graphics\textures\design** folder for **bluetile.bmp**. You'll find the folder and file name immediately following each graphics image.

\design\bluetile.bmp

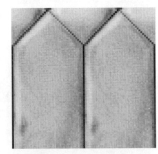
\design\browntal.bmp

\design\greenma0.bmp

\design\greenmar.bmp

\design\ivorybat.bmp

\fabrics\bluecanv.bmp

\fabrics\blueherr.bmp   \fabrics\brnmodel.bmp   \fabrics\brnwool.bmp

\fabrics\darkline.bmp   \fabrics\darkpurp.bmp   \fabrics\graywool.bmp

\fabrics\grnbrown.bmp   \organic\grnbark.bmp   \organic\sandystu.bmp

\paper\brnpaper.bmp   \paper\grayspot.bmp   \paper\lttextur.bmp

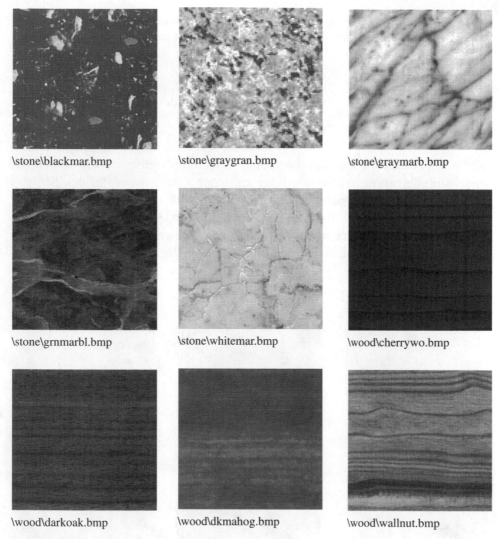

\stone\blackmar.bmp

\stone\graygran.bmp

\stone\graymarb.bmp

\stone\grnmarbl.bmp

\stone\whitemar.bmp

\wood\cherrywo.bmp

\wood\darkoak.bmp

\wood\dkmahog.bmp

\wood\wallnut.bmp

Background Images for Casual Business Web Pages

While some may prefer to project a conservative, formal presence on the Web—perfectly consistent with a conservative institution such as a bank or financial services company—others may prefer a more personable, friendly tone. The images in this category retain some of the formality you may find appropriate for a business web page but also suggest approachability, accessibility, and friendliness. You may find some of these images also appropriate for use on pages that are for personal, informal use.

REMEMBER: *The images listed earlier in the "Background Images for Formal Business or Personal Web Pages" section may be equally appropriate for use in casual pages.*

Each of these images can be found in their respective folders within the **\corel\suite8\graphics\textures** folder on your Corel WordPerfect Suite 8 CD-ROM. The image name will be listed here with the folder first, like this: **\design\brownche.bmp**. To find that image, for example, you'd look in the **\corel\suite8\graphics\textures\design** folder for **brownche.bmp**. You'll find the folder and file name immediately following each graphics image.

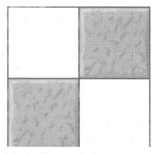

\design\brownche.bmp

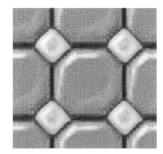

\design\browntil.bmp

\design\greenbat.bmp

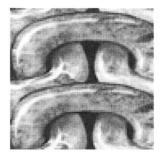

\design\marblech.bmp

\design\spottile.bmp

\fabrics\bluetwed.bmp

\fabrics\brncarpt.bmp

\fabrics\brnknit.bmp

\fabrics\brownele.bmp

\fabrics\brwnherr.bmp

\fabrics\graystrp.bmp

\fabrics\grnwrnkl.bmp

\fabrics\btblcanv.bmp

\fabrics\whitefir.bmp

\fabrics\wrinkleo.bmp

\nature\bluewave.bmp

\oil\fallswrl.bmp

\oil\redbark.bmp

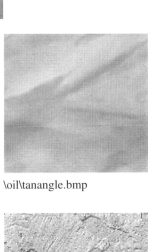

\oil\tanangle.bmp

\organic\brwnhtch.bmp

\organic\brwnplas.bmp

\organic\scrpdstu.bmp

\organic\tanstucc.bmp

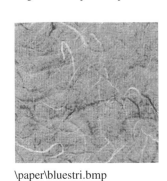

\paper\bluestri.bmp

\paper\brownrhi.bmp

\paper\grayfibe.bmp

\paper\graytext.bmp

\paper\sandpapr.bmp

\paper\tantextu.bmp

\paper\whiteele.bmp

\paper\whitespo.bmp	\paper\wrnkpapr.bmp	\stone\goldslat.bmp
\stone\pinkmarb.bmp	\wood\lightoak.bmp	\wood\ltpine.bmp
\wood\ltpoplar.bmp	\wood\spruce.bmp	\wood\sugarmap.bmp

Background Images for Personal (Informal) Web Pages

When you don't have to project any image but your own—when you're not trapped under a corporate style guide—you can choose whatever image you prefer. In fact, depending on the purpose of your personal web page, you could choose just about any image in this appendix. However, certain images are well-suited for use on a more informal web page that you'd place on your personal web site. They're not so wild as to render your pages unreadable but are still casual or whimsical enough to evoke a personal feeling.

 REMEMBER: *The images listed in the previous sections may be equally appropriate for use in personal pages.*

Each of these images can be found in their respective folders on your Corel WordPerfect Suite 8 CD-ROM in the **\corel\suite8\graphics\textures** folder. The image name will be listed here with the folder first, like this: **\design\bluestar.bmp**. To find that image, for example, you'd look in the **\corel\suite8\graphics\ textures\design** folder for **bluestar.bmp**. You'll find the folder and file name immediately following each graphics image.

\design\bluestar.bmp

\design\honeycom.bmp

\design\purpvine.bmp

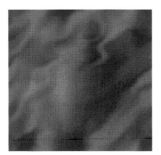
\design\redflame.bmp

\design\smallcro.bmp

\design\smallpur.bmp

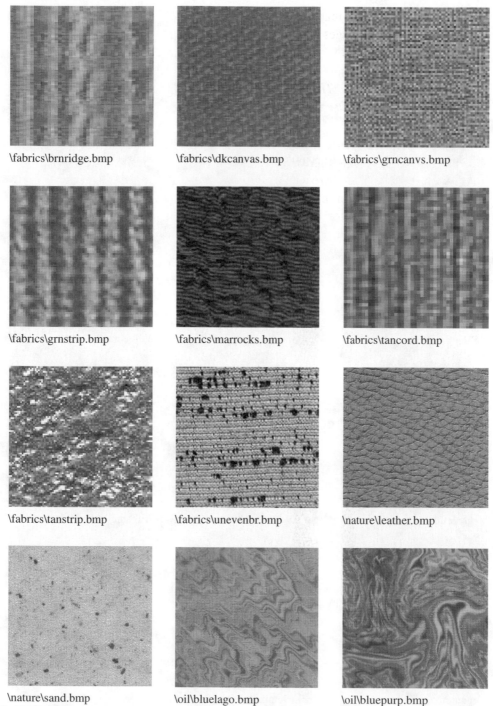

\fabrics\brnridge.bmp

\fabrics\dkcanvas.bmp

\fabrics\grncanvs.bmp

\fabrics\grnstrip.bmp

\fabrics\marrocks.bmp

\fabrics\tancord.bmp

\fabrics\tanstrip.bmp

\fabrics\unevenbr.bmp

\nature\leather.bmp

\nature\sand.bmp

\oil\bluelago.bmp

\oil\bluepurp.bmp

\oil\blueviol.bmp

\oil\firestrm.bmp

\oil\goldred.bmp

\oil\mtnstrea.bmp

\oil\ochermar.bmp

\oil\redorang.bmp

\organic\blueclay.bmp

\organic\bluecubi.cmp

\organic\candyice.bmp

\organic\frznrain.bmp

\organic\glasspan.bmp

\organic\gryplast.bmp

\organic\whtlace.bmp

\paper\purplweb.bmp

\paper\tanstrin.bmp

\stone\bgmarble.bmp

\stone\bluespot.bmp

\stone\brushmar.bmp

\stone\rockwall.bmp

\stone\rustclou.bmp

\stone\rustmarb.bmp

\stone\whipmarb.bmp

Background Images for Themed Web Pages

If you're creating web pages that revolve around a specific theme, this category's for you. Be careful: these images are strong enough that they must reinforce the theme of your web pages, not overshadow it. You'll also want to experiment carefully: these images make page layout difficult because it's hard to read text placed on top of them.

Each of these images can be found in their respective folders on your Corel WordPerfect Suite 8 CD-ROM in the **\corel\suite8\graphics\textures** folder. The image name will be listed here with the folder first, like this: **\design\fallwind.bmp**. To find that image, for example, you'd look in the **\corel\suite8\graphics\textures\design** folder for **fallwind.bmp**. You'll find the folder and file name immediately following each graphics age.

\design\fallwind.bmp

\design\softrain.bmp

\fabrics\brwnbrlp.bmp

\fabrics\delicate.bmp

\fabrics\multicol.bmp

\food\candy.bmp

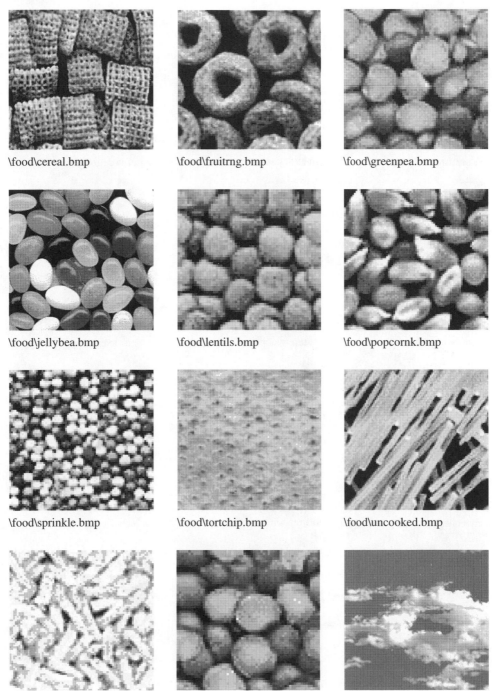

\food\cereal.bmp

\food\fruitrng.bmp

\food\greenpea.bmp

\food\jellybea.bmp

\food\lentils.bmp

\food\popcornk.bmp

\food\sprinkle.bmp

\food\tortchip.bmp

\food\uncooked.bmp

\food\whitrice.bmp

\food\yellwpea.bmp

\nature\circloud.bmp

\nature\ftrcloud.bmp

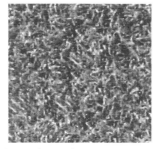

\nature\grass.bmp

\nature\oregongr.bmp

\nature\purplila.bmp

\nature\woodchip.bmp

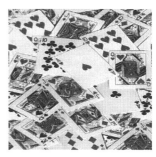

\objects\cards.bmp

\objects\cdroms.bmp

\objects\circuit.bmp

\objects\floppy.bmp

\objects\golftees.bmp

\objects\marbles.bmp

\objects\purpglas.bmp

\objects\pushpins.bmp

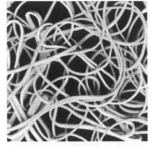

\objects\rubbrbnd.bmp

\objects\screws.bmp

\objects\uscoins.bmp

\organic\gldnuggt.bmp

\organic\goldplat.bmp

\stone\brnbrick.bmp

\stone\ltdkbrck.bmp

\stone\redbrick.bmp

\stone\whitbrck.bmp

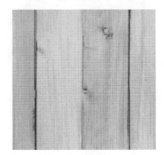

\wood\pinefenc.bmp

\wood\redwood.bmp

Background Images You Can Use at Your Own Risk

Let's face it. A few of these images are a little too, well, too garish for general use. They might be a little too busy, or be composed of colors that will make it difficult to read any text placed on top of them. You may find that one of these is perfect for your web pages but, as they say in the fine print, "actual mileage may vary," "don't try this at home," "no warranty is expressed or implied," and so on.

Each of these images can be found in their respective folders on your Corel WordPerfect Suite 8 CD-ROM in the **\corel\suite8\graphics\textures** folder. The image name will be listed here with the folder first, like this: **\design\aztctile.bmp**. To find that image, for example, you'd look in the **\corel\suite8\graphics\ textures\design** folder for **aztctile.bmp**. You'll find this folder and file name immediately following each graphics image.

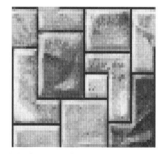

\design\aztctile.bmp

\design\formalde.bmp

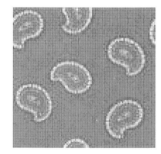

\design\redpaisl.bmp

\design\redplaid.bmp

\design\twisting.bmp

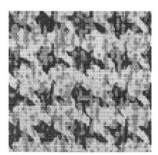

\fabrics\brnhound.bmp

\fabrics\drkplaid.bmp

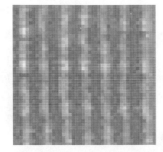

\fabrics\ltblcord.bmp

\fabrics\mauvetwd.bmp

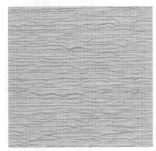

\fabrics\pinkelep.bmp

\fabrics\purplean.bmp

\fabrics\redplaid.bmp

\fabrics\tancarpt.bmp

\fabrics\violetca.bmp

\nature\blueflwr.bmp

\nature\blueiris.bmp

\nature\grnplant.bmp

\nature\pansies.bmp

\nature\purplpan.bmp

\nature\thckflwr.bmp

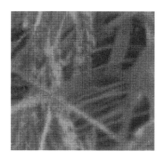

\nature\wheat.bmp

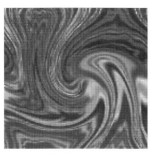

\oil\redwhite.bmp

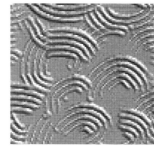

\organic\bluerake.bmp

\organic\grnsquig.bmp

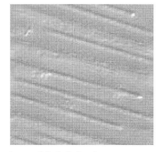

\organic\pinkclay.bmp

\organic\pnktwist.bmp

\organic\purpfibe.bmp

\organic\redrust.bmp

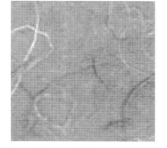

\paper\purpstri.bmp

\organic\waspnest.bmp

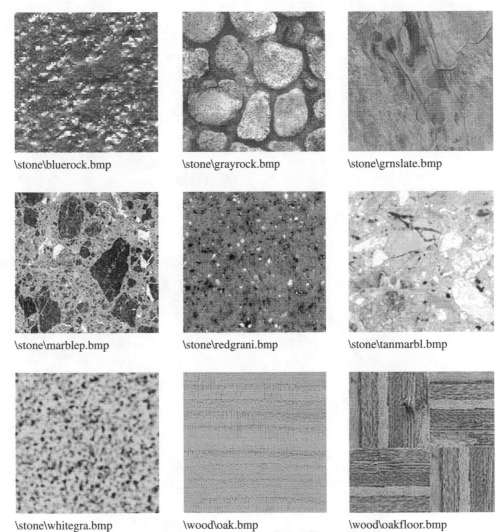

\stone\bluerock.bmp

\stone\grayrock.bmp

\stone\grnslate.bmp

\stone\marblep.bmp

\stone\redgrani.bmp

\stone\tanmarbl.bmp

\stone\whitegra.bmp

\wood\oak.bmp

\wood\oakfloor.bmp

Corel Barista: Frequently Asked Questions and Answers

I f you're a relatively experienced Corel Barista user, you may find the material presented earlier in the book to be insufficient for your advanced questions. Thanks to Corel Corporation, you'll find here their frequently asked questions and answers (FAQ) list for Corel Barista.

Corel Barista Basics

Q. What is new or changed in Corel Barista 2.0?

A. For version 2 we made the following improvements:

- Increased the speed
- Added a new toolbar to make Corel Barista features easier to use (see Figure C-1)
- Added, to the toolbar, a direct link to the Corel Barista home page (also shown in Figure C-1)
- Made transitions accessible through the application programming interface (API)
- Added support for sound (AU files) and bitmap graphics
- Added printer driver special effects for web slide shows

Q. What is a Corel Barista file?

A. A Corel Barista file is an HTML file that contains a Java applet named Barista.class. Web browsers give control to the applet when they encounter the applet type. The Barista applet then reads the rest of the HTML file and uses the additional information to render the document using Java technology.

Go to the Corel Barista home page on the Web

Return to the first page in the Corel Barista document

Go back one page

Go forward one page

Jump to the last page in the Corel Barista document

Jump to the previous position in the document

Jump directly to a specific page
from the pull-down menu

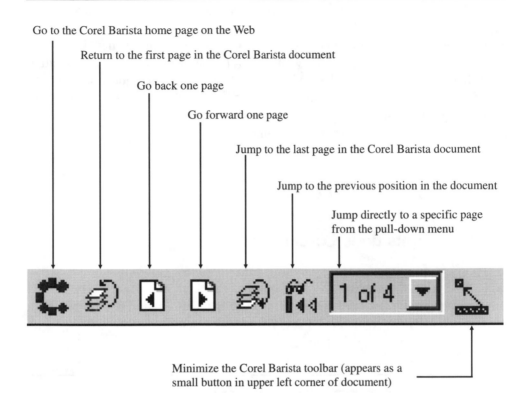

Minimize the Corel Barista toolbar (appears as a
small button in upper left corner of document)

FIGURE C-1   Corel Barista 2.0's new toolbar makes page navigation easy

NOTE: *Corel Barista documents are made up of multiple files. It is important to understand that when you create a Corel Barista file, not all the information is contained in one file. This is not unusual for web documents. Most web documents are made up of several files. For example, when you load an HTML document with graphical pictures, those images that make up part of the display are stored in separate files. When you view a web document, the browser reads through the initial file and finds information in it that tells the browser where to locate additional files that contain the pictures that complete the display of the document. You may have noticed that the text in some web documents displays before the pictures do. This is because the browser is still retrieving those additional files that contain the pictures.*

The Corel Barista document contains information that tells the browser where to get each external file. If you move a Corel Barista document from the location where you created the document, you must also move the image files and sounds associated with the Corel Barista document at the same time to the same relative path. If you do not, you will have to edit the Corel Barista document and identify where you have put the additional files. Sometimes there is a subfolder associated with the Corel Barista document (it will have the same name as the document) that has all of the associated parts of the document in it.

Corel Barista and Fonts

Q. What fonts does Corel Barista 2.0 support?

A. Corel Barista 2.0 supports the standard fonts that Java 1.0 supports. These fonts are Courier, Helvetica, and Times Roman. Note that Figure C-2 shows both Helvetica and Times Roman in a Corel Barista document.

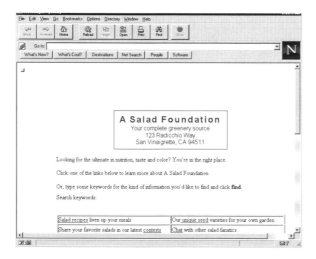

FIGURE C-2 Corel Barista can display fonts supported by Java 1.0, including Helvetica and Times Roman, shown here. Note that the Corel Barista toolbar has been minimized to the small button at the upper left.

Q. Why did Corel ship Bitstream TrueDoc fonts with Corel Barista 1.0 and not with Corel Barista 2.0?

A. Corel Barista 1.0 included Bitstream TrueDoc technology, which allowed you to embed fonts that Java 1.0 does not support. Corel discontinued support for font embedding and eliminated the shipment of Bitstream TrueDoc fonts for two reasons. First, they wanted Corel Barista to be 100 percent Java-compliant. Second, embedding TrueDoc fonts into a Corel Barista document forced anyone who wished to browse the documents to install the TrueDoc font technology on the individual machine. Corel prefers not to force users to install or to configure their local machine before they read Corel Barista documents on the Web.

NOTE: *Netscape Communicator 4.0 now includes support for font embedding using Bitstream's TrueDoc technology. Microsoft has also announced a similar technology for Internet Explorer 4. You can read more about these technologies at these companies' web sites (**www.netscape.com** or **www.microsoft.com**) or read an interesting discussion of the two by Daniel Will-Harris (accessible through **www.will-harris.com**).*

Q. Can all browsers view Corel Barista documents?

A. Corel Barista documents are Java applets. Not all browsers are Java-enabled yet. Earlier versions of browsers such as Netscape Navigator 2.0 and Microsoft Internet Explorer 2 did not support Java technology. Netscape Navigator 2.01 was the first version to be Java-enabled. Corel recommends Netscape Navigator 3.0 and Microsoft Internet Explorer 3.0 or later versions be used when viewing Corel Barista documents.

Corel Barista and Web Browsers

Q. How do web browsers handle Corel Barista files?

A. When you view a Corel Barista file, the browsers such as Netscape Navigator and Microsoft Internet Explorer pass control of the viewing process over to the Java interpreter that is distributed with the browser. The Java interpreter, in turn, runs the Corel Barista applet to display the web page.

Q. Why doesn't the search button on my browser work when I am viewing a Corel Barista document?

A. Web browsers today still have some improvements to make in handling Java applets. Current browsers pass complete control of the browsing process to the Java interpreter. They do not always enable communication between the search buttons of the browser and the Java interpreter.

Q. On a similar note, when I move my mouse cursor over a hypertext link, why doesn't the cursor change to the pointing hand that shows I can jump to a new location?

A. As mentioned in the previous answer, your browser's Java interpreter is not communicating with its cursor handling. In fact, in testing, Corel found that when the Java applet told the browser it was over a hypertext link and that it should change the cursor to a pointing hand, the browser would do so, but then would immediately change it back to the arrow cursor.

Q. Can I do a text search on a Corel Barista document?

A. Not yet, but soon. Web browsers' search buttons do not work with the Java interpreter. If Java 1.1 technology does not support this enhancement, Corel plans to add a search button to the Corel Barista toolbar.

Understanding Corel Barista's Class Files

Q. What are "class" files?

A. Corel Barista documents rely on "class" files. The files that comprise Corel Barista documents aren't just graphics, animation, and sound. Since Corel Barista is Java-based, like other Java applets, it relies on external files known as class files that support its special features. These classes contain instructions for the Java interpreter on how to handle Corel Barista information.

Q. Where are the class files stored?

A. When you install Corel Barista from Corel WordPerfect Suite 8 setup program using the default directory structure, you will find the class files in the following folder: C:\Corel\Suite8\Shared\Barista*.class. (These files will be easy to identify because they all have the extension of CLASS.)

Q. Can I put these class files on other web servers?

A. Absolutely. Otherwise, those individuals who do not have the Corel Barista software installed cannot view the Corel Barista files.

Distributing Corel Barista Documents

Q. How do I put my Corel Barista documents on a server for others to view?

A. There are few steps to making sure others can view your Corel Barista documents. First, and probably the most obvious step, is to make sure that all BMP, JPEG, GIF, and other image files are moved to the same folder as your Corel Barista document.

NOTE: *You can edit the Corel Barista file in an ASCII editor to change where you put your images and sound files. However, be cautious when doing this. It is easy to make errors when changing these file paths.*

You'll then need to make sure that the Corel Barista class files can be located by other browsers. (Not all browsers behave the same when searching for the class files for the Java interpreter.) Two "variables" (special values) tell the browser where to look for the class files. These variables are CLASSPATH and CODEBASE. Browsers also generally look in the same folder as the Corel Barista document.

Q. What are the CLASSPATH and CODEBASE variables?

A. In its initial release (version 1.0), Corel Barista's installation added a CLASSPATH setting in the autoexec.bat file. Unfortunately, this made Corel Barista 1.0 not completely Java-compliant: not all operating systems use an autoexec.bat file. Corel Barista 2.0 doesn't use the autoexec.bat file. In fact, Corel recommends that those who installed Corel Barista 1.0 remove the CLASSPATH setting from their autoexec.bat file.

CODEBASE is an optional attribute value that can be in the HTML tag called <APPLET>. The CODEBASE attribute value tells the browser where to look for the Corel Barista Java class files. Note that the path stored in this setting may not be the first place the browser looks for the classes. Here is an example of what the HTML tag might look like:

```
<APPLET code="Barista.class" width=00816 height=01084
codebase="\\US1\Barista20">
```

(where \\US1\Barista20 represents the path, or folder, where the Corel Barista class files are stored on your web server.)

If you find many people are having difficulties viewing your Corel Barista documents, first advise them to delete any CLASSPATH settings they may have in their autoexec.bat files. Corel then recommends you place all Corel Barista documents in the same directory as the class files on your web server.

If you decide to organize your server so that Corel Barista documents are distributed in multiple directories, and you want to locate the CLASS files in one directory, make sure you add the CODEBASE attribute to all Corel Barista documents' <APPLET> tag.

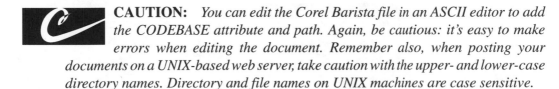

CAUTION: *You can edit the Corel Barista file in an ASCII editor to add the CODEBASE attribute and path. Again, be cautious: it's easy to make errors when editing the document. Remember also, when posting your documents on a UNIX-based web server, take caution with the upper- and lower-case directory names. Directory and file names on UNIX machines are case sensitive.*

Using Corel Barista's Special Effects

Q. What are the new, special effects in the Corel Barista 2.0 printer driver, and how do I use them?

A. The Corel Barista 2.0 printer driver for Windows 95 supports new special effects for slide transitions and sound effects. For example, you can have the pages in your Corel Barista file turn automatically. Or you might have transitions between pages

as you would in an electronic slide presentation. From *any* application that prints on Windows 95 you can create a simple slide show with sound effects. When you choose File | Print, then select the Corel Barista printer driver, select the printer properties to see a special effects tab (see Figure C-3). Click the special effects tab, then select the Slide Show check box.

From here, you can specify several options in the Transitions group box. If you'd like to automatically advance from one page to the next, choose Time from the Transition On pull-down menu. (Specify the time—in milliseconds, or one-thousandths of a second—between pages in the Time text box.) If you would like people to be able to advance manually between slides, choose User Input from the Transition On pull-down menu. To advance pages in the document when it's displayed, you can either click the mouse button or press PAGE UP or PAGE DOWN.

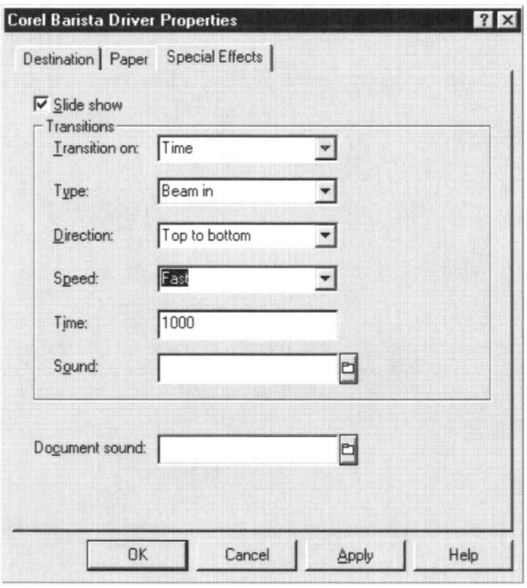

FIGURE C-3 You can print to Corel Barista from any Windows 95 application, complete with between-page transitions and sounds. You can even select a sound file to play whenever the document's being viewed.

In the Transitions group box, you can also specify the type of between-page transitions you want (only one transition type per document). Choose the transition style you prefer from the Type pull-down menu. Choose the direction from which the transition begins in the Direction menu as well as its speed from the Speed menu. If you want a sound file to play as you transition between pages, you can specify that file in the Sound text box.

Regardless of whether you're using between-page effects, or slide show effects, you can also specify a sound file to be played when the Corel Barista document is displayed. Specify that file in the Document Sound text box.

Q. What type of sound file formats do the special effects support?

A. Java currently supports only AU sound files. (AU files are commonly used on the Web as sound files that can be played on any platform or operating system.) You can find utilities on the Web to convert sound files in other formats to AU format. Of course, if you embed a sound clip (in any supported format) in a Corel WordPerfect document and publish the document to Corel Barista, it automatically converts the sound clip to AU file for you.

Additional Corel Barista Details

Q. Will my Corel Barista 1.0 documents work with the new Corel Barista 2.0 class files?

A. Yes. You can replace all your Corel Barista 1.0 class files with Corel Barista 2.0 class files.

Q. In a web browser, can you download a graphic from a page published to Corel Barista?

A. Any graphic that appears on a Corel Barista page is downloaded when you view the page. They are downloaded to whatever directory the browser uses to save their temp files (often called a "cache" folder). This, however, does not make the files easily accessible. You cannot click on a graphic on a Corel Barista page and get a save dialog to save just the graphic image or to view just that graphic as you can with standard HTML documents. Industrious or particularly dedicated users, however, can get around this by searching in the browser temp directory while they're viewing a Corel Barista document and copy the graphic image before the viewer destroys the temporary files. Realistically, few users will bother to go to the trouble—thereby adding a measure of protection one step beyond that found in a standard HTML document.

Q. The graphic images do not display with my Corel Barista documents when I view them locally with Microsoft Internet Explorer 3.01 or 3.02. What is wrong?

A. The problem is that IE 3.02 will not let you run Java applets locally and still open images. Apparently it returns an error for illegally accessing files and won't display them. This problem does not occur with Internet Explorer when the document is viewed from a web server.

You can still get Internet Explorer to view these documents and graphics during "local" page testing. Although it's not recommended for general use, just set the CLASSPATH variable in your autoexec.bat file to point to the latest Corel Barista class files. For example, if you installed the Corel Barista classes to the default folder, you would add a line in the autoexec.bat file like this:

```
SET CLASSPATH=C:\COREL\SUITE8\SHARED\BARISTA
```

Consult your Windows 95 documentation for information on editing system files such as autoexec.bat. Remember, it's not 100 percent Java-compliant to rely on the autoexec.bat file to find the class files, so Corel does not encourage this practice.

Corel Barista and Document Security

Q. Can a user cut and paste from my Corel Barista file?

A. No. Java does not support cut and paste.

Q. Can you set security options when you publish to Corel Barista so that viewers are denied or granted permission to copy selected text, graphics, etc.?

A. No. However, you don't need such restrictions because Java does not allow the user to cut and paste text from a Corel Barista file being viewed by a browser. In theory, someone could save the file and have access to all the text in it, because it is just an HTML file. But the text is not formatted and would require a lot of work to make it look good.

Corel Barista File Format Reference

D

In this appendix, you'll find Corel's language reference information to help you decipher and troubleshoot Corel Barista files. If you're an extremely advanced user and want to take advantage of Corel Barista's Java classes, you can also access additional information from the developer section of their web site. They include complete Corel Barista software development kit (SDK) information, from which some of this information has been drawn.

If you read the Corel Barista questions and answers in depth (Appendix C), you may have gleaned that Corel Barista creates files that are in HTML format. However, if you were to look at a Corel Barista document, you would see that it's largely comprised of codes and tags that seem indecipherable. If you're curious, or trying to troubleshoot a Corel Barista document, you may want to do some deciphering.

That's where this appendix comes in. You can use this as kind of a Corel Barista-to-English dictionary. It can help you discern the structure of your Corel Barista documents and better understand how they work. Remember, Corel Barista consists of two components: Java-based classes and the documents themselves. The Corel Barista Java classes load into the browser to translate the documents into their displayed form.

NOTE: *For more information on the Corel Barista Java classes, you can consult a complete reference on the Web (Corel's made their Corel Barista software development kit freely available). Visit **www.corel.com** and explore the developer area for details.*

As you peruse your Corel Barista documents, you'll notice that the contents are largely contained within certain HTML tags. These tags begin with <APPLET CODE= *barista.class*>, where *barista.class* is one of the parameters listed in this appendix; are followed by the definitions; and end with an </APPLET> tag. The parameters describe the information needed for page layout, as well as how to represent each object stored on a page.

Insider Tip

If you're bold enough to change these values, you'll need to

- Retain the case of all parameters and values. Java is case sensitive.

- Make sure all positions and dimensions are in display units (pixels).

Color Representations

Throughout this section, you'll come across parameter values that list a color value. In Corel Barista, color is represented using a 4-byte value that isn't case sensitive. The definition, with all values in hexadecimal format, is

Byte 1 (Color Type)	Byte 2 (Red)	Byte 3 (Green)	Byte 4 (Blue)
00 hex—Solid	00 - FF	00 - FF	00 - FF
01 hex—Transparent			
02 hex—Gradient			

For example: A solid color red would be 00ff0000, solid green 0000ff00, solid blue 000000ff, and solid black 00000000.

The Applet Tag

All Barista HTML documents begin with the tag: <APPLET CODE="Barista.class" WIDTH= x HEIGHT= x > (where x defines the size of the window in pixels). This is followed by a series of parameters and their values using the syntax: <PARAM NAME= parameter name VALUE= " parameter value ">. These parameters are described later under "Corel Barista Parameters." An Applet code ends with the HTML tag: </APPLET>.

EXAMPLE:

```
<APPLET CODE="Barista.class" WIDTH=816 HEIGHT=1106 >
<PARAM NAME=Version VALUE ="1000">
<PARAM NAME=Background VALUE="00FFFFFF">
</APPLET>
```

Corel Barista Parameters

As you learned in the previous section, between the <APPLET> paired tags, a Corel Barista document consists of parameters and their related values. The sections that follow describe these parameters and their values. Note that not all of these parameters will appear in any given Corel Barista document. For example, Corel WordPerfect will take advantage of certain Corel Barista features, Corel Presentations will take advantage of others, and the Corel Barista Windows 95 printer driver will use still others.

Document Parameters

Document parameters apply to the entire Corel Barista document—to each page within the document. They're what are sometimes called "global" parameters.

Version

This is an integer that is used for version control purposes. The version number in the document will have to follow the Barista version number (currently at version 2.0.0.21).

EXAMPLE:

PageDir

PageDir is used to define the directory for a file per page document. For a multiple page document you can have all pages defined in one HTML file, or you can have each page defined in a separate HTML file. You do not need to define this parameter if you are storing all pages within a single file. If you are using multiple files, the directory defined by PageDir will be used to locate all subsequent pages. These pages will be identified using Pn.htm (where n represents the document's page number). The subdirectory is relative to the directory of the current HTML file. By default, it is the same name as the Barista HTML file name. Corel recommends using multiple files if you have a large document with many pages; otherwise, you should use a single page.

   EXAMPLE:

```
<param name=PageDir value="MyPageDirectory">
```

Background

Background is used to define the background color used by all pages. This parameter will take a color or an image. The background color of the Applet window has to be in hexadecimal RGB format (see "Color Representations" earlier in this appendix). The image can be tiled or centered.

   EXAMPLE:

```
<param name=Background value="FFFFFF">
<param name=Background value="image.gif 0">
```

(where the graphics image "image.gif" is a tiled background).

BookmarkList

This is a list of bookmarks that can be jumped to by the Graphics Objects Jump to Bookmark action. Each bookmark in the list is followed by a page number and an X-Y position on the page to be jumped to.

   NOTE: *Java currently does not support jumping to a location on a page: the X and Y parameters are for future use only.*

   EXAMPLE:

```
<param name=BookmarkList  value="Bookmark1, P3, 30, 50,
Bookmark2, P1, 10, 50,">
```

NumOfPages

This parameter specifies the number of pages contained within the document.

EXAMPLE:

```
<param name=NumOfPages value="10">
```

DisplayToolBar

This parameter is used to hide the toolbar in multipage documents. The default value is "1", which allows the toolbar to display. A value of "0" will hide the toolbar. This is useful for slide shows where the author does not want any user input or visual "distraction" from the presentation.

EXAMPLE:

```
<param name=DisplayToolbar value="0">
```

AutoScroll

The document should be automatically scrolled to make it easier to move through it. The scrolling can be done by time, by pressing PAGE UP/PAGE DOWN or the mouse button, or by audio clip/time. If enabled, automatic scrolling will not start until the first page of the document has been completely drawn on the screen. This parameter tells Corel Barista to turn automatic scrolling on or off (if the parameter's not found, default is off), while the Ax parameter is used to indicate the type of automatic scrolling and transitioning to be done per page. If no Ax parameter is found on a page and Auto Scrolling is on, default scrolling and transition values will be given for that page. If an Ax parameter is found on a previous page (up to the beginning of the document), the scrolling and transition values for the previous page will be applied to the new page. If an Ax parameter cannot be found on any previous page, the new page gets default scrolling and transition values of events, immediate, undefined, fast (see the "Ax" section later in the appendix).

EXAMPLE:

```
<param name=AutoScroll value="1">
```

(Turns auto scrolling on.)

XYDPI

This parameter specifies the resolution of the display context in DPI; by default it is 96.

EXAMPLE:

```
<param name=XYDPI  value="96">
```

Px

The contents of a page are included in a parameter list following a >Px= name. At this time there are basically 5 different types of objects that may be contained in a page:

Text	denoted by Tx
Graphics	denoted by Gx
Tables	denoted by Bx
Sound	denoted by Sx
AutoScroll	denoted by Ax

EXAMPLE:

```
<param name=P1 value=T1 G1 T2 T3 G2 B1 S1 A1">
```

Objects will be displayed in the order in which they are expressed. One page sound is allowed per page. If present, it will be played after the objects are drawn. One auto scroll object is allowed per page. If present, it will begin after all the objects on the page are drawn. Each type of object will be covered in detail separately.

Graphic Parameters

These Corel Barista parameters are used to control the appearance of graphic images in Corel Barista documents.

Gx

The >x= represents an integer to distinguish each individual object. The parameters are as follows:

Type	TLX	TLY	Width	Height	Color
1	2	3	4	5	6

- Element 1   Refers to the type of graphical shape. The following values of Element 1 determine the shape of the graphical object:

Value	Shape
0	rectangle/square
1	circle/ellipse
2	polygon
3	round rectangle/square
4	polyline
5	arc
6	image
7	polycurve
8	polypolygon
-1	XOR fountain fill

- Element 2   The top-left X coordinate of the bounding rectangle in display units, relative to the position of the bounding box.

- Element 3   The top-left Y coordinate of the bounding rectangle in display units, relative to the position of the bounding box.

- Element 4   The width of the bounding rectangle in display units, relative to the position of the bounding box.

- Element 5   The height of the bounding rectangle in display units, relative to the position of the bounding box.

■ Element 6   Always set with 4 bytes xxxxxxxx, where the leftmost
    byte represents the color model, the remaining 3 bytes represent the
    RGB color:

First byte	Model	Last 3 bytes
ff	indexed color (not implemented)	the index number
00	solid RGB color	the RGB representation
01	no color—transparent	000000
02	special fill	000000

n **NOTE:** *The rectangle in this GraphObj class is the bounding box of the
object. For some types of this object, such as Rectangle, Square, Circle,
Ellipse, Rounded Rectangle, Arc, and Image, the bounding box is the
parameters of the shape itself, therefore, the ShapeObj classes of these types do not
carry the parameters. The other types, Polygon, Polyline, and Polycurve, have their
own shape parameters to describe the shape, therefore, the rectangle of this
GraphObj is purely an invisible bounding box. The purpose of this bounding box is
for clipping, location positioning, and fountain fill. This bounding box doesn't have
to be the exact profile box of an object, it can be larger than the object to fulfill the
special fountain fills. All the polygon, polyline, and polycurve points are related to
the top-left corner of their bounding boxes (0, 0), which allows you to move an
object without changing all the points in a polygon, etc.. Some applications do not
have the concept of bounding boxes for their objects; they simply enter 0 0 0 0 as x,
y, width, and height, which the Barista would take as "NO BOUNDING BOX," and
process it with an absolute coordinate— using the top-left corner of the window as
(0, 0).*

EXAMPLE:

```
<param name=G1 value=@0 100 100 50 50 00FF0000@>
<param name=G1 value=@0 100 100 50 50 0200000@>
```

(Because there is a fountain fill, a G1F parameter needs to be added, so the final
three bytes have no meaning.)

```
<param name=G1 value=@0 100 100 50 50 01000000@>
```

(Because there is no color, no fill, and it is transparent, the final three bytes have no meaning.)

GxL

This parameter defines the outline of the object. If it is not present, no outline will be present.

Thickness	Color	Style	Line-Type	Line-End
1	2	3	4	5

- Element 1   The thickness of the line, expressed in display units, relative to the position of the bounding box.

- Element 2   The color of the line, expressed in RGB and hex format.

- Element 3   The line style. (Refer to the "Line Styles Listing" section later in this appendix.)

- Element 4   The line-join type: 0 - miter, 1 - round, 2 - bevel.

- Element 5   The line-end type: 0 - flat, 1 - round, 2 - square.

EXAMPLE:

```
<param name=G1L value=@5 000000ff 0 0 0">
```

GxS

This parameter defines the shape of the object, therefore contents of this parameter will be different for each type of object.

Type 0 (Rectangle)   No parameters required.
Type 1 (Circle/Ellipse)   No parameters required.
Type 2 (Polygon)   (See details, next.)

#Points	X	Y	X	Y	X	Y	X	Y...
1	2	3	2	3	2	3	2	3...

- Element 1 The number of points in the polygon.

- Element 2 The X coordinates of each point, expressed in display units, relative to the position of the bounding box.

- Element 3 The Y coordinates of each point, expressed in display units, relative to the position of the bounding box.

 NOTE: *If a bounding box is being defined, all the X and Y coordinates are related to it, with the top-left corner of the box as (0, 0).*

If the rectangle of the GraphObj is 0 0 0 0 as x, y, width, and height, it will be "NO BOUNDING BOX"; the point (x, y) is an absolute coordinate—use the top-left corner of the window as (0, 0).

EXAMPLE:

```
<param name=G1S value=@3 10 0 20 10 0 20">
```

Type 3 (Rounded Rectangle)

ARCWIDTH Expressed in display units, relative to the position of the bounding box, this parameter is the horizontal diameter of the arc that will be forming the corners.

ARCHEIGHT Expressed in display units, relative to the position of the bounding box, this parameter is the vertical diameter of the arc that will be forming the corners.

EXAMPLE:

```
<param name=G1S value=@50 30">
```

Type 4 (Polyline)

N1	N2	#Points	X	Y	X	Y	X	Y	X	Y...
1	2	3	4	5	4	5	4	5	4	5...

- Element 1   Beginning arrowhead type: 0 - no arrowhead; 1,2,3,4,5,6,7 - arrowhead types.

- Element 2   Ending arrowhead type: 0 - no arrowhead; 1,2,3,4,5,6,7 - arrowhead types.

- Element 3   Number of points in the polyline.

- Element 4   The X coordinates of each point, expressed in display units, relative to the position of the bounding box.

- Element 5   The Y coordinates of each point, expressed in display units, relative to the position of the bounding box.

NOTE: *If a bounding box is being defined, all the X and Y coordinates are related to it, with the top-left corner of the box as (0, 0).*

If the rectangle of the GraphObj is 0 0 0 0 as x, y, width, and height, it will be "NO BOUNDING BOX"; the point (x, y) is an absolute coordinate—use the top-left corner of the window as (0, 0).

EXAMPLE:

```
<param name=G1S value=@0 0 3 100 100 200 200 300 300">
```

Type 5 (Arc)

START_ANGLE	INCREMENT_ANGLE
1	2

- Element 1   The starting angle of the arc (expressed in degrees).

- Element 2   The amount the arc will rotate and the direction (expressed in degrees; counterclockwise is +).

EXAMPLE:

```
<param name=G1S value=@90 90">
```

Type 6 (Image)   No parameters required.
Type 7 (Polycurve)

N1	N2	X	Y	C	X	Y	X	Y	X	Y	L	X	Y	C	X	Y	X	Y	X	Y...
1	2	1	2	3	4	5	4	5	4	5	3	4	5	3	4	5	4	5	4	5...

- Element 1   Beginning arrowhead type: 0 - no arrowhead; 1,2,3 - arrowhead types.

- Element 2   Ending arrowhead type: 0 - no arrowhead; 1,2,3 - arrowhead types.

- Element 3   Start X coordinate, expressed in display units, relative to the position of the bounding box.

- Element 4   Start Y coordinate, expressed in display units, relative to the position of the bounding box.

- Element 5   The type of bezier object: L - Line node, C - Curve node, M - Move to node. A curve requires 3 control points. The following table describes how the type of Element 5 affects Elements 6 and 7:

Object type of Element 5	Element 6	Element 7
L	The X coordinate of the end of the line, expressed in display units, relative to the position of the bounding box.	The Y coordinate of the end of the line, expressed in display units, relative to the position of the bounding box.
C	The X coordinate of the control points, expressed in display units, relative to the position of the bounding box.	The Y coordinate of the control points, expressed in display units, relative to the position of the bounding box.
M	The X coordinate of the start point of a new polygon, expressed in display units, relative to the position of the bounding box.	The Y coordinate of the start point of a new polygon, expressed in display units, relative to the position of the bounding box.

NOTE: *If a bounding box is being defined, all the X and Y coordinates are related to it, with the top-left corner of this box as (0, 0).*

If the rectangle of the GraphObj is 0 0 0 0 as x, y, width, and height, it will be "NO BOUNDING BOX"; the point (x, y) is an absolute coordinate—use the top-left corner of the window as (0, 0).

EXAMPLE:

```
<param name=G1S value=@0 0 100 100 L 200 200 C 300 200 400
300 400 400">
```

Type 8 (PolyPolygon)

#P1 P2 P3	M	X	Y
1 2 3	4	5	6

- Elements 1,2,3   Indicate the number of points in each polygon.

- Element 4   The letter M is used to indicate the start of points.

- Element 5   The X coordinates of each point for all polygons, expressed in display units, relative to the position of the bounding box.

- Element 6   The Y coordinates of each point for all polygons, expressed in display units, relative to the position of the bounding box.

 NOTE: *If a bounding box is being defined, all the X and Y coordinates are related to it, with the top-left corner of this box as (0, 0).*

If the rectangle of the GraphObj is 0 0 0 0 as x, y, width, and height, it will be "NO BOUNDING BOX"; the point (x, y) is in absolute coordinate—use the top-left corner of the window as (0, 0).

EXAMPLE:

```
<param name=G1S value=@3 4 M 10 10 30 10 30 30 40 30 40 15 60
15 60 30">
```

In the previous example there are two polygons. The first has three vertices, and the second has four vertices. The first and the last vertices are automatically connected. The character 'M' is simply a delimiter. Then the next elements are a group of X and Y coordinates that denotes the vertices of the polygon. As the first polygon has three vertices, subsequently the first three pairs of numbers are the coordinates of the polygon's three vertices: (10, 10), (30, 10), and (30, 30). As the next polygon has four vertices, the next four pairs of numbers are the coordinates of the next polygon's four vertices.

Gxl

This parameter is only present for an object of type 6 (image). It contains the filename to be displayed. At this time, it may only be a GIF or JPG (check GxB for bitmap [BMP] display). Images can be scaled but cannot yet be clipped.

EXAMPLE:

```
<param name=G2I value=@ball.gif@>
```

GxB

This parameter is only present for an object of type 6 (image). It contains the filename of the BMP file to be displayed. Bitmap images can not yet be clipped.

EXAMPLE:

```
<param name=G3B value=@car.bmp@>
```

GxF

Corel Barista will perform a special fill on the object if this parameter is present.

Type	Method	#Colors	Cn	Pn	X	Y	Angle	Numsteps	Pad
1	2	3	4	5	6	7	8	9	10

■ Element 1 Must be 2 for fountain fill, 240 for transparent fill.

If Element 1 is 2, then:

- Element 2   The method that will be used to perform the fill:

     1 = LINEAR FOUNTAIN FILL
     2 = RADIAL FOUNTAIN FILL
     3 = CONICAL FOUNTAIN FILL
     4 = SQUARE FOUNTAIN FILL

- Element 3   The number of colors in the fill (minimum value of 2).

- Element 4   A color, expressed in RGB and hex format.

- Element 5   The position of the color.

 NOTE: *First position is* always *0, last position is* always *100.*

- Element 6   The X offset of the fill. (Default 0). Must be in the range of -100% to 100%.

- Element 7   The Y offset of the fill. (Default 0). Must be in the range of -100% to 100%.

- Element 8   The angle of the fill expressed in degrees (-360 to 360). (Default 0).

- Element 9   The number of steps in the fill (2 to 255). If 0, then 255 is used.

- Element 10   The edge pad of the fill: 0 to 45 degrees.

If Element 1 is 240, then:

- Element 2   Color to be used.

- Element 3   The percentage of transparency (can be 50%, 25%, or 12%).

EXAMPLE:

```
<param name=G1F value=@2 1 2 000000ff 0 00ff0000 100 35 0 30
0 0 0">
<param name=G1F value=@2 2 3 000000ff 0 0000ff00 40 00ff0000
100 35 0 30 0 0 0">
<param name=G1F value=@240 ff0000 50">
```

GxA

This parameter associates an action string, which is executed when the graphic object is clicked.

 NOTE: *This is optional—specified only for graphic objects that have actions associated with them, such as hyperlinks, or for playing sound files.*

Type	String
1	2

- Element 1   Refers to the type of action.

    Action Type=1 Operand(Element2) - external URL string e.g. *www.corel.com*.
    Action Type=2 Operand(Element2) - Goto Page (Px) eg. 2 P5.
    Action Type=3 Currently not used.
    Action Type=4 PopUp Footnote text.

- Element 2   Name of the parameter that gets the rest of the information.

POPUP FOOTNOTES   If it's a pop up window, the next element contains basic information and a pointer to the Text parameter.

X Width	Y Width	X Height	Y Height	Fore-ground color	Back-ground color	Font Face	Bold	Italic	Point Size	Parameter name with text
1	2	3	4	5	6	7	8	9	10	11

- Elements 1,2,3,4   x, y, width, and height for pop-up window.

■ Elements 5, 6   Foreground and background colors.

■ Elements 7,8,9,10   Font face, bold, italic, point size.

■ Element 11   Name of parameter with text.

Text Element - contains the text for the footnote:

■ Element 1   Text

Sound Files

Action Type=5   Currently not used.
Action Type=6   Currently not used.
Action Type=7   Currently not used.
Action Type=8   Currently not used.
Action Type=9   Currently not used.
Action Type=10 Play a sound file.

If you've chosen Action Type 10, these elements apply:

■ Element 2   Sound file type (currently only type "0" supported - .au).

■ Element 3   Sound action (0 = stop, 1 = play, 2 = loop).

■ Element 4   Sound file string ("sndfiles/playme.au").

Other Actions, Including E-Mail

Action Type=11   Operand(Element2) - Jump to Bookmark e.g.
                 MyBookmark.
Action Type=12   Operand(Element2) - Clear Component text - no other
                 operands.
Action Type=13   Send Component eMail. e.g. toddler@fictitious.com,
                 Auto Callback Info

■ Element 2   e-mail addressee

■ Element 3   e-mail subject

NOTE: *A comma separates the e-mail addressee from the subject.*

Sound Parameters

Only one page sound is allowed per page. The following parameters apply:

Sx

The >x= represents the page number associated with each individual object. Only one page sound is allowed per page.

EXAMPLE:

```
<param name=S1 value="0 1 sndfiles/mysound.au">
```

- Element 1   Sound file type (currently only type "0" supported - .au).
- Element 2   Sound action (0 = stop, 1 = play, 2 = loop).
- Element 3   Sound file string ("sndfiles/mysound.au").

Text Parameters

These parameters define how text is displayed on a Corel Barista page. If text objects are present, then the following parameters must exist:

FontnameList

This parameter defines a list of all font names within the document. Font names are delimited with commas.

 NOTE: *Because the Java language currently only supports five fonts, this parameter can be ignored unless you are using some add-on font technologies such as Bitstream TrueDoc.*

EXAMPLE:

```
<param name=FontnameList value="Times New Roman, Snell">
```

FontRatio

This parameter defines a list of the maximum pixel height of the previous fonts when set to 72 points. This accounts for the Java bug that does not properly set the point size of fonts. There must be an equal number of elements in this list as there were in the FontnameList parameter.

EXAMPLE:

```
<param name=FontRatio value=108, 114">
```

J3FontnameList

This parameter defines a list of all font names within the document after they have been mapped to Java system fonts.

NOTE: *Only three fonts (Courier, TimesRoman, Helvetica) are present in Java 1.0. Different font names are comma-delimited.*

EXAMPLE:

```
<param name=J3FontnameList value="TimesRoman,Helvetica">
```

FontRefList

This is a lookup table of information about the fonts. All elements in the tables are space delimited, as are the tables themselves.

Font	Size	Style	Color
1	2	3	4

- Element 1   A 0-based reference to a font in the FontnameList table above.

- Element 2   Point size the font is to be displayed in.

- Element 3   Font style:

   0 = normal
   1 = **bold**
   2 = *italic*
   4 = <u>underline</u>
   8 = ~~strikeout~~
 16 = <u>double underline</u>
 32 = overscore
 64 = highlight

NOTE: *Attributes can be used together (for example, 6 = <u>italics and</u> <u>underline</u>). The highlight attribute requires the* Txh *parameter to be set if the highlight color is other than yellow.*

- Element 4   RGB color the text is to be displayed in, expressed in hexadecimal notation.

EXAMPLE:

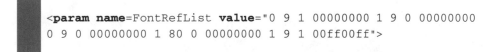

```
<param name=FontRefList value="0 9 1 00000000 1 9 0 00000000
0 9 0 00000000 1 80 0 00000000 1 9 1 00ff00ff">
```

The previous example contains five tables (0 - 4).

Tx

The >x= represents an integer to distinguish each individual object. The value of this object is the actual string that is to be displayed.

EXAMPLE:

```
<param name=T1  value="Corel Barista is really nifty.">
```

Txh

This is a table that defines the highlight colors to use when text is highlighted. If this entry is not found and the highlight attribute is set, the highlight color will default to yellow. If a color other than yellow is desired for the default highlight color, then a single color entry should be used. For multiple highlight colors, the desired color must be entered each time a highlight is encountered. The entries are RGB values.

EXAMPLE:

To set the default highlight color to blue:

```
<param name=Txh value="000000ff"  >
```

The first highlighted the text red, the second green, the third red, the fourth magenta:

```
<param name=Txh value="00ff0000 0000ff00 00ff0000 00ff00ff "  >
```

Txr

This is a lookup table that describes the font that each character of the string is to be displayed in. All elements in the tables are space delimited, as are the tables themselves.

Fontref	#Chars
1	2

- Element 1   A 0-based reference to a table in the FontRefList parameter.

- Element 2   Display this many characters using the previous font.

EXAMPLE:

```
<param name=T1r  value="0 13 1 17">
```

In the previous example, the first 13 characters of the text object are displayed using Font Reference table 0 in the Font Reference List, and the next 17 characters are displayed using Font Reference table 1 in the Font Reference List.

Txp

This is a lookup table that describes where each character of the string is to be positioned on the display. All elements in the tables are space delimited, as are the tables themselves.

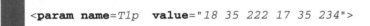

#Chars	ABS-X	ABS-Y
1	2	3

- ■ Element 1   Print this many characters, starting at position 2,3.

- ■ Element 2   The absolute X position at which printing will start (expressed in pixels).

- ■ Element 3   The absolute Y position at which printing will start (expressed in pixels).

EXAMPLE:

```
<param name=T1p  value="18 35 222 17 35 234">
```

In the previous example, the first 18 characters of the text object are displayed from location (35, 222), and the next 17 characters are displayed from location (35, 234).

Autoscroll Parameters

These parameters control the transitions among pages in Corel Barista documents.

Ax

The >x= represents an integer to distinguish each individual object. The value of this object indicates the scroll and transitions values to use for one or more pages.

EXAMPLES:

```
<param name=A1  value="1 2 5 3 2000">
<param name=A1  value="2 9 11 2">
<param name=A1  value="3 28 3 3 4000 sound.au">
```

■ Element 1   Indicates what action should trigger the scrolling/transition:

1 - Scroll/transition on time amount found in Element 5.
2 - Scroll/transition on page up/page down/mouse events whenever they happen.
3 - Scroll/transition on sound and time found in Elements 6 and 5.

■ Element 2   Indicates the type of transition to occur while scrolling to the next page. These transitions are currently based on slide show transitions found in Corel Presentations:

1 - Transition with Beam In
2 - Transition with Blinds
3 - Transition with Blocks
4 - Transition with Blocks Stack
5 - Transition with Burst In
6 - Transition with Burst Out
7 - Transition with Circles Small
8 - Transition with Circles Large
9 - Transition with Clock
10 - Transition with Diamonds Small
11 - Transition with Diamonds Large
12 - Transition with Dissolve
13 - Transition with Fade
14 - Transition with Immediate
15 - Transition with Lines
16 - Transition with Lines Skip
17 - Transition with Lines Sweep
18 - Transition with Mosaic
19 - Transition with Mosaic Dissolve
20 - Transition with Mosaic Wave
21 - Transition with Photo Lens In
22 - Transition with Photo Lens Out
23 - Transition with Push Away
24 - Transition with Puzzle
25 - Transition with Rectangles
26 - Transition with Roll In

27 - Transition with Roll Out
28 - Transition with Slide In
29 - Transition with Slide In From Corner
30 - Transition with Slide In Close
31 - Transition with Slide Out
32 - Transition with Slide Out To Corner
33 - Transition with Slide Out Open
34 - Transition with Spiral
35 - Transition with Spiral Away
36 - Transition with Stars
37 - Transition with Stretch
38 - Transition with Stretch From Corner
39 - Transition with Stretch From Center
40 - Transition with Stretch To Corner
41 - Transition with Stretch Open
42 - Transition with Stretch Close
43 - Transition with Sweep
44 - Transition with Sweep Around
45 - Transition with Sweep From Corner
46 - Transition with Sweep From Center
47 - Transition with Sweep To Center
48 - Transition with Sweep Open
49 - Transition with Sweep Close
50 - Transition with Triangles
51 - Transition with Wave
52 - Transition with Weave
53 - Transition with Windmill

NOTE: *Corel Barista currently supports all these transitions: Beam In, Blinds, Blocks, Burst In, Burst Out, Circles Large, Circles Small, Clock, Diamonds Large, Diamonds Small, Dissolve, Immediate, Lines Skip, Lines Sweep, Photo Lens In, Photo Lens Out, Push Away, Puzzle, Rectangles, Slide In, Slide In Close, Slide In From Corner, Slide Out, Slide Out To Corner, Slide Out Open, Spiral, Stars, Stretch, Stretch From Center, Stretch From Corner, Stretch Open, Sweep, Sweep Around, Sweep Close, Sweep From Center, Sweep From Corner, Sweep Open, Sweep To Center, Triangles, Wave, and Windmill.*

■ Element 3   Indicates the direction for the transition to go (if it's a transition that can go in any particular direction):

   0 - Direction is Undefined (used when transition has no direction)
   1 - Direction is Left to Right
   2 - Direction is Right to Left
   3 - Direction is Top to Bottom
   4 - Direction is Bottom to Top
   5 - Direction is Horizontal
   6 - Direction is Vertical
   7 - Direction is Left and Down
   8 - Direction is Right and Down
   9 - Direction is Left and Up
  10 - Direction is Right and Up
  11 - Direction is Clockwise
  12 - Direction is Counter Clockwise

■ Element 4   Indicates the speed for the transition:

   1 - Speed is slow
   2 - Speed is medium
   3 - Speed is fast

■ Element 5   Indicates the amount of time in milliseconds to wait after page is completely drawn before scrolling/transitioning to the next page. This element is not needed when Element 1 has a value of 2 (scroll/transition on page up/page down/mouse events).

■ Element 6   Indicates the audio clip (.au filename) to play before scrolling/transitioning to the next page. It was originally intended that Corel Barista would wait until the audio clip was done playing before scrolling/transitioning to the next page. However, since there is currently not a way in Java to tell when an audio clip is finished playing, Corel Barista uses the time indicated in Element 5 to determine how long to wait before scrolling/transitioning to the next page. It is expected that the time indicated in Element 5 will be the time needed to play the audio clip in this element. If in the future Java provides a way to determine when an audio clip is done playing, the dependency of having to have a time to go along with this audio clip file will be removed. If there is a current audio clip being played, this audio clip will be stopped before the new one is started.

Table Parameters

These parameters define how tables are displayed in Corel Barista documents.

BxB

This parameter gives the points of the lines that make up the table (Border, Horizontal, and Vertical rules) and defines the line thickness, its style, and in which color it will be drawn. These sets of seven (or four, since the last three are optional) parameters are separated by commas.

X1	Y1	X2	Y2	Thickness	Color Style	X3	Y3	X4	Y4	X5	Y5	X6	Y6
1	2	3	4	5	6	7	1	2	3	4	1	2	3

- ■ Element 1   The X coordinate of the start point expressed in display units, relative to the position of the bounding box.

- ■ Element 2   The Y coordinate of the start point expressed in display units, relative to the position of the bounding box.

- ■ Element 3   The X coordinate of the end point expressed in display units, relative to the position of the bounding box.

- ■ Element 4   The Y coordinate of the end point expressed in display units, relative to the position of the bounding box

Optional Parameters: If these parameters are not present, the values of the last specified entry are used for drawing the succeeding lines. (That is, until the chain is broken by a new set of thickness, color, and style.)

- ■ Element 5   The thickness of the line, expressed in display units, relative to the position of the bounding box.

- ■ Element 6   The RGB color value expressed in hex.

■ Element 7 The Line Style value (refer to "Line Styles Listing" section later in this appendix).

EXAMPLE:

```
<param name=B1B value=@10 10 60 60 12 FF 1, 60 60 60 100, 60
100 10 100 10  FFFF 4, 10 100 10 10">
```

Line Styles Listing

0	SOLID
1	DOTSSPACE
2	DOT
3	DOTLSPACE
4	SDASHSSPACE
5	SDASH
6	SDASHLSPACE
7	DASHSSPACE
8	DASH
9	DASHLSPACE
10	LDASHSSPACE
11	LDASH
12	LDASHLSPACE
13	DASHDOTSSPACE
14	DASHDOT
15	DASHDOTLSPACE
16	DASHDOTDOTSSPACE
17	DASHDOTDOT
18	DASHDOTDOTLSPACE
19	LDASHDASH
20	DOTDOTLSPACE
21	DOTDOTLSPACEDOT
22	DASHDASHDOT

23	DASHDASHDOTDOT
24	DASHDASHDASHDOT
25	DOTDOTDOTDASHDASH
26	DASHDASHDASHDOTDOT

The following are line styles specifically requested by Corel WordPerfect:

27	LDASHDASHDASH
28	LDASHLDASHDASH
29	LDASHLDASHDASHDASH

Arrowhead Type Listing

Arrow Head Number	Arrow Head Style
1	◁
2	◁
3	◁
4	◁
5	◁
6	◁

Arrow Head Number	Arrow Head Style
7	▯

Graphics Group Parameters

Graphical objects can also be grouped together in a group, represented by:

Kx

The 'x' represents an integer to distinguish each individual object. The parameters are as follows:

TLX	TLY	Width	Height	Gx1 Gx2 Gx3...Gxn
1	2	3	4	5...n

- Element 1   The top-left X coordinate of the bounding box in display units, relative to the position of the applet bounding box.

- Element 2   The top-left Y coordinate of the bounding box in display units, relative to the position of the applet bounding box.

- Element 3   The width of the bounding box in display units.

- Element 4   The height of the bounding box in display units.

- Element 5...n   The graphical objects that belong to this group.

EXAMPLE:

```
<param name=K1 value="100 100 200 200 G3 G4 G5 G6">
```

The previous example represents a group of objects contained in the bounding box whose top-left coordinates are 100,100 and which has a width and height of 200, 200. This group contains graphic objects G3, G4, G5, and G6.

Page Component Parameters

PxL

The components on a page are included in a parameter list following a >PxL= name.

EXAMPLE:

```
<param name=P1L value=C1 C2 C3 C4 C5 C6 C7">
```

All components have the format: Cx

The >x= represents an integer to distinguish each individual object. The components will be displayed in the order in which they are expressed.

■   Element 1   Refers to the type of component. There are 11 different types of components available at this time that may be contained in a page (two of the 13 types below are unused):

Component type:

1 = Label
2 = Button
3 = Text Field
4 = Check Box
5 = Radio Button
6 = Combo Box
7 = List Box
8 = Text Box
9 = unused
10 = Image Button
11 = Corel WEB.MOVE Animation
12 = GIF Animation
13 = unused

The component type (Element 1) is followed by six standard parameters:

■   Element 2   X position

- Element 3   Y position
- Element 4   Width
- Element 5   Height
- Element 6   Foreground color
- Element 7   Background color

Each component will now be covered in more detail.

Component Type 1 = Label

Element 8   Label text

Component Type 2 = Button

Element 8   Button text
Each *Cx* button should be associated with a *CxA* entry in the HTML file. The *CxA* parameter specifies what action will occur when the button is pressed. (See the "GxA" section earlier in this appendix for the *CxA* format specification. The *CxA* format is identical to the *GxA* format.)

Component Type 3 = Text Field

Element 8   Default text (optional).

Component Type 4 = Check Box

Element 8   Check state (0 = unchecked, 1= checked).

Component Type 5 = Radio Button

Element 8   Button state (0 = unselected, 1 = selected).
Element 9   Button group name.
Element 10   Button text.

Component Type 6 = Combo Box

Element 8   Active item index (zero based)
Element 9   Item text
Element 10   Item text
Element 11 ...

Component Type 7 = List Box

Element 8   Number of visible items.
Element 9   Multiple select active (0 = false, 1 = true).
Element 10   Default selected item (zero based).
Element 11   Item text.
Element 12   Item text.
Element 13 ...

Component Type 8 = Text Box

Element 8   Number of rows.
Element 9   Number of columns.
Element 10   Default text (optional).

Component Type 10 = Image Button

Element 8   Button type (0 = plain, 1 = 3-D pushbutton, 2 = 3-D pushbutton "note").
If type = 2 (footnote, endnote, etc.) and Corel Barista cannot find the specified GIF file, it will load an internal GIF image for the note button display.
Element 9   Normal image (e.g. image1.gif).
Element 10   Pressed image (e.g. image2.gif).
Element 11   Disabled image (e.g. image3.gif).
Element 12   Highlighted image (e.g. image4.gif).
Element 13   Button text.

Each *Cx* button should be associated with a CxA entry in the HTML file. The *CxA* parameter specifies what action will occur when the button is pressed. See the section "GxA" earlier in this appendix for the *CxA* format specification (parameters and elements are identical).

Component Type 11 = Corel Web.MOVE Animation

Element 8   "Animationlib.animator"—Corel animator class name.

There are three parameters that can be specified when using a Corel Web.MOVE Animation component:

Parameters:

- Cx_INPUTFILE   Allows you to specify the name of the Corel Web.MOVE Java file that contains the animation to display.

- Cx_LOADING   Allows you to specify a message to be displayed while the animation file is being loaded.

- Cx_PROGRESSIVE   If this value is true, the animation will draw progressively, with the first frame fading in while the other frames are being loaded. If this value is false, the LOADING message will be displayed while the all of the frames are being loaded.

EXAMPLE:

```
<param name=C1  value="11,700,500,200,200,000000,000000,
 animationlib.animator">
<param name=C1_INPUTFILE value="cheetah.cjw">
<param name=C1_LOADING value="Loading CorelWEB.MOVE Animation">
<param name=C1_PROGRESSIVE value="true">
```

Component Type 12 = GIF Animation

Element 8   "Animationlib.GIFAnimator"—GIF animator class name.

There are several parameters that can be specified when using a GIF Animation component:

Parameters:

- Cx_IMAGES   Specifies the list of GIF files that will be displayed in the frames of the animation, and the order in which they will be displayed. Images can be used more than once in this list. The images in the list are separated by commas.

- **Cx_IMAGESOURCE**   Specifies the directory where the GIF images that will be displayed in the animation can be found.

- **Cx_STARTUP**   Specifies a GIF image to be displayed at the startup of the animation (while the other images for the animation are still being loaded).

- **Cx_BACKGROUND**   Specifies a GIF image to be displayed as the background for the other images of the animation.

- **Cx_BACKGROUNDCOLOR**   Specifies the background color of the animation. The color is specified in BGR format (i.e. 0x00FF00 = Green).

- **Cx_PAUSE**   Specifies the global pause or frame rate in milliseconds. This is the amount of time that the animation will wait between drawing frames. If this value is not specified, the default frame rate is 50 milliseconds.

- **Cx_PAUSES**   Specifies a separate pause in milliseconds for each individual frame of the animation. This is the amount of time that the animation will wait before drawing the next frame. The pauses are separated by commas. A blank field means that the global pause (or the default pause) will be used.

- **Cx_REPEAT**   Specifies whether the animation will loop continuously or will play through once and stop. If this parameter is set to true, the animation will loop.

- **Cx_POSITIONS**   Specifies the position (relative to the animation boundaries) at which each frame will be drawn. This allows animations to move around on the screen (i.e. a running puppy). The positions are specified as X,Y coordinates. Each X,Y pair is separated by commas.

- **Cx_SOUNDTRACK**   Specifies an AU file that will be played while the animation is displayed. This soundtrack will loop continuously while the animation loops.

- **Cx_SOUNDS**   Specifies AU sound files that are associated with a given frame and will be played while that frame is active. The sound files in the list are separated by commas. A blank entry means that no sound (nor the soundtrack) will be played with that frame.

■   **Cx_SOUNDSOURCE**   Specifies the directory where the AU sound files
(SOUNDS or SOUNDTRACK) that will be played during the animation
can be found.

EXAMPLE:

```
<param name=C1
value="12,475,485,255,68,000000,000000,animationlib.GIFAnimator">
<param name=C1_IMAGES value="T1.Gif,T2.Gif,T3.Gif,T4.Gif,T5.Gif">
<param name=C1_IMAGESOURCE value="DukeGifs">
<param name=C1_STARTUP value="Start.Gif">
<param name=C1_BACKGROUND value="BackGnd.Gif">
<param name=C1_BACKGROUNDCOLOR value=" 00990000">
<param name=C1_PAUSE value="3900">
<param name=C1_PAUSES value="250, , 750, 50,50">
<param name=C1_REPEAT value="true">
<param name=C1_POSITIONS value="0 0,20 0,40 0,60 0, 80 0,100 0">
<param name=C1_SOUNDTRACK value="Duke.au">
<param name=C1_SOUNDSOURCE value="sounds">
<param name=C1_SOUNDS value="barmusic.au, , , batman.au ,duke.au ,">
```

INDEX

J

K

L

Q

R

S

ORDER BOOKS DIRECTLY FROM OSBORNE/McGRAW-HILL

For a complete catalog of Osborne's books, call 510-549-6600 or write to us at 2600 Tenth Street, Berkeley, CA 94710

 Call Toll-Free, *24 hours a day, 7 days a week, in the U.S.A.*
U.S.A.: 1-800-262-4729   *Canada:* **1-800-565-5758**

Mail *in the U.S.A. to:*   *Canada*
McGraw-Hill, Inc.   *McGraw-Hill Ryerson*
Customer Service Dept.   *Customer Service*
P.O. Box 182607   *300 Water Street*
Columbus, OH 43218-2607   *Whitby, Ontario L1N 9B6*

Fax *in the U.S.A. to:*   *Canada*
1-614-759-3644   **1-800-463-5885**
                                     Canada
                                     orders@mcgrawhill.ca

SHIP TO:

Name _____

Company _____

Address _____

City / State / Zip _____

Daytime Telephone *(We'll contact you if there's a question about your order.)*

ISBN #	BOOK TITLE	Quantity	Price	Total
0-07-88				
0-07-88				
0-07-88				
0-07-88				
0-07-88				
0-07088				
0-07-88				
0-07-88				
0-07-88				
0-07-88				
0-07-88				
0-07-88				
0-07-88				
0-07-88				

Shipping & Handling Charge from Chart Below		
Subtotal		
Please Add Applicable State & Local Sales Tax		
TOTAL		

Shipping & Handling Charges

Order Amount	U.S.	Outside U.S.
$15.00 - $24.99	$4.00	$6.00
$25.00 - $49.99	$5.00	$7.00
$50.00 - $74.99	$6.00	$8.00
$75.00 - and up	$7.00	$9.00
$100.00 - and up	$8.00	$10.00

Occasionally we allow other selected companies to use our mailing list. If you would prefer that we not include you in these extra mailings, please check here: ❏

METHOD OF PAYMENT

❏ Check or money order enclosed (payable to Osborne/McGraw-Hill)

❏ AMERICAN EXPRESS   ❏ DISCOVER   ❏ MasterCard   ❏ VISA

Account No. | | | | | | | | | | | | | | | | |

Expiration Date _____

Signature _____

In a hurry? Call with your order anytime, day or night, or visit your local bookstore.

Thank you for your order   Code BC640SL